1866.

EUGÈNE BOUDIN

14 July regatta at Honfleur, 1858

EUGÈNE BOUDIN

G. JEAN-AUBRY

with Robert Schmit

207 illustrations, 50 in color

New York Graphic Society Ltd. Greenwich, Connecticut

TRANSLATED FROM THE FRENCH
BY CAROLINE TISDALL

Standard Book Number 8212-0355-X
Library of Congress Catalog Card Number 69-20244

Original version of text published 1922 by Editions Bernheim-Jeune, Paris
Reprinted by kind permission of Messieurs Jean and Henri Dauberville,
Editions Bernheim-Jeune

Printed in Switzerland

CONTENTS

Part One LIFE

The Amazone, *the fifty-gun frigate on which the painter's father Léonard-Sébastien Boudin was serving as a gunner in 1811 when she sailed for Martinique in company with another vessel, the* Élisa, *and was intercepted by a British flotilla. The* Élisa *was sunk, and the commander of the* Amazone *beached his ship near Cherbourg.*

Léonard-Sébastien Boudin in 1870. Portrait in the Musée du Havre

Le Havre, Bassin du Commerce, c. 1860. Photo M. Sirot

Honfleur: the quayside, c. 1860. Photo M. Sirot

Constant Troyon (1810–65)

Jean-François Millet (1814–75)

Claude Oscar Monet (1840–1926)

Trouville harbour at low tide, c. 1850. Photo M. Sirot

Honfleur: the first steamship to ply regularly between Le Havre and Honfleur. Photo M. Sirot

Childhood · The stationer's shop
Millet, Troyon and Couture
First stay in Paris and journey to Belgium
The municipal study grant · First visit to Brittany
Boudin meets Courbet and Baudelaire · Saint-Siméon

Le Havre: harbour entrance at high tide. Photo M. Sirot

Le Havre: sailing ships in harbour

Chapter 1 1824-1861

Louis-Eugène Boudin was born in Honfleur, in the Rue Bourdet, on 12 July 1824.

His parents were of humble origins. His father, Léonard-Sébastien Boudin, was born in 1789 into a family of sailors in Honfleur. After naval service in the Napoleonic wars, he returned to Honfleur. He sailed with the fishing fleet for Newfoundland, and, on his return at the end of the 1816 fishing season, married Marie-Félicité Buffet in Honfleur. He later became master of a small cargo boat which sailed between Honfleur and Rouen, and which, because of its instability, was derisively called the *Polichinelle* ('Punchinello'). In 1835 Léonard Boudin and his family moved to Le Havre, to 51 Grand Quai. At first he served on ships of the Albrecht company, plying between Le Havre and Hamburg, the *Hambourg* and the *Le Havre*, then on a barge between Le Havre and Paris, and finally in 1838 as a deckhand on the *Français*, one of the first steamships to sail regularly between Le Havre and Honfleur. His wife was a stewardess on the same run. This service had been maintained for a long time by two large sloops which anchored in Le Havre in the Anse des Pilotes, which at this time still looked very much as it does in old engravings. Sailing ships unloaded sugar there, and the quayside was blocked by rows of wine casks and crowded with coopers, for whom it was a meeting-place.

It was into this modest family, whose links with the sea were so strong, that the future painter of seascapes was born.

Contrary to general belief Louis-Eugène Boudin never in fact undertook a long sea voyage, and the actual nautical experience of this marine painter was very limited.

When he was about ten years old Eugène was cabin boy aboard the *Polichinelle*, the small boat captained by his father. He had a natural love of ships and the sea, and with his small friends he used to wander happily around the docks and ships at Honfleur. One day he was playing on the *Polichinelle* with the other cabin boys, when he lost his balance and fell into the harbour. Luckily a sailor who was standing nearby talking to his father saw what had happened, and rescued the child just in time. That is the full extent of Boudin's adventures at sea. His mother, alarmed by the occasions on which the *Polichinelle* had capsized, put an end to his maritime career.

It was, however, in the little cabin of the *Polichinelle*, in the margins of a volume of Abbé Raynal's *Histoire philosophique*, which he used to read aloud to his father and the ship's mate, that Boudin the cabin boy made his first drawings.

Nothing in his environment seemed to favour his artistic instinct, and no one encouraged him. His parents could not afford to give him any training in the elements of painting, and his education, which at this stage was of course very rudimentary, did not fill in the gaps. For these reasons Boudin is one of the most interesting examples of instinctive creativity, a painter who demonstrates the uselessness of schools and rules, and the supreme virtue of personal effort, long patience, and a steadfast gift.

When the Boudin family moved to Le Havre in 1835, Eugène, who was then eleven years old, was enrolled in a school run by monks, the Ecole des Frères, in the Rue Saint-Jacques, where he stayed for just one year. All that is known of this year is that he won a prize for handwriting, and began to draw birds and leaves in his textbooks and exercise books.

At the end of the scholastic year he became a clerk for Joseph Morlent, a publisher and printer, whose workshop in the Place de la Comédie was the meeting place of all the literary figures living in or visiting Le Havre. It is probable that it was through Morlent that Boudin met Alphonse Karr, who was to give him his support in the municipal council in 1851. After a short time with Morlent, Boudin left to join Alphonse Lemasle's stationery firm in the Rue des Drapiers. He was engaged as a clerk, but Lemasle appreciated his intelligence and methodical mind, and employed him in a vague secretarial capacity.

When not at work he was already consumed by his passion for drawing, and sketched enthusiastically. His employer discovered him drawing one day and gave him his first box of paints. Boudin stayed with Lemasle until he was eighteen, when he left to set up his own business with Acher, one of Lemasle's foremen. The company was founded in Acher's name in 1844, and their stationery shop was opened at 18 Rue de la Communauté. Orders poured in and the business flourished. The qualities of order and attention to detail which were to distinguish Boudin's whole life and his work were already apparent, and contrasted greatly with the irresponsibility and disorder of most of the painters of his time.

The little shop was well situated in a street which at that time was one of the busiest in the town. From time to time, canvases by artists visiting Le Havre were shown in the window. In fact the painters who regularly stayed in Le Havre or in the countryside around it included some of the best of the period, and they all asked Boudin to display and sell their work in his shop. In this way Boudin met successively Eugène Isabey, Constant Troyon, who made several visits to Normandy at this time, Thomas Couture, and Jean-François Millet.

Boudin himself wrote of Millet's visit:

> In about 1846 [in fact this date is wrong, since Millet was in Le Havre from 1844–5, and in December 1845 the young family moved to Paris], Millet, who had just finished studying in Paris under Delaroche, was looking for 'work' as he described it, and came to Le Havre to do a series of portraits in oil and pastel at a minimum price of 30 francs. The artist who was to paint the *Angelus* was scarcely known then; he had married a short time before, and had come from Cherbourg. Because he had forfeited the small pension granted to him by Cherbourg as his adopted town, he was forced to execute drawings of various types and styles, *vert-vert*, little boys fishing, their naked bodies dappled with sunshine in the manner of Diaz and Couture. He was searching for a style. It was Millet, who had produced so many beautiful drawings, who corrected my first attempt, a landscape in the style of Troyon, whose pastels I had so often been able to frame and sell.
>
> From that moment on I felt I had finished with framing and stationery. When Millet recognized my intention to 'join in,' as he put it, he was unable to hide his concern for my future. The impoverished master's path had not been strewn with roses, and his life exemplified the trials I would have to undergo. He himself was going through such a difficult period that, although he had intended to stay in Le Havre only for a short time, he was forced to stay there for nearly two years. (*L'Art*, XLIII, 1887.)

Yet Millet at this time had already been noticed at the Salon when he exhibited *Woman carrying a jug* and *Riding lesson*. He executed a considerable number of portraits in Le Havre, though none remains in the town, except a *Portrait of a man* which was left to the museum. Portraits of naval officers done during this period can be seen in the museums of Rouen and Lyons.

In 1846 Boudin was obliged to dissolve his partnership with Jean Acher. He was called up for military service and had to withdraw his 2,500 francs from the business to pay a substitute. This of course led to friction with Acher. The number Boudin had drawn would have condemned him to the infantry for seven years, which was certainly not how he wished to spend his time. In 1850 Acher transferred his shop to 99 Rue de Paris, as the *Almanach du commerce* of that year records. He died that same year, and since his widow carried on the business, it is very probable

Three figures in the harbour

that it was there, in 1859, that Courbet first noticed some of Boudin's work.

Boudin's struggles and ill-fortunes had began; he was determined to follow his vocation, and the early years were extremely difficult. He would set off in the morning taking a piece of bread and cheese, and would stay out sketching until the evening. He drew on both sides of the paper, noting details of rigging, indicating groups of fishermen on the quayside with a stroke of his pencil; using a few pastels bought at great sacrifice, he began the studies of the sky which were to be his great passion, and in which he was soon to aquire an undeniable mastery. Two short extracts from notebooks written at this time give some idea of the situation:

> What a miracle! Who would have thought it? What a stroke of luck! Two pictures sold at the same time. Admittedly it's not for 1,000 francs, or even 500, but two mere *cent-sous* pieces. But when your assets are nil any minute sum seems like a fortune. (18 June 1847.)
>
> Work is a true consolation. It seems to me that one fulfils all one's duties by working, whatever the result. (6 July 1847.)

He met several art-lovers, among them M. Wanner, the Swiss consul, who had commissioned a portrait from Millet, and an underwriter called Valls who was already buying works by Isabey and Camille Corot. Perhaps it was he who, in 1810, had paid 500 francs for Corot's *Monk* at a Le Havre painting exhibition. But these were the only patrons Boudin found, apart from Mr Taylor, the United States vice-consul in Le Havre, who helped Boudin over a long period, in spite of his own modest means. In a notebook Boudin indicates that in 1851 he executed two portraits for Mr Taylor for forty francs each.

At this time Eugène Boudin was living with his family at 51 Grand-Quai. The ground floor of the house was rented to a man called Audièvre, who had a restaurant there. Then as now, there were many restaurants along the quay, since the Honfleur boats and the animated life of the port were already a tourist attraction. There were then monkey- and parrot-sellers' shops which gave the quay an exotic atmosphere which it has now lost, but which it is still easy to imagine. Painters were not alone in their appreciation of this quarter of Le Havre, for one day a man eating at Audièvre's with his wife and child asked the restaurant owner whether he knew any local painters. 'Upon my word,' replied Audièvre, 'there's one in this very house,' and he took them up to see Boudin. The traveller's name was Théodule Ribot, and this was the beginning of a long and close friendship. Ribot, who had been employed by a building speculator in Algeria, had returned to Paris and had been successively a sign and store painter and a book-keeper. He painted borders decorated with birds for a frame-maker, illustrated novels, was employed by the painter Auguste-Barthelémy Glaize to paint in the architectural backgrounds in his canvases, and copied paintings by Lancret, Boucher, and Watteau for a manufacturer. He was not to exhibit in the Salon until 1861.

Boudin was working relentlessly, and the study of nature occupied all his time, though his slender resources would not permit him to set up on a grand scale. He took a studio on the fourth floor of a house on the Grand-Quai. The days were too short for the amount of work he would have liked to do, although he was out every morning to catch the sunrise and did not return until sunset. He sketched the characters on the quayside, and caught on paper the picturesque corners of the town, especially Le Perrey, the old quarter of Le Havre, with its logettes, windmills, moats, the boats beached on the shingle, and the Tour François Ier. He tried all the media he could afford to buy: watercolour, sepia ink and pastel. His mother set aside small amounts of her housekeeping money for him and with this, and the money he earned from the sale of flower paintings and still-lifes at ridiculously low prices, Eugène set off for Paris in 1847.

In spite of the contacts he had made among the Parisian painters as a stationer and framer in Le Havre, he was too shy to visit any of the artists who were to become the greatest of their generation. He worked alone, spending entire days in the Louvre, and learning by study of the old masters an art whose rudiments he already knew by instinct.

The revolutionary upheaval of 1848 brought good fortune to Boudin. He had a letter of introduction to Baron Taylor, royal commissioner for the Comédie-Française in 1824, inspector-general of fine arts in 1848, associate member of the Académie des Beaux-Arts. The baron gave him the job of accompanying the sculptor Louis Rochet (1813–78) on a mission to the north of France and to Belgium to sell tickets for a national subscription in the form of a lottery to help writers and artists, many of whom had fallen on hard times as a result of the unstable political situation.

Boudin wrote to Baron Taylor as follows:

> Left Le Havre on 20 August 1849, as requested by the sculptor M. Rochet. After setting up the exhibition at Dieppe, left for Arras where I met up with Rochet again. From Arras went to Lille to help Rochet organize the exhibition, which will be open until the 13 October. From Lille proceeded to Valenciennes, then to Condé and Saint-Amand, where we took approximately a thousand francs. From there into Belgium, then to Tourcoing, Roubaix, and finally Orchies.

This fortuitous turn of events enabled Boudin to study the works of the Flemish masters in Belgium, and to see some fine examples of the Dutch landscape and marine schools whose tradition he was to continue.

He began to paint a great many copies of the old masters at this time, and these copies, apart from more or less ensuring him a livelihood, enabled him to examine in greater detail the techniques of the great painters of the past. In this way he copied paintings by Paulus Potter, Van der Velde and Ruysdael, artists with whom he already had a certain affinity. He is also known to have done copies of Teniers and Boucher at this time. A letter which Baron Taylor sent to Boudin on 14 November 1849 commissioned him to copy Van Ostade's *Travellers' rest*, and paintings by Watteau, Lancret, and Joseph Vernet, the choice of which he left to the artist. These copies reveal a painter already sure of his technique.

He returned to Le Havre, where visiting artists could see and judge for themselves the young man's talent. Among these visitors were Isabey and Couture, who had inspired his first works. In 1850 Boudin sent several canvases to the exhibition of the Société des Amis des Arts, which was held once every two years in Le Havre. The buying committee of the society acquired two of the works submitted by Boudin. The report describes them in this way:

'The committee included in their choice two works by an unknown and unsupported young man, works which reveal a genuine talent which attracted their attention. To their great surprise, the committee learnt that this painter, already remarkable for his skill, was completely untaught, had never left Le Havre, and had no other teacher than Nature and a certain feeling for his art. In disclosing its opinions on the subject, the buying committee requested that the outstanding qualities of M. Boudin be brought to the notice of the municipal council.'

With this end in view, a petition dated 19 September 1850 was sent to the municipal council, and the matter was referred back to the committee on 16 November; then, on 6 February 1851, the chairman, M. Millet Saint-Pierre, who was also one of the administrators of the Société des Amis des Arts, presented a very vigorous report to the municipal council, recommending that Eugène Boudin be given a study grant of 1,200 francs per annum for three years. To support his request the chairman quoted letters from two extremely valuable witnesses; one was from Couture, who wrote:

'I am happy to certify that M. Boudin is a gifted artist with excellent prospects. I congratulate the municipal council of Le Havre on its wish to help a young man who will one day, I am quite certain, be one of the triumphs of our modern school' (Paris, 6 December 1850).

The other letter was from Troyon:

'I am very glad to have been asked to give my opinion of M. Boudin's talent, and I can say from the bottom of my heart that Boudin is not only destined to be a great painter, but can already be considered on a level with the young painters of our new school. Believe me, I should be very happy if my opinion were to carry some weight in the decision made by the municipal council, both in the interest of the arts, and in that of a young man in whom one cannot help but take the liveliest interest.'

This turned out to be an accurate prophecy. Alphonse Karr, the writer, and Adolphe-Hippolyte Couveley, the director of the Musée du Havre from its founding on 1 January 1815 until 27 April 1867, both supported the request, which was granted. According to Boudin himself, Alphonse Karr was the instigator of these measures; he had been living near Le Havre, at Sainte-Adresse, since 1841. Eugène Boudin left for Paris on 30 June 1851 with a three-year grant, 1,200 francs to be paid each year, on condition that every year he sent a number of original paintings or copies to the town of Le Havre, which would give a representative idea of his work, and enrich the city museum.

In fact Boudin spent much of these three years in Honfleur, preferring to work there, but he used the time he was in Paris as part of a careful and methodical search for his own personal style. For him, as for all truly original artists, contact with the old masters in the Louvre, or with living painters, only served as a measure of his own independence, and as an incentive to rely on his own temperament.

This is how he wrote to his brother at the time:

> I have already told you of the sheltered life I have been leading. The little that does reach me I learn through hearsay, so that I know a word or two about everything and nothing in depth. The best time for study, my dear brother, is when one is sitting quietly by the fire with no human complications to trouble you, for only then can one devote paternal love and care to one's little creations. I won't tell you any more about myself, for I work a great deal, but progress very slowly. (To Louis Boudin, 21 February 1853.)
>
> It is essential to have a long-term idea of one's ambitions, and not rush into acquiring a reputation too early. Personally I would prefer not to be forced to produce works before I have overcome the difficulties I encounter at every step. To be obliged to produce is a terrible torture which can only bring discouragement with it. (To Louis Boudin, 4 March 1853.)

From this time onwards, Boudin's letters contain the charming mixture of simplicity, refinement, and calm determination that he continued to show right up to his death. Occasionally his letters contain comments like these:

I'm becoming an expert shopper. What would Father say if he saw me in my slippers, my basket full of lettuce and leeks for soup, and my pockets bulging with eggs!... There was no cupboard in my room, so I've made one out of a crate. (To Louis, 21 February 1853.)

But the self-critical eagerness with which he approached his work was not to the taste of his fellow townsmen, nor did they approve of the new direction in which his painting seemed to be developing. The little interest his work aroused in most of the citizens of Le Havre is evident in several passages from his letters:

Valls is here and is plaguing me to give him some paintings to take to confound the people of Le Havre, who are hot on the heels of poor Boudin. (To Louis, 4 March 1853.)

The following letter was sent to him at this time by the curator of the Musée du Havre, and shows just how out of favour Boudin was with the town that had given him money:

'*My dear Boudin,* 16 March 1853

'I was sent for yesterday by the Mayor, who wants to know what you are doing before the budget committee meets. It seems that someone has been trying to turn the municipal council against you.

'I think the reasons for this are the same as before, because the Mayor told me that you are hardly ever in Paris, and more often in Caen, Rouen, or Le Havre. I put him right on this, and told him that you only came to Le Havre once every three months to collect your pension, and that in the summer you have to work from nature, since you have chosen to be a landscape painter. He wants to know which studio you are attending. I replied that you are under the guidance of Troyon. When you come you would do well to bring a written confirmation of this, which Troyon will be pleased to give you.

'I told him also that you were busy doing a copy of a Ruysdael for us, so do hurry up and get on with that as soon as possible.

'I think I've managed to counter your friend Ochard's influence this year, for I feel sure that all this can be traced back to him.'

During his years in Paris, Boudin sent to Le Havre a copy of a *Meadow* by Paulus Potter, and one of a *Brook* by Ruysdael, followed soon after by a still-life. The copy of the *Meadow* is especially fine, treated with an exactitude, and at the same time an independence of technique, that are delightful. All three works are still in the Musée du Havre.

There also exists a *Still-life* painted during this early period in Paris, which Boudin sent to Le Havre, but which for some unknown reason was not accepted by the museum. Some thirty years later the painting was sold to a collector, who showed it to a friend of his who was well acquainted with Boudin's style. He was amazed to see at the bottom of the canvas the signature 'Couveley'. When Boudin was consulted he had no difficulty in recognizing his own work, and restored his signature. He said on seeing it that one of the partridges in the still-life had never been finished, and gave the reason. At that time Boudin hired his 'models' from a nearby butcher who allowed him to keep them for forty-eight hours, but on this occasion the butcher had come to reclaim them too early.

It seems that neither the public officials nor the art-lovers of Le Havre were satisfied with the painter they were supporting financially. Le Havre for Boudin was like Cherbourg for Millet. In spite of the efforts that were made on his behalf, it proved impossible to extend the young painter's grant. Boudin's tentative and patient search for a style was too far removed from the facile and impersonal execution which is always hailed by the majority of those who congratulate themselves on being discerning art-lovers, and who in fact only encourage mediocrity. Some years later a request for a grant was submitted

Shepherds

to the same municipal council by M. Monet on behalf of his son Claude, and remained unanswered.

Here is Boudin's own account of the business:

My pension had ended. The town of Le Havre owed me nothing, but it had been disappointed. They had hoped that after three years I would return from Paris like a phoenix of art. In fact I came back more confused than ever, perturbed by the famous painters of the day, from [Théodore] Rousseau, who enchanted me, to Corot who was opening up a new direction to me. My most precious years, and those of many other young painters like me, were spent in this way, exploring the field and trying for years on end to find a formula to please the public, that sole arbiter of fame. We were all searching for our own styles, and for all our efforts we succeeded only in spoiling whatever element of originality there was in each of us. There are so many painters around who have gone astray, and who really deserved a better fate.

If Corot, with his great talent, had such a tremendous struggle to establish himself, what would I, his poor follower, have to go through? Grey painting was little appreciated at that time, least of all in seascapes. [Théodore] Gudin reigned supreme, Isabey's use of natural colour was pushing his prices up, Le Poittevin and others were all the rage with their 'chic' painting. It was hardly the right moment to bring in grey, which no one wanted at any price. The only solution was to withdraw from Paris and wait for more favourable times. That is why I did not return there for nearly fifteen years. [But see Chronological Table, p. 184.] (*L'Art*, 1887.)

Boudin continued to paint, setting up a small studio in the Rue de l'Orangerie, and then in a garret in the Rue Séry, painting portraits, 'dining-room pictures, watercolours, landscapes, in fact anything that might bring in a little income.'

It was during this period that the earliest positively datable works by Boudin were painted. These are few, and a lack of evidence makes it difficult to establish their authenticity. Quite apart from this, these early works are not usually signed, and the style is often imitative of the leading painters of the day. The paintings consist in the main of little landscapes very strongly influenced by Rousseau, although the way in which the sky is painted in some of them is already highly characteristic of Boudin's style.

There is, for example, a large panel in Le Havre, dating from 1855. This is a landscape depicting a view of Rouelles (Seine-Inférieure). While it is true that the foreground is reminiscent of the manner of Rousseau and Troyon, the execution of the trees outlined against the sky, and of the sky itself, is typical of Boudin's early style.

Although his output during these early years was large, most of the works have by now disappeared, though some evidence for their existence remains. In 1852, when he was already in Paris, eleven canvases by Boudin were listed in the catalogue of the biennial exhibition of painting, sculpture, and *objets d'art* at the Musée du Havre. One of these, *Kettle*, was sold for 175 francs, another, *Willows*, fetched 100 francs. Also from this period date the two little panels which were given to the Musée du Havre in 1893 (see p. 25). One of these bears the title *Le Havre, town hall, glacis, Tour François-I*er*, Porte du Perrey*, and the other, *Le Havre, Tour François-I*er. The rather dry handling in the first of these panels must owe something to the influence of Isabey, although once again the sky is painted in the characteristically delicate manner which was to typify Boudin's later style.

It is in his notebooks that the struggles and hesitations Boudin experienced when young, his difficulties in realizing his aims, and his patient attempts to do so, become most clearly apparent. For these notebook jottings, intended as they were, only for himself, reveal most fully what was going on in his mind:

1854. Sunday 25 March. Walked to Saint-Vigor. Nature is richer than I represent it.

March. Perfection, elusive perfection: it is not exactly perfection that I seek, but what eternal unrest! I turn things over and over in my mind; here the land is too cramped, there the sky too near, and then again the balance is lost. I am irked by my technique which becomes dull and heavy; and then I find that what has been lost is the light. What ardour one has to put into it; how many discouragements must be borne. It is a miserable life, a life entirely within myself. Nature, which I look at continually, and never see. Must this be the price I pay for peace? Sometimes, in the course of a melancholy walk, I look at the light which floods the earth, trembles on the water, and plays on human garments, and my courage fails me at the thought of how much genius is needed to grasp so many difficulties, how limited is the human spirit, unable to hold so many things in its consciousness at once; and more strongly still I sense that poetry is there, and how it can be extracted. I sometimes glimpse what needs to be expressed.

Are all these anxieties the sign of impotence, or the result of a mind which cannot easily find satisfaction? I'm sure that it is only by labouring at my panels that I can hope to express even the tiniest particle of poetry, yet this process is so slow, so painful. To create a balance between the hard realities of daily life and the realization of dreams is a difficult task for a man of my temperament, and one which nevertheless has to be achieved.

6 April. I'm terribly afraid that being in a state of perpetual struggle with myself, as I am at the moment, might fatally damage my talent. What is it that is lacking in my painting? Almost nothing, and yet everything, for the effect is inaccurate and the colour weak. Today I took a large picture and put it alongside several paintings in the museum, which was consoling and made me aware of a number of defects in my work. My handling is clumsy, my colour dim, and I lack liveliness in my execution – I shall have to study each of these things all over again.

Friday 6 April. I'm still worrying about not being able to sell my work. I must work faster and try to *be brilliant.*

Saturday 7 April. What beautiful points to capture if only I had the nerve. I must rise above trivialities.

15 April. I've just sent off three little pictures at last. What effort went into producing these mediocrities! It is clear that I shall have to persist stubbornly to achieve an output, and yet I do feel that I am making progress. Nature often speaks to me, but my gropings are terribly laborious. And then my head, my poor head, is full, so full.

June. I am in such a dreadful state of confusion. I feel I must shake myself out of this muddle, for I think I am on the brink of great inspiration. I read books which contain the spark, and yet I do not take fire. I have a conviction of my own powers that nothing, neither intensive effort nor sloth, can shake, though perhaps I am wrong about this. On the other hand, it's true that genius is a natural gift and cannot be cultivated. Yet I never feel uplifted, because I cannot always find my ideal in Nature herself. I lack two things: faith and passion – two qualities which the cold wind of calculation extinguishes, and which nevertheless constitute a powerful lever. Besides this I am tormented by the need to earn my daily bread. And yet alongside or underlying all this, there is a dominant idea.

Nature will appear more abundant, more luxuriant, and I must find the means of preserving the luminous power which is the essence of her charm. I must put into it so much abandon, so much luxury, that it will do one good to see Nature in my paintings just as it does in reality.

18 July. Left for Honfleur.

6 October. I'm not going to complain about public inertia, although I'm in the homeland of indifference; I'm only too

Breton costumes

aware of my unimportance. Nevertheless it's cruel, my strength often fails me.

I have unpacked my sketches, and am more satisfied now that I can see that I have made some progress towards a mature style, but all this is nothing compared to what I would like to achieve.

22 October. I've returned from Honfleur for good, discouraged, and yet in good form. I hope to God that I'll be free of suffering for some time.

Sunday 29 October. I've lost all my energy. I have not a penny in the world, I have absolutely nothing. There's a little picture I want to do, but I can see that it will take so long that I am overcome by disillusion, and can achieve nothing. I began a large landscape, and here I am in this state. Before midday it's too dark to do any work at all in this rotten studio, still I don't pay anything for it, and it is heated. I am disgusted by everything I do. On first perceiving a subject I am carried away on a wave of inspiration, but as soon as I begin to work on it I lose sight of my vision, and end up like this, utterly discouraged. Nothing can take my mind off it, even my moments of leisure are a burden.

Sunday 12 December. This morning began working on my picture again, and, like everything I undertake, it's going badly. I can feel the expansiveness, the delicacy and the brilliant light which turns everything under my eyes into enchanted groves, yet out of all this I can only produce colours like mud. I am forced to admit that my mind, or rather my hand, is incapable of the inspired vigour that would give expression to my ideal, or even a tiny part of it. Yet I still have a feeling that I'll get there in the end, but it's such a slow process, and I'm already thirty. Besides, I'm in such a stupid environment here.

I went out this afternoon, and the sun was glorious. It was a holiday, and I did well to go out and enjoy it, for it led me to think up all sorts of ideas about painting, for example, how light in paintings always looks weak and sad. For the twentieth time I have tried to convey the delicacy and charm of the light which plays over everything. As the weather was so cool the light was soft, changeable, and a little pink. The sea was superb, and the sky soft, *velvety*. Later on everything turned to gold, and then to a warmer tone.Finally as the sun set it threw beautiful purple shadows over everything, and the fields and ditches echoed this colour.

Only paintings by Claude Lorrain have, with their freshness, achieved this delicacy of tone. Occasionally Corot caught it in his clear and soft range of nuances, but these were clumsy attempts and the subject must be tackled again. The Eure marsh with its soft violet-blue lights was so beautiful, transparent and matt at the same time. One always makes things too crude.

31 December. I finished this year utterly discouraged.

1856. 6 January. I must look at my paintings with an eye to the future as well. After some struggle with myself, this is what I've decided: I must try to earn something from everything I do, above all, to be single-minded about making money; so there is not a moment to lose. I will frame every successful canvas and price it at 25 to 30 francs. Besides this, I must try to break in on the Paris market, so I will direct most of my efforts towards producing really nice and accomplished works. Later I'll find a way to get my work shown in Paris, but at the moment the most essential thing is to work with energy, above all at seascapes....

By the grace of God I have realized that energy is the thing which will enable me to create, not with the wholehearted assurance which confidence guarantees, but with an element of doubt which is not without its virtue, since it incites one to greater efforts.

23 February. At last I am beginning to gather some fruits from my patient labours. People are beginning to visit me, and I'm no longer treated like a miserable failure. I've been given enough commissions to keep me going for some time.

Mathieu has helped me a great deal by making me aware of my potential, for I feel that I could develop the poetic side of myself considerably.

I'd like to note in passing something Mathieu said. This was that the romantics have had their day and that now we must search out the simple beauties of nature. I was happy doing just that, and will continue to do so with ardour. The phase in my life which is now coming to a close will, I think be decisive. I have always had a feeling that I might succeed. I wonder if this will happen? At last I can see my goal clearly, despite my tormented mind. It's quite clear: nature seen in all her variety and freshness, I am eager to see the fulfilment of my untaught inclinations.

15 June. For some time now this journal has remained silent, for I no longer feel the need to confide to it all my miseries and desires. At last I'm in a position to cope with my most urgent needs, though I'm in for a lot more worries of all kinds, but the material necessity which stultified me has disappeared.

Friday 14 November. I'm feeling very sad and unsociable. I cannot live even one day in peace, and yet must keep up my courage and persevere. I feel the need to leave this part of the country and seek my fortune elsewhere.

Saturday 15. With my last *quarante sous* piece I bought some fruit and vegetables to paint.

Wednesday 26. I am obsessed with the idea of leaving. I must travel, for that would probably relax me.

Tuesday 3 December. To bathe in the depths of the sky, to express the gentleness of clouds, to balance these masses far,

far away, from the grey mist, to set the blue of the sky alight, I can feel all this within me, poised and awaiting expression. What a joy and yet what a torment! But if I was at peace in my heart, perhaps I would never be able to plumb the depths. When in the past have they done better? Did the Dutch painters find the poetry in the clouds for which I search? or the tenderness in the sky which I admire to the point of adoration – and I am not exaggerating. (Unpublished notebook.)

Boudin followed his own advice. With the unceasing patience that was to serve him throughout his artistic career, the young painter continued his study of nature, and the self-examination manifest in his notebooks, forcing himself to simplify his means of expression, and building up a wealth of sketches and studies.

All the tortured hours of unrewarded and lonely work went unnoticed by those who began to take an interest in the young painter, and they mistook his hesitancy and delays for negligence and idleness. The following letter from an early patron illustrates this attitude clearly enough, while at the same time it provides interesting information about picture prices at this time, about 1855:

'My dear M. Boudin, Paris 18 May 1855

'Exactly one month ago, I commissioned a painting of fish and vegetables from you and you have not your canvas yet. To judge by your apparent eagerness to proceed, the end is nowhere in sight; I could have made two visits to Paris in the time. But let us not talk of this matter, which tends to make me lose my temper, but concern ourselves with you instead. You could rise to fame so quickly, if you would only profit by your youth, and apply yourself with energy, whereas my only claim to fame lies in having appreciated you. These disagreeable thoughts have long been familiar, but in view of what is happening now they become more and more relevant.

'Modern painting is getting increasingly popular, and the number of patrons is rapidly multiplying; prices of certain artists whom we like have almost tripled, and they are enriched with fame and fortune. Despite the war and general unrest, their pictures are worth their weight in gold.

'At the recent Halphen sale, two little Rousseaus fetched 226 and 470 francs; the first was a very rough sketch, the other, more finished, was less attractive. Two works by Jules Dupré of the same size, 485 and 655 francs. A Millet, as always anti-heroic in content, this time of an ugly girl searching her bedclothes for fleas, and painted on thick cardboard, was considered to be worth 40 francs. A Rosa Bonheur, heavily handled, horribly coloured and dry in treatment, fetched 720, though I wouldn't have given 10 francs for it. A Delacroix *Tiger in the Atlas Mountains*, a beautiful work by the great master which I am happy to say was knocked down to me at 505 francs (it's about 30 cm by 50 cm). Ten pathetic little figure pieces by Meissonier, some mere pen lines and others in pencil, achieved fantastic prices, ranging from 50 to 760 francs. Five Troyons, on the whole old works, fetched from 425 to 1,360 francs.

'Apart from the Delacroix and the Diaz bought in the sale, I'm in the running for an old Diaz which he has recently retouched, and also for a little Troyon which has just been completed.

'Your devoted friend, *J. Valls*.

'Don't tell anyone that I'm buying pictures, as this could do me a great deal of harm.'

By this time Boudin was beginning to attract a few patrons, and he held a sale which, although the prices were still very low, raised enough money to cover the cost of a visit to Brittany, the first of a number he was to make to the region, culminating in his journey to Douarnenez and Pont-Aven in 1897.

The first journey to Brittany occurred in about 1857, although at this time Boudin showed scant enthusiasm for a countryside to which he was later to return with such pleasure. In a letter to his brother, dated 12 July 1857, he wrote:

I'm in good health, and exploring every nook and cranny of Finistère without finding one corner which really suits me, or which stands up to anything on our coast. I stayed for a few days at Brest, a stupid sort of town, where I saw one or two old tubs of boats painted grey. The shipping roads are rather fine, I suppose, but apart from this the place is just not up to our region....

I am writing to you from Chateaulin, a little town between some very steep mountains which must look very much like the villages in the Pyrenees – pretty, but not really to my taste.... I suppose I might grow to like the place once I'm by the sea.

Two days later he wrote again from Quimper:

I've found a little river with lovely banks, but I could have found far better at Caudebec, or by the open sea.... As for the beaches, I have been robbed. Sainte-Adresse and Trouville are far prettier than these.... The only interesting things are the beautiful costumes worn by the peasant women.

It seems that at this time it was not so much the sea itself as the picturesque quality of the inhabitants that attracted him. He made innumerable sketches of costumes, watched processions, weddings, and other ceremonies at which costume was worn; he painted women in front of church doors, and men clustered round carts on market days. He wrote to his brother:

I have just attended the famous pilgrimage of Sainte-Anne-la-Palud. I have come to appreciate this place too late; it is what I have been dreaming of, and I shall return. (14 July 1857.)

This letter was written from Douarnenez; he did in fact return there several times, and it was the place he went to on one of his last visits outside Normandy in the year before his death.

There is a charming reminiscence of his impressions in a letter of this period written to his brother:

You asked me in your last letter if the countryside around Cornouailles is wooded or flat, and if the farms are open or enclosed, etc.... Since I've a quarter of an hour to spare, I shall try to give you an idea of it. It is impossible to feel homesick for Normandy here, for it is perhaps even more beautiful. Seen from the hills above it looks like one huge garden divided up by fences: every field has its own little rampart, and every farm (or 'village,' as they call them here) is surrounded by tall trees, just as in Normandy, and round these are orchards or well-tended gardens. In addition to this most of the farms are old manor houses, and this gives them a rather monumental and interesting atmosphere.... There are also some simple cottages built of granite blocks. Soft granite forms the soil of the region and is there for the taking. The cottages seem to be more scattered than in Normandy. They are always more numerous around the towns, and thatched, again as in Normandy, so that, apart from the people and the teams of horses, you could easily imagine you were at home, so similar are the trees, the grass, and the thousand plants that grow in the ditches and on the roadsides. I haven't really paid much attention to the landscape, since it offers nothing very unusual, but they do say it's quite different near the mountains; I can't say, because I haven't seen much of it. But the people themselves are what interests me. Various features distinguish them from our peasants, though basically there is a great deal of the Norman in these hulking *brayons* who come to market every Saturday, one with a cow, another with a couple of pigs or calves. You should see them there, squabbling and wrangling, one to make something out of it, and the other to get some sort of concession. They'll harangue for hours to make a deal. They drink prodigiously and curse before accepting the *cent-sous* piece which some scarecrow holds out. When the market shuts, the drinking continues.... after each market day the roads are filled with victims of the Divine Bottle returning to their villages, led by their animals, which seem to have enough intelligence for both of them. The women don't go short either, and usually roll home well loaded with alcohol. Brandy rules supreme in this place. During the week their life is fairly hard – black bread, gruel, and water to drink – that's all they have, and I must admit that when it comes to second helpings, I prefer to fast.

The women are surprisingly vain of their appearance, and dress like queens. They spend their lives working in the fields or looking after the animals, and have little opportunity to show themselves off. But they often have weddings which are like huge picnics, since everyone contributes four francs. I have been spending the last few days at a really beautiful one, though it wasn't very gay, because the bride was bedridden and died the next day, during the second day of feasting. The costumes were quite magnificent; we drank, danced and ate in the open to the playing of bagpipes, most melancholy music. The men are not very chivalrous – they all sat on the same side of the table. The bride and groom were placed on a sort of dais, which was beribboned in the most ridiculous fashion.

When the sun set the bagpipes wheezed to a halt, and everyone went to bed to prepare for the next day's hard work. (24 September 1857.)

Boudin brought back a number of sketches, and the catalogue for the 1858 exhibition of the Société des Amis des Arts of Le Havre contains references to a number of Breton landscapes: *Breton farm (Finistère)*, *Landscape*, *The afternoon rest*, *The manor* (this was a farm outside Quimperlé), a *Pilgrimage* near Quimper, as well as a number of landscapes of Rouelles (Seine-Inférieure) and a still-life of a hare which is now in the Musée du Havre, and which already shows the solid yet delicate qualities which gradually emerge in Boudin's work.

Boudin used the studies made during the two visits to Brittany in 1857 and 1858 to compose a large canvas *The pilgrimage of Sainte-Anne-la-Palud* (see p. 26). This painting is significant both for its size, which is exceptional in the work of the artist, and also because it was the first work he sent to the Salon. (One of Boudin's notebooks shows that this picture was bought by the city of Le Havre for 500 francs, inclusive of the frame, on 20 April 1860). It was an ambitious attempt at formal composition by a painter who, up to this point, had concentrated almost exclusively on summary sketches. That Boudin himself was far from satisfied with the work is indicated in his notebooks:

25 January 1859. My picture (the *Pilgrimage*) is full of defects; I had certainly visualized something better. There is too much in it, yet nothing that would specifically characterize Brittany; the colour and light are lacking in something. I must try to achieve more clarity, more luminosity and more refinement. Still, despite my depression and all these setbacks, I have already achieved quite a lot. But this picture lacks the ideal quality of transformation, there is no central point of interest, and not a single figure stands out.

27 January. I sent the *Pilgrimage* off today. I am afraid my heart was not in it at the end; it has no breadth, no flexibility, no originality – it's a beginner's work. I have in my mind a very different perfection. To send it off, I had to borrow three francs.

I've spent a sickening day. It really makes me lose heart to think that, however hard I try, I can't earn a penny by my painting. I've just finished four sketches and am going to offer them to old man Taylor. I hope to God he doesn't refuse them.

Times were obviously hard for the thirty-five-year-old painter, and the future seemed just as gloomy. His notebooks reveal his struggles with himself and with his poverty:

28 May 1859. Nature is so beautiful that when I'm not tortured by poverty I'm tortured by her splendour. How fortunate we are to be able to see and admire the glories of the sky and earth; if only I could be content just to admire them! But there is always the torment of struggling to reproduce them, the impossibility of creating anything within the narrow limits of painting. A reflection of these marvels, however enfeebled, must surely be worth something, when I think of the thousands of wretches whose lives are spent doing such petty things, and who nevertheless make money out of them! The important thing is to keep trying, to aspire towards the sublime, for one day one's efforts and aspirations will be recognized and appreciated.

The isolation which Boudin had suffered during these years was about to end, for he was soon to meet some of the people who were to influence his life directly or indirectly, and who were to be among the great painters of the century. One of the important turning-points in the history of modern French painting, the meeting between Boudin and Monet, occurred at about this time.

Claude Monet, or Oscar Monet as he was still called, had already become quite famous locally for caricatures and cartoon portraits, some of which can still be seen in private collections in Le Havre. He was already thinking seriously about painting, though admittedly his ideas on the subject differed from Boudin's.

This is how Monet himself described their meeting and their differences when I talked to him at Giverny.

'I remember our meeting as if it were yesterday. I was in the framer's shop where I often exhibited the pencil caricatures which had won me some notoriety in Le Havre, and even a little money. I met Eugène Boudin there. He was then about thirty, and his expansive and generous personality was already apparent. [In fact, Boudin was thirty-five, and Monet eighteen.] I had seen his work on several occasions, and I must admit I thought it was frightful. "These little things are yours, are they, young man?" he asked. "It's a pity you don't aim higher, for you obviously have talent. Why don't you paint?"

'I confess that the thought of painting in Boudin's idiom didn't exactly thrill me. But, when he insisted,

Le Havre, town hall, glacis, Tour François Ier, Porte du Perrey, 1852

Le Havre, Tour François Ier, 1852

The Pilgrimage of Sainte-Anne-la-Palud, Finistère, 1858

Study for the painting 'The Pilgrimage of Sainte-Anne-la-Palud', *c.* 1858

I agreed to go painting in the open air with him. I bought a paintbox, and we set off to Rouelles, without much enthusiasm on my part. I watched him rather apprehensively, and then more attentively, and then suddenly it was as if a veil had been torn from my eyes. I had understood, I had grasped what painting could be. Boudin's absorption in his work, and his independence, were enough to decide the entire future and development of my painting.'

'If I have become a painter,' Monet said to me on two occasions, 'I owe it to Eugène Boudin.'

It is a tribute to Boudin's greatness that, apart from the beauty of his own work, he was able to awaken the genius of one of the greatest and most original of modern painters.

It is very probable that the meeting between Boudin and Monet occurred in 1858, since two letters have come to light in the town archives of Le Havre, one of which is dated that year. They were written by Monsieur A. Monet, who requested that the town of Le Havre should award a study grant to his son Oscar (Claude Monet) to enable him to go to Paris to study painting. The first, dated 6 August 1858, just says: '...my son, Oscar Monet, has studied painting with Messieurs Ochard and Vasseur,' whereas the second, dated 21 March 1859, elaborates this: '...my son, Oscar Monet, has studied with Messieurs Ochard, Vasseur and Boudin.'

While his father was waiting for a reply, Monet, who did not even know of his request, was able to go to Paris for a month, in May 1859. His letters to Boudin described what he saw, and urged him to leave Le Havre as soon as possible, but Boudin felt that this would still be unwise in view of his shaky financial position. Nevertheless, Monet sent him this letter on 19 May 1859:

'I've visited several painters, beginning with M. [Amand] Gautier, who asked me to send you his regards, and hopes to see you back in Paris soon. That's what everyone says. You will only get discouraged if you stay in that stuffy old town. Troyon has talked to me a great deal about you: he is absolutely amazed not to have seen you back in the capital before now. He told me to ask you to send a dozen of your most finished paintings, grey seascapes, still-lifes and landscapes. He wants to see whether they are better finished than those you sent him last time. He advises you very strongly to come to Paris.'

But despite his pupil's persistence, Boudin stayed in Le Havre, and continued his steady development alone, though from time to time he was able to widen his circle of acquaintances, sometimes quite profitably. Thus in 1859 he met two people who were to play an important part in his life: Gustave Courbet and Charles Baudelaire.

Courbet and Schanne, the 'Schaunard' of Murger's *Vie de Bohème*, had decided to visit Le Havre to be by the sea, and to do a little 'botany' on the coast. In a shop window in the Rue de Paris the master of Ornans noticed a display of carefully executed little seascapes which immediately aroused his interest. He asked for the painter's address, and was sent to Boudin, who was delighted to meet the great Courbet. He showed the two visitors round Le Havre, then took them to Honfleur, and found them lodgings half way between the two towns, *chez* Mme Toutain on her farm at Saint-Siméon. Courbet recorded this visit in *Mme Toutain's garden*, and it seems that it was Boudin who persuaded him to paint the Channel. Works painted by Courbet during his visit include among others: *Cliffs at Honfleur*, *Mme Toutain's garden*, *Sunset on the English Channel*, and *View of the Seine estuary* (in the Musée de Lille).

Walking round the harbour one morning, the three friends were surprised to meet Baudelaire, who was on holiday with his mother. In spite of their protests and their informal dress, he insisted on taking them to dinner. They were introduced to his mother, and Courbet gallantly offered her his arm as they went into the dining-room, although she was so tiny that he had to bend double to do so. The meal was delightful, and afterwards they drank coffee on the balcony, among the rare plants, and with the sea before them. At nine o'clock they took their leave, quite overcome by this unexpected pleasure. Baudelaire accompanied them as far as the harbour, then to Le Havre, and finally returned with them to Paris, saying that he hated the country when the weather was fine because it reminded him too much of India. He much preferred the gentle sky of Paris, with its ceaseless changes, the captive water running by the embankments, and his favourite walk along the banks of the Ourcq canal.

This meeting with Courbet increased Boudin's admiration for him, and laid the foundations of a friendship that was to remain unshaken even later in life, when everyone else so stupidly turned against Courbet. On 2 January 1872, when Courbet was taken, as a political prisoner on parole after his part in the Commune rising of 1871, to Dr Duval's convalescent home at Neuilly, Boudin sent him an affectionate letter, written on behalf of Monet and Gautier as well. Courbet was painting still-lifes to pass the time, and in reply sent Boudin a small canvas of *Red apples*. When Courbet died, Boudin wrote this letter to a friend:

Poverty holds quite a few painters in its grasp, but death takes its quota too. Mathieu had hardly been laid to rest beneath the roses in the little cemetery at Bois-Le-Roy, when Courbet died in exile, practically abandoned by his friends, and suffering from the most profound sadness. The first news we heard on New Year's Day was that he had died. There are some people to whom one is drawn by an inexplicable affinity. There are some natures which more or less subjugate one. Courbet was one of these people.

Although we were never very intimate friends, I loved his character, so strong, yet at the same time so naïve, which had struck me even at our first meeting twenty years ago when I was still receiving a grant from Le Havre. [One of the frequent chronological errors in Boudin's letters. His grant had expired in 1854, four years before he met Courbet.]

His death caused me very deep sorrow, particularly since at my age it is so difficult to make friendships involving both feeling and admiration. They are passing illusions which fade one by one and leave only the sad memory of vanished loved ones. Like several of his friends, I deeply regret never sending any sign of friendship to relieve his solitude, no remembrance of those who had not forgotten him. (12 January 1878.)

At the time of their first meeting Courbet had just begun his career as a seascapist with a series of studies of the Mediterranean painted at Palavas-les-Flots, Maguelonne and in the Camargue, and had finished works that were to be shown at the Exposition Universelle in 1867, among them *The Mediterranean at Maguelonne*. The strong, unsettled and passionate side of Courbet's nature had already been aroused by the attraction of the sea and the sky, but it was a very different matter when he was confronted with the sky at Honfleur; for all the strength of his art, he never succeeded in capturing the elusive subtlety and variety of its continual changes. The sturdy inland painter from the Franche-Comté despaired at his inability to seize the fugitive magic of these northern skies. It is understandable, therefore, that one day when confronted with Boudin's soft, repeatedly broken outline and sensitive calligraphic shorthand, Courbet, who was preoccupied with solid matter expressed in precise contours, and firm composition, should have exclaimed: 'Good Lord, Boudin, you must be an angel, certainly only you know what the sky is really like.'

Quite by chance I was lucky enough to find the exact page, torn out of a notebook written by Boudin in 1859, on which he described his meeting with Courbet:

16 June 1859. Courbet visited me. He liked everything he saw, at least I hope so. If I took him at his word, I would certainly consider myself to be one of the major talents of our era. He found my tone rather lacking in strength, and that, broadly speaking, is perhaps true. But he assured me that few people paint as well as I do.

18 June. Returned to Honfleur with Courbet. Spent a wonderful evening at the Dreuils' house with Courbet and Schanne. The noise there was absolutely deafening. Overheated brains were spinning, and reason was reeling. Courbet confided his beliefs to us, though not, of course, in a very lucid way. There were beautiful moments. We sang, wept and were so rowdy that dawn found us still glass in hand. We came back shouting and

Le Havre harbour, *c.* 1863–5

singing through the streets, which was certainly not very dignified, and slept in my poor dear parents' bed. This morning our heads were leaden, but we managed, nevertheless, to admire many of the beautiful things we saw, so much so, in fact, that I've decided to stay there this summer, if I can. Courbet has already given me some courage, and I shall try to do some paintings, working on a larger scale and paying more attention to tone. At last I am really committed to painting, and I must have courage.

We watched Courbet at work. He really is a vigorous man. His approach is broad, and perhaps I could adapt this to my own work, yet at the same time I find it very coarse, and his attention to detail, very summary and rather styleless. I feel that there is a truer and surer way to paint. And yet he taught me something. I must say, he has great strength of will, but also a certain stubbornness, born of his desire to make of this an eccentricity.

Obviously, Courbet's arrival raised Boudin's spirits, but the shrewd Norman in him was not dazzled by Courbet's admiration, nor by his compliments.

The meeting between Baudelaire and Boudin was not to lead to any close or lasting connection. Baudelaire does not mention Boudin in his correspondence, and Boudin's letters, published or unpublished, refer only once to Baudelaire:

So far I have met only Baudelaire, who wrote quite well of me in a review he was editing at the time, and which has recently ceased publication. (To Louis, 2 February 1861.)

Since Baudelaire often visited Honfleur, at least during that year, it is probable that he was able to meet Boudin again on several occasions, since Boudin too was spending a certain amount of time there. Baudelaire's *Salon de 1859* contains a lasting tribute to their meeting. In it Baudelaire devotes a page of warm, and often prophetic, praise to the painter of skies (see p. 32).

Baudelaire had just arrived in Honfleur, though he should have been there from the 10 June 1858 onwards. On 14 May he had written to Poulet-Malassis: 'When you receive this letter, I shall already be at my mother's house, where I shall be from the tenth of June onwards. Just 'Honfleur' will be sufficient for the address. The house stands on its own not in a street. But if you like add *chez Mme Aupick*.'

Baudelaire was detained in Paris, partly by his financial difficulties, but more particularly, this time, by the illness of his mistress Jeanne Duval; for he managed to visit Honfleur only for a few days in October. On 3 November 1858, he wrote to Poulet-Malassis: 'I am preparing my two new houses, one in the Rue Beautreillis and one in Honfleur. I have been to see the place; it is perched above the sea, and even the garden looks like a miniature stage set. Everything is calculated to amaze the eyes, and that is what I need.'

That was indeed exactly what he needed, for on 21 February 1859, he wrote to Sainte-Beuve: 'Here, thanks to the rest I have been taking, my fluency has returned.'

This was quite true, for among other things, Baudelaire published at this time *Le Goût du Néant*; *Le Possédé* (*Revue française*, 20 January 1859); Poe's *Eleonora* (*Revue française*, 20 March 1859); *Théophile Gautier* (*Artiste*, 19 March 1859); *Sisina*, *Le Voyage*, *L'Albatros* (*Revue française*, 10 August 1859); *La Chevelure* (*Revue française*, 20 May 1859); and the *Salon de 1859* (*Revue française*, 10 and 20 June, 1 and 20 July 1859). Among the many pages Baudelaire wrote in the first months of 1859 was an account of the Salon, and the page devoted to Boudin illustrates the penetrating understanding of one of the most gifted critics of art of all time.

The *Salon de 1859* first appeared in the *Revue française*. As Baudelaire wrote in a letter to Nadar: 'Before publishing my *Curiosités* [*Esthétiques*], I am writing a few more articles about painting (the last) and am now working on an account of the Salon without even seeing it. But I have got an official guide book. Apart from the effort required to identify the pictures, this is an excellent method, and one I recommend to you. One is always afraid of praising or condemning too strongly, and this is the way to achieve impartiality.'

Trouville beach, 1863

Admittedly, in a second letter to Nadar (16 May 1859), he added: 'Alas, I lied to you a little about the Salon, but only very slightly. I did visit it once to seek out any new talent, but found very little, and I can rely on my memory, aided by the guide book, to write about all the old or well-known names. This method, I repeat, is not a bad one, as one is quite sure of one's opinions.'

For a critic other than Baudelaire, this method would be of dubious validity, to say the least, but in any case he did not apply it to Boudin. In fact, apart from a few short visits to Paris the poet spent most of 1859 in Honfleur, and probably did more justice to Boudin than to any other painter in the Salon. He wrote less of his rather careful Salon exhibit than of his hundreds of improvised pastel studies of the sea and the sky: 'these studies, so quickly and so faithfully sketched from the elements in nature which are the most inconstant and elusive in form and colour: waves and clouds.' And these lines are strangely prophetic: 'I have no doubt that in time to come he will capture the magic of air and water in finished works as well as sketches.'

This passage by Baudelaire (reprinted in full on p. 231 of this book) was the first homage paid by a critic to Boudin's talent, and all the praise he was later to receive did nothing to diminish the pleasure it gave him.

That Baudelaire did in fact see the sketches in Honfleur is made clear in a letter written by Boudin:

I was living in my garret in the Rue de l'Homme-de-Bois, isolated from the world by thirty-six stairs, which was all my slender purse could afford.

Many famous men, now dead, came to visit me there... among them Courbet and Schaunard of *La Vie de Bohème*, and Baudelaire, who saw my pastel skies there. Mathieu read me his symphonies, Troyon spent many hours there and so did Français. Isabey was my neighbour and encouraged me, and the great Jongkind often visited, and left intoxicated with the view of the Seine estuary, with our intimate chats, and with our good old Norman cider.

Poor little garret, where I spent my penniless years. (Letter to M. Soudan de Pierrefitte, 25 October 1896.)

The events recalled in these excerpts occurred over a period of six or seven years, from 1859 to 1866, when he was spending his time in Le Havre, Honfleur, and, from 1862, Paris. These were the most difficult years of his life, and he was often overcome by poverty and discouragement, particularly in 1862. One winter, apparently, he burned his furniture for fuel, and he certainly wrote this letter to Gustave Mathieu from Honfleur on 27 January 1862:

This year I had once again resolved to go to Paris, to try to scrape by with the help of my friends there, including yourself. But the accounts I have heard of the situation in Paris at the moment alarm me, all the more so since I have no money in hand and would have to depend entirely on the all-too-occasional sale of my paintings.

I must admit that here I lose all desire to go on living. I really must find somewhere else. I am going to retreat to some remote part of the country round here, to concentrate on improving my style. I am sick of begging people to buy my work for such paltry sums, and have been forced to turn out formless daubs to suit the tastes of ignorant buyers. A painter's life is certainly a hard one.

Another letter, to his friend Martin, throws more light on his situation:

I don't think I should sell these pictures for less than 60 francs, because Lebas, a dealer in Le Havre, paid me that even when they had no mounts. But if I could get a hundred francs for the two of them it would probably be advisable to let them go, since times are hard and penury pressing. (To Martin, 30 June 1862.)

But Boudin was never discouraged for long. Fundamental to his character were unshakable perseverence, patient resistance, and a sort of 'adventurous equability', qualities which may seem contradictory, but which are the only ones which can describe accurately the character of Eugène Boudin the archetypal *Honfleurais*.

Poverty and solitude, however, were not Boudin's only company during this period, for the artists' meetings at Saint-Siméon took place at this time and were to be among the milestones in the history of nineteenth-century French painting.

Just as the painters of Barbizon and Fontainebleau have been labelled 'schools', so the artists of Honfleur could be grouped together, except for the fact that the interest and charm of their meetings on the Côte de Grâce were enhanced by a variety of styles and approaches representing both the present and future of painting.

At this time Saint-Siméon was just a group of farm buildings, belonging to Mme Toutain, half way along the Côte de Grâce, sheltered and half hidden among the grass and trees. Even now, the view is one of the most peaceful and unspoilt imaginable: the sandy estuary of the Seine bordered with trees that stretch right down to the water's edge. This was the time when artists were discovering the picturesque aspects of France, when Etretat and Deauville were soon to be 'invented', and when an extraordinary number of painters were attracted by the grace and charm of the French countryside.

On 6 August 1864, Johan Barthold Jongkind wrote to Boudin: 'In my opinion, Honfleur is an admirable place in which to live and work.' And Boudin later wrote in a letter to Soudan de Pierrefitte:

> One could make a beautiful legend out of the inn at Saint-Siméon. So many famous people went there after I had discovered it. I took Français there one day with Gustave Mathieu, my old friend the poet, who afterwards spent a long time there with his friend [Amédée] Achard. The master of the masters: Harpignies. Old Achard couldn't paint the sky, so claimed it did not exist. On another occasion, I took Troyon and Van Marek there to drink cider. They are both dead now: Troyon tragically early, and then Van Marek, his pupil, though he had time to benefit from Troyon's development. I nearly forgot to mention Claude Monet, my pupil.
>
> Diaz and I played many a game of skittles there. He's still going strong, and aimed with an energy that made short work of the skittles and usually won him the game. There's another great man for you.
>
> Many other less famous painters visited Saint-Siméon: Amand Gautier, Ménard, Rémy and Mathon, not to mention the most recent like André Gill and dear [Adolphe-Félix] Cals.

On 21 August 1858 Boudin had received the following letter from A. Dubourg, a painter who deserves to be better known:

'*My dear friend,*

'I was walking between Villerville and Trouville when I came across the most wonderful stretch of country, slightly back from the coast. I am quite sure you don't know of it. Some parts are absolutely admirable, wild and hilly like Salvator Rosa's landscapes, others stretch smoothly for twenty miles down to the sea. Do come with me next time I go there, to see the countryside where Daubigny spent the summer. He has just left, and must have had a fair number of paintings to take back: apparently he did a great deal of work here.'

Other painters, unmentioned by Boudin, who stayed there included Jongkind, Courbet, who produced two beautiful works there, Paul Huet, Jules Dupré, Camille Flers, Charles-François Daubigny, Ernest Duez, Nicolas Charlet, Butin, Dantan, Renouf, Levillain, Defaux, Fischer and Bagaluboff.

Perhaps no other corner of France has sheltered so many painters, and the tradition continues, and will do so as long as there are landscape painters who can respond to the richness and delicacy of nature, the subtlety of the sky, and the particular atmosphere of a landscape close to the sea.

From 1859 onwards, it was at Saint-Siméon that Boudin added steadily to what Baudelaire called 'his collection of skies', though at the same time the works and theories of masters like Isabey, Courbet, Troyon and Daubigny certainly had some effect on his formation, and on the free expression of his own nature. All this time his young friend Monet was clamouring for Boudin to join him in Paris; Monet had managed to persuade his parents to prolong his stay, and eventually to allow him to live there permanently. He sent his impressions of the Salon to Boudin in a letter dated 3 June 1859, and added shrewdly: 'I would add that there is a total lack of

Breton festival, *c.* 1864

marine painters, and it's up to you to set off on the road which will lead you far.'

On 20 February 1860 he wrote: 'Do come, you can't fail to do well. You know that Jongkind is dead as an artist; he has gone completely mad, and he was the only great marine painter we had. All the artists are contributing to a fund that's been set up to care for him. His place is empty and you could fill it.... Every day I see our good friend Gustave Mathieu, who sends his kindest regards, and so does Amand Gautier. They are all very worried about you, and feel that dirty old Le Havre will have a stultifying effect on your painting.'

He wrote to Boudin again on 20 April 1860: 'Do come, I would be so happy to see you and to ask some advice about my work.'

These letters show how persistently Boudin's young pupil urged him to go to Paris, and how highly he rated him, even after seeing the works of the great painters of the day.

Study for the painting 'Breton festival,' 1864

Trouville: the Le Havre packet sails from the Quai de Joinville, 1880.
Photo Neurdein, Bibliothèque Nationale, Cabinet des estampes

Jean-Baptiste Camille Corot (1796–1875)

Bordeaux: the quayside, c. 1875. Photo M. Sirot

Johan Barthold Jongkind (1819–91)

Le Havre: three-master with tug, the semaphore and the pier. Photo M. Sirot

Charles Daubigny (1817–78)

Gustave Courbet (1819–77)

Théodule Ribot (1823–91)

Eugène Boudin in 1874. Photo F. Mulnier, Paris

Boudin moves to Paris · Works for Troyon
Corot, Courbet and Ribot · Sale at Caen · Jongkind
Marriage · He sketches Deauville beach society
Visits Brittany · Opinion of Claude Monet
Le Havre exhibition

Study of figures, 1865

Chapter 2 1861-1870

At times despair and the poverty that weighed him down seemed to overwhelm Boudin, who was still groping tentatively in his search for a style, and was still in the grip of poverty. His notebooks provide ample proof of this:

15 January 1860. Restarted work on my picture [the *Pilgrimage*]; more heartbreak. I shall have to repaint it completely, but poverty is pressing.

5 March 1860. Great deal of difficulty in squeezing a miserable 500 francs out of the town council for my *Pilgrimage*.

15 December 1860, Honfleur. I must be very dejected. As I walk through the streets I am sometimes shaken by a despair that brings tears to my eyes. And yet we have just spent days filled with anguish down there in our 'castle,' but it's not all over yet: I shall have to settle it all so that I can leave. Leave, but even then, what will happen to me down there? Perhaps I shall find a few kindly souls who will help me to live, to put a little hope back into my heart and cure me of this terrible disease of discouragement that has taken root in me.

He was still hesitant about facing the struggle of Parisian life and leaving the countryside to which he was attached by stronger bonds than memory. His friends in Paris, however, were urging him to join them, among them the sculptor Jules Bonnafé:

'*My dear Boudin*,

'I was glad to receive your letter. Since then I have been to see old Aubourg, who thinks as highly of you as I do. He does not know of any empty studios at the moment, but advises you to come, and to take any sort of room for the first few days. He says that Troyon would be only too happy to let you use his studio. So do come, and you'll see that things will go well. In a short time you'll have no difficulty in finding a studio.

'Do come, my dear Boudin, leave that hellish hole of a town, inhabited only by idiots: your place is here.

'Bring all the canvases and sketches you possess, and come soon.'

Encouraged in this way, Boudin at last decided to go to live in Paris, at 66 Rue Pigalle. He started a way of life that he was to continue until his death, living in Paris during the winter months only, then hurrying off to the coast of Normandy, Brittany or Holland, or to the South, so that he managed to keep his vision perpetually fresh far from the unrest of Paris and the professional cliques which he always warily avoided.

After all sorts of trials, I have at last managed, after a fashion, to set up my studio, and furnished with my two chests and a borrowed easel it doesn't look too bad. From my window I can see the windmills on top of the Butte de Montmartre.

I never go out at all, except to see the pictures in the auction rooms by painters who interest me. I can see that times will be rather hard at first, but with a bit of courage, I feel hopeful that I can overcome all that, and take my place in the sun like so many others, and do my little bit of gold-digging....

I can't tell you very much about what is going on in the art world. So far I have only seen Troyon and some exhibitions which confirmed my belief that I know more about painting than many of the artists who are in fashion now, but that my work lacks a little of this and that, particularly of breadth and boldness. (To Louis, 2 February 1861.)

The most difficult part of his life in Paris was at the beginning. If the present was hardly encouraging, the future held little reassurance. Boudin was thirty-seven, and this time he arrived in Paris no longer, as ten years previously, provided for by a pension, however small, but depending entirely on his painting for a living, and scarcely any better known in the dealers' world that he had been on his first stay. As he wrote to his friend Martin:

I have had to go out to search for dealers, the brokers of painting (for they exist in art just as in other trades), and found it all far from reassuring. In fact I was dumbfounded. Just imagine my position. One man would say, 'Your painting is too artistic, you must find a way of appealing to the buying public,' another: 'I don't want even to hear the word "painting." I've squandered forty thousand francs in two years on you artists.' And another would exclaim: 'Oh, that's beautiful, but first of all you need to have had a successful exhibition. (To Martin, 20 February 1861.)

That is the fate reserved to beginners, particularly when they have some definite personality of their own, but Boudin was no longer a young man. Nevertheless, his basic gaiety, reinforced by the high spirits of his 'little companion', as he called the girl with whom he now lived, Marianne Guédès, shone through in spite of all, and he finished his letter in this way:

After all that, let it be shouted aloud that Paris is a marvellous place, and that Boudin sparkles brilliantly there; that the city could not survive without him, and that at last the great marine painter has appeared whose arrival was heralded for so long like that of a comet. Amen. (To Martin, 20 February 1861.)

However modest his requirements, this new beginning was to prove difficult. He was already nearly forty years old, and had a very precise idea of his own worth. He just managed to scrape by.

By dint of scratching out and 'wasting more than forty francs worth of paint' [Marianne speaking], I have at last managed some brightness and light, and, thanks to some buyers, have actually sold half a dozen small pictures which have restored a few coppers to our long-empty purse, and some hope to the heart of the painter, which had long been discouraged, though he was loath to admit it. (To Louis, 12 April 1861.)

He was to find moral and financial help from one of the most admired painters of the day, who had been one of the first to appreciate his rare qualities. This was Troyon, who ten years previously had warmly supported him in a letter to the municipal council of Le Havre.

At this time Troyon was at the peak of his talent and his fortune. He had just exhibited the *Departure for market*, and the *Return to the farm* of 1859, now in the Louvre. He could no longer keep up with the commissions that flooded in; he exhibited everywhere, in Bordeaux, Antwerp, Brussels and The Hague, and everywhere his pictures were given pride of place. But in 1861, at the time when Boudin met him again, the painter's hand was weakening, his vision was losing its delicacy, and decadence was setting in. Yet he continued to work indefatigably, perhaps even too much so, since slaving over the easel resulted in a mechanical touch and encouraged a slickness which is obvious today in many of his works, and which was already regretted by Baudelaire. Troyon went too far in putting into practice his dictum: 'There is no such thing as chance in painting,' and often his unparalleled skill would have been well replaced by sincere spontaneity. In 1860 we find Monet telling Boudin that Troyon's works 'just don't bear comparison' with those of Delacroix, Decamps, Rousseau and Dupré which were hung next to them at the Salon.

But Boudin, at any rate, benefited from Troyon's overproduction.

In spite of my poverty, which I hide carefully, I had a charming welcome from my fellow painters: Troyon, for instance, in spite of the work which leaves him scarcely the time to see and eat, urged me to bring my attempts to him so that he could add the highlights and patches of colour that the public demands. I must admit that to crown it all I'm not on a pitch with all those fellows, and that I must learn to howl with the pack. (To Martin, 20 February 1861.)

But Troyon did not stop at retouching and advising, he saw too what he could get out of Boudin. Two months later, on 12 April, Boudin notified his brother of a turn of events to his financial benefit: he was stretching Troyon's large compositions for him, and often painting in the entire sky.

Last week I visited Troyon, who hardly has time to do any painting, because he's so upset and busy trying to help his unfortunate fellow painters, who pester him to correct their mistakes and help them earn a subsistence. He suggested something to me this week and I really do wish he'd thought of it earlier – he would have saved me many a cold sweat and agony of depression. Anyway, I'm even more delighted with this

Walking on Trouville beach, *c.* 1864

windfall since it will ensure me a day's work, and also because working on large canvases will relax my hand. I will prepare the pictures using his preliminary sketches, and he will add the finishing touches. Don't say anything about this to Casinelli [a painter in Le Havre of Boudin's generation; a few pictures exist which are signed by both of them], nor to Couveley, for people are all too ready to slander those who accept help. Teaching is impossible in the provinces, since one has neither the advantage of the masters' presence, nor of their example; quite apart from the fact that, here, excellent men – like Corot, the wisest of all – take pleasure in visiting even the humblest; and even Troyon, after acquiring skill and fame, has realized rather late that one must help one's fellow painters, and that that is really the triumph of talent, and the only real enjoyment it can bring. (To Louis, 12 April 1861.)

This passage shows clearly Boudin's insight, for he was neither deceived nor dazzled by Troyon's reputation and wealth. He retained his independence of thought, yet was able to assess Troyon's virtues just as accurately as his weaknesses. His moral and material position in 1861 is apparent in another letter to his brother which shows both his obstinacy and his scruples, and at the same time the lucidity and the scrupulous fairness, both to himself and to others, of which his letters provide continual evidence.

My day doesn't actually begin at dawn because I haven't yet been able to force myself to that extreme, but I do get up as early as I possibly can, and, apart from half an hour for supper, I keep my palette in hand all day. I can assure you that by the evening I've only enough courage left for a stroll on the Boulevard to stretch my limbs and take a little air before bedtime. All this is an effort to make up for lost time. I've already told you about the terrible mental state I was in for two months, though now that I'm back to my normal self I can laugh about it. But just imagine a budding writer arriving from the provinces with his little notebooks and being confronted by M. Hugo with his coloured verse, or M. Lamartine with his massive lungs. Think of this poet, frightened by so much colour, by so many bold images and such skill, hurriedly hiding his little jottings, or if forced by necessity and rage, sharpening up his miserable quill and throwing all his energy into his poetry. I was rather like this, terrified by all the difficulties, without stopping to consider that I too would one day achieve my little corner of perfection, which would in turn frighten the next generation. At last all that is over; I still go to see what the others are doing, out of curiosity, and also to benefit from the good in their work, for perfection is a collective achievement: without X, Y would never have reached perfection. You see old troupers like Jules Dupré, who were among the first in the arena, worrying about the progress their pupils are making, and ending up imitating them....

You ask me to define my position, which is rather difficult to do, particularly since the unforeseen plays its part in it. I've been working for Troyon for about a week, and he gave me a 100-franc note. With Mathieu's help I've also sold a few small seascapes, and at the moment I'm finishing off all the works I had started so that I can sell them all off to some dealer for a very modest sum. You can imagine that I shall have to wind up everything here and put something aside for my journey. I had undertaken to do some pictures for 75 francs a dozen, and I shall be forced to carry out the agreement. It certainly is very tiresome, but it won't take long, and it is a good opening. As you can see, all this doesn't quite add up to a hundred thousand francs a year, but nevertheless it's quite something to have found an honest solution, for the beginnings in this profession are difficult. And then I can't really grumble since I haven't yet produced anything worthwhile. (To Louis, 3 May 1861.)

Life in Paris could not satisfy Boudin for long when what he really needed was to be face to face with nature again and to put to good use the teaching and advice that had been showered on him from left and right, at sales and exhibitions, or during conversations with writers or painters. He had often chatted to friends like Mathieu, and he often saw Champfleury, at whose house he was to meet Baudelaire again, though he could equally well have met him at Courbet's. He had also met Théodule Ribot, who had exhibited for the first time that year. Any one of these could have confirmed Troyon's advice. Boudin had become bolder, or perhaps all these meetings had given him courage; at any rate he had the basic obstinate indolence of the citizens of Honfleur. He disliked seeking recommendations or advice, and was better at beginning canvases afresh than at paying visits.

He did meet Corot, however. The great painter was at last achieving fame, and had just exhibited the wonderful landscape with figures which is now known as *La Toilette* (1859). It was ten years since Corot had begun his beautiful series of landscapes with nymphs. He was then sixty-five years old and was beginning to sell. Besides, Napoleon III had overruled the uncomprehending animosity of Nieuwerkerke, the superintendent of the Beaux-Arts, by buying *Souvenir of Marcoussis* (1855), so that Corot, in his good natured, mocking way, knew of the incompetence with which talent is bound to clash, and of the patience needed for the painful undertaking of self-realization.

Besides, the old man knew the countryside that was dear to Boudin. At the time when Boudin was born, the young Camille Corot was painting his first landscapes in the countryside round Rouen, in 1824. A little later, in 1830, he painted Honfleur, and then in 1834 the harbour at Rouen. In spite of his fame, age and long struggle, he was sensitive to the delicate qualities of a painter who loved the sky and air with a similar fervour. Looking at Boudin's pastels, water-colours and rough sketches, Corot could not remain unmoved; for it was he who had said of cloud: 'You must caress it like a woman's shoulder.'

Boudin, however, tore himself away from a situation that looked as if it could be profitable to him, and returned to the shore he loved. He spent the winter of 1861–2 living in Honfleur itself, in the garret in the Rue de l'Homme-de-Bois. He wanted to return to Paris and inquired of Troyon if there was any work he could do there:

On Deauville beach, 1864

Monsieur Troyon, Honfleur, 20 January 1862

I did not have the pleasure of seeing you this summer, although the Michaud ladies often announced your visit. Couveley tells me you found Villers a charming place from the picturesque point of view, but it seems on the other hand that it has had an unfortunate effect on your health. The sea coast obviously does not suit your constitution.

You were kind enough to ask after me, and I thank you sincerely. I would not like to bore you with a description of my misfortunes in the midst of my indifferent fellow-citizens. I would like very much indeed to spend some months of this year in Paris, so as not to lose the few contacts I made last year, but everyone is unanimous in painting such a sombre picture of the situation there that I am hesitating before leaving, in spite of the precarious state of my poor finances here.

I thought that if I could be useful to you, if your work would allow you to employ me to do some rough sketches, even if only for a short time, this assurance of a period of work would enable me to look around for some other source of income.

If you would be kind enough to let me have two lines in reply, I could make my arrangements a little in advance, if you can make use of my hands for any sort of work.

Yours very sincerely, *E. Boudin.*

But Troyon, though full of sympathy and kindness towards the unfortunate painter, did not encourage him to go to Paris.

'My dear Boudin, Paris, 29 January 1862.

'I am terribly sorry not to be able to encourage you to come to Paris at the moment. As you say in your letter, the situation here is difficult, and the artists generally are dissatisfied. As for me, at the present moment I have nothing on hand that you could help me with. I do not want at all to dissuade you from your purpose. I just give you my advice: think carefully. The poor young folks have some reason to complain. Do rest assured that I will always do all I can to be of help to you.' *'Troyon.'*

And Boudin resigned himself to not going to Paris that year. That there were still difficult moments is shown not only by the letter to Mathieu quoted above, but also the one that follows, which is not lacking in beauty and picturesqueness despite its sombre tone. In June 1862, after several visits to Trouville, which was already beginning to be very

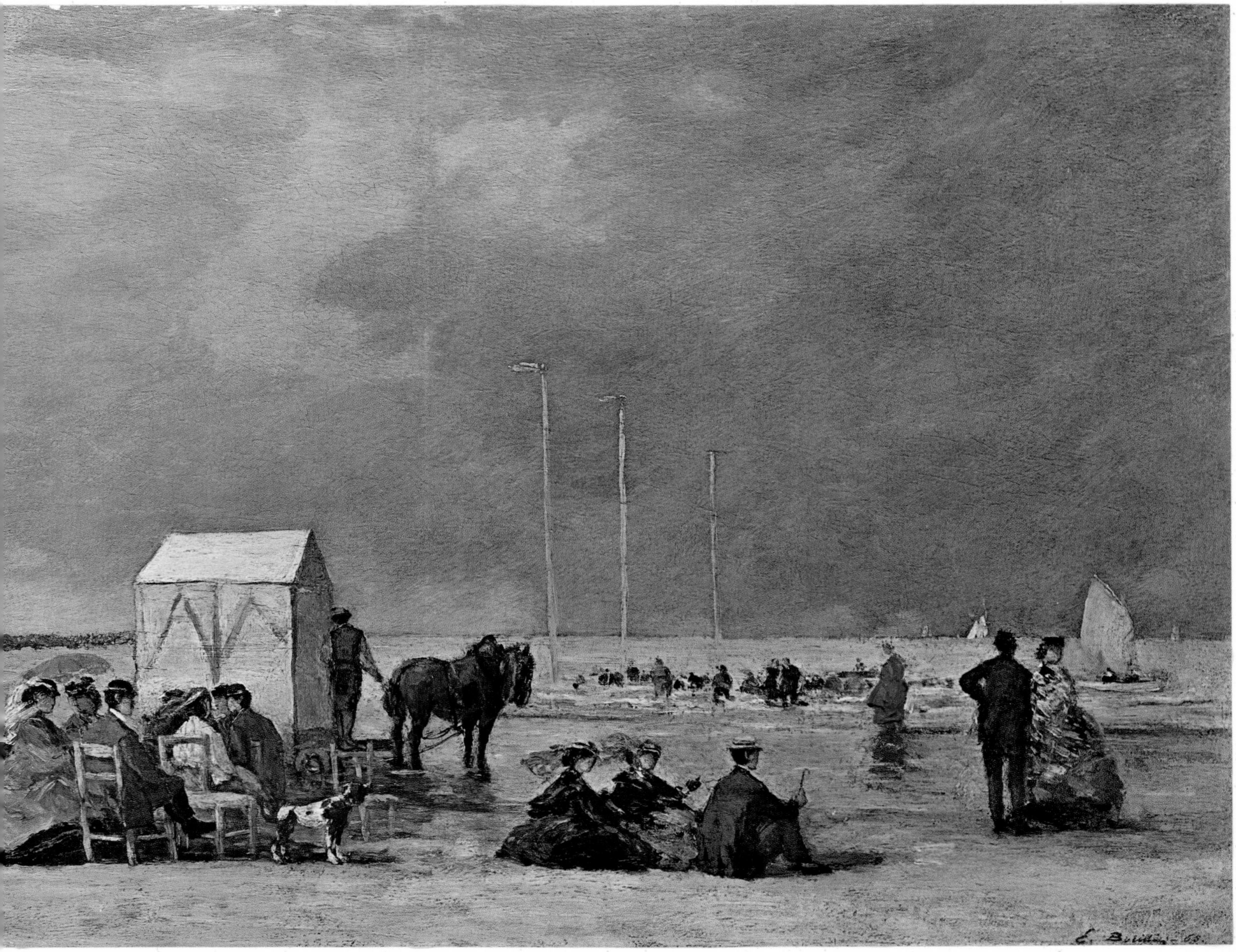

Bathing time on Deauville beach, 1865

popular, he and Dubourg tried to organize a sale of their work at Caen. He wrote this letter from Caen itself on 26 June 1862, immediately after the sale, to his friend Martin:

My dear old friend,

You made me promise to send you news of the result of our enterprise. Since I have a half hour of security left, and my legs are too weary to support me, I shall narrate our odyssey to you in a few words that will calm my thoughts.

I could sum it all up in two words. It was a complete fiasco, but so complete that there wasn't even a battle, for lack of combatants. Dubourg and I had come here last week with our canvases, and after spending an entire week in preparations and conferences with the president of the Société des Beaux-Arts, they finally lent us a hall usually reserved for learned meetings. This hall, though quite beautiful, did not bring us luck, but I doubt whether we would have had more success in the catacombs of the auction rooms. Finally, worn out by tiredness and lack of money, we had returned to spend two days in solitude, and had decided that I (certainly as the braver of the two) should return to face the sale and rake in the 'proceeds.' Well, at exactly eleven o'clock, an hour before the sale, I was at the auctioneer's giving him our last instructions. During this fatal hour, which was followed by one yet more fatal, I sat not far from our stall to keep an eye on it. The clock struck twelve, I redoubled my attention and craned my neck to see around me. The whole place was deserted. The sun was beating down on the square, and I felt as if I were in the middle of the Sahara. That was a terrible moment for me. And still the doorway, through which all the art lovers should have been streaming, remained empty. One shamefaced visitor did come in, then the auctioneer and his assistants, until there were six people in the room. When I saw the agonizing state of our poor sale, I went up to the auctioneer, in rather a temper, and asked him to stop the proceedings. A few bidders offered prices that barely covered the price of the frames, and perhaps even less. I started to take down the pictures. A few people strolled in at about four o'clock, looking for bargains, and after that silence reigned again. I forgot to eat all day, and was sorely tempted by the waters of the Orne. (To Martin, 26 June 1862.)

It was at about this time that Boudin met a man he had long admired, an expansive, warm and friendly character who gave proof, on many occasions, of his sincere affection, a painter whose influence on him was to be greater than that of Daubigny or Troyon,

Cover of catalogue of Caen sale, 1862

TABLEAUX MODERNES.

EXPOSITION & VENTE

DE

40 TABLEAUX

ET DESSINS.

EXPOSITION PUBLIQUE

AU PAVILLON

Les Dimanche 22 et Lundi 23 Juin 1862, de midi à quatre heures.

VENTE PUBLIQUE

Dans la salle de l'exposition

Le Mardi 24 Juin 1862, à midi précis

Par le ministère de Me MAINFROY, Commissaire-Priseur.

CAEN

1862.

List of Boudin's works in Caen sale, 1862

TABLEAUX.

E. BOUDIN.

1. — Nature morte. — Homard.
2. — D°. — Huîtres.
3. — Fleurs et Fruits.
4. — Fleurs et Fruits.
5. — Paysage. — Le berger.
6. — Paysage. — Effet d'automne.
7. — Le Pardon de sainte Anne-la-Palue.
(Esquisse du Tableau acquis par le musée du Havre.)
8. — Pardon dans le Finistère.
9. — Buveurs de cidre.
10. — Marché à Honfleur.
11. — Marine. — Jetée d'Honfleur.
12. — Marine. — Port d'Honfleur.

Trouville beach, 1865

and who was to show him the way to a greater freedom: Johan Barthold Jongkind.

Reference will be made later to Jongkind's influence on Boudin and to their artistic affinities. At a time when Boudin, discouraged by material difficulties, had need at least of artistic certitude, his friendship with Jongkind came as a precious gift.

Jongkind was an old pupil of Isabey's, and had been to Trouville a few times to visit his master, and then spent part of the summer and autumn of that year in Le Havre. He executed a whole series of studies at Sainte-Adresse.

One morning Monet was on a farm near Phares-de-La-Hève, sketching a cow which would not stay still for one minute. An Englishman who was passing by and whose interest was aroused by the scene, came to hold the model still, started a conversation with Monet and asked him if a painter called Jongkind had any talent. Monet had already admired several of the artist's pictures and watercolours, and assured the Englishman that Jongkind had indeed great talent. The next day Monet was doubly pleased to hear of the presence of Jongkind in Le Havre. The Englishman invited both of them to dine with him. It was through Monet that Boudin was to meet Jongkind several days later. The two marine painters were quick to recognize each other's talents. Boudin wrote the great Dutchman a letter, now unfortunately lost, to which he replied on 3 December 1862; 'I will tell you that I consider your letter to be an article full of poetry and reverie.' All the passion and the ingenuous, grave sensitivity of Jongkind, whose spiritual qualities have not to this day been explored, are apparent in the final words of this letter to Boudin: 'I desire that you should find peace in painting out of love.'

Boudin continued to work patiently in Honfleur, trying in solitude to vanquish his worries.

Apart from this I feel that one cannot paint all on one's own, and Paris is beginning to attract me. (To Martin, 9 December 1862.)

In answer to Boudin's requests, his friend Bonnafé again urged him to return to Paris (26 December 1862):

'You wrote of your wish to return here. You know the gospel I've always preached – Paris is the place to temper one's talent.

'The other day I saw Isabey the jack-in-a-box. I told him I had news of you and that you were coming. At that he started to gesticulate like a Punch and Judy show and said that you were mistaken to consider Paris. I would not have confidence in that acrobat, my dear Boudin. Gather your confidence together, take courage, and you will succeed, because you have in you the necessary qualities for success. Don't let yourself become dull in Trouville, but come here.'

In January 1863 Boudin married, though this did not change his life to any great extent. He married the 'companion' he had mentioned in his letters since 1860. Marianne (or Marie-Anne) Guédès was a neatly built and highly organized Breton girl who made his life calm and sweet. The quiet serenity of her uncomplex nature added to Boudin's patient perseverence. They lived side by side, released from social and worldly cares, in continual concord. Their life was sometimes difficult, but without great upheavals. (Marianne's capital amounted to 2,100 francs, left to her in 1862.)

The letter in which he writes of his impending marriage shows the basic kindliness and bluntness of this Norman sailor's son.

You have made a very praiseworthy effort to reconcile your friends with the moral code, and to put them straight as regards society. As soon as my conscience is stilled, the relatives satisfied, and my friends happy, I would like to send the bridal pair away, to prevent people complimenting them, etc.... but I'm afraid that our good families will decide that a ceremony with the mayor has not made us *sufficiently married*, and that they will plague us to be married by the priest. That's a ceremony I would dearly love to avoid, since I'm not very devout and dislike the idea of banns and everything that smacks of ceremony. It's like going to pay for your trading-licence, but the tiresome thing is the dressing up needed, the gloves and what not. We old sinners can be forgiven much, but we also have much to hide. (To Martin, 31 December 1862.)

In January 1863 Boudin returned to settle in Paris, at 27 Avenue Trudaine, 'in a marvellous new house as high as the tower of Cordouan' (as he wrote to his brother on 1 February 1863), at the end of the garden of Troyon's house. Boudin was still working for him, managing to live on this work and a few sales.

He wrote to Martin:

You can have no idea how disastrous the situation in the art world is. The big names have only the heartbreak of seeing their work sold at 50 or 60 per cent. reductions, but the martyrs can't sell for anything at all. Some of them, like [Jean-Louis] Hamon who was praised so highly by the newspapers, are resolutely

Quays at Trouville, *c.* 1865

painting plates. [François] Bonvin, who welcomed Whistler's *Piano lesson* into his studio after its refusal at the 1859 Salon, an excellent painter in Chardin's manner, and scarcely less of a painter, has been lucky enough to find a job as a clerk in a market at a rate of 1,500 francs, and is very happy about it. Some of them are colouring prints, good painters as well as hopeless ones. Jongkind, who has just left me, would have been in hospital by now had he not found a charitable soul to save him.... Just now poor Jongkind clasped my hand and said: 'I cannot do anything else, but have courage, dear Boudin,' and as he said that I saw tears swimming in his eyes. (To Martin, 12 February 1863.)

The hardship of his life in Paris, and then the death of his father in June 1863, brought about Boudin's return to Le Havre. He left to Jongkind's care a picture he was exhibiting at the Salon, *Honfleur harbour*. The official catalogue for 1863 does not mention Boudin's submission, but the phrasing of Jongkind's letter is unambiguous, and cannot refer to the Salon des Refusés. Jongkind wrote, 'I have seen your picture, it's quite well placed, and very good.'

In that same year the Salon des Refusés was held at the request of Napoleon III, and among those who exhibited were Antoine Vollon, Théodore Fantin-Latour, Edgar Manet, Camille Pissarro, Cals, Cazin, Jongkind, Harpignies and Whistler, that is, nearly all those whom Boudin was to appreciate most among the painters of his generation. It was in that year too that the Salons, which up till then had been biennial, became annual events.

Boudin left to spend the summer at Trouville. The previous year too the marine and landscape painter had tried his hand at portraying daily life.

A great number of elegant people were beginning to frequent Trouville, and were naturally disposed to welcome paintings depicting the colourful, picturesque excitement of the town: studies of the beach, the casinos, the regattas or the races.

And so Boudin executed a number of pencil sketches of groups of elegant women and fashionable people on the beach (see pp. 55-8, 69, 77, 197). The colours are indicated by watercolour washes, or simply by written notes.

These charming sketches form part of the same group as Boudin's studies of fishermen on the quaysides, or boats in the harbours, but apart from this they constitute as artistically valuable a documentation of the fashions of an epoch as those of Constantin Guys. It is regrettable that all these sketches have been scattered, since a choice of them would have composed a charming album of feminine fashion on the beaches during the heyday of the Second Empire.

He did not confine himself to jottings, nor to rough sketches, for these were only the preliminaries for large compositions, beach scenes as he called them. Among them are the great canvas *Trouville beach* (see p. 31), exhibited at the Salon of 1864; *Inauguration of Deauville Casino*, in which Mmes de Metternich, de Galliffet and de Pourtalès are portrayed; regatta scenes at Trouville, and the *Deauville races* (see p. 51).

They love my little ladies on the beach, and some people say that there's a thread of gold to exploit there. I am working on a regatta scene for the next exhibition. (To Martin, 12 February, 1863.)

If the large-scale compositions of this sort did not bring him the success he expected, at least the picturesque, and, one must admit, rather anecdotal side of these beach scenes did attract some buyers.

Our little business affairs continue to go well. I shall return with enough commissions to occupy part of the summer. (To Martin, 1 June 1864.)

And the winter of 1864 which he spent in Paris at 14 Rue Durantin, was less severe and more encouraging. Painters were coming to see his studies, and dealers were beginning to suspect the presence of an artist, and to scent possible business. Cadart was the first to realize the practical interest of Boudin's studies, and others in the art world followed his example. By March he could say:

Even the most exacting artists foretell a great future for me, and are convinced that I shall soon take my place among the big names of art. I myself feel a renewed eagerness to study and will make haste to oil my skates to chase the perfection I feel. (To Martin, 3 March 1864.)

Deauville races, 1866

It was not difficult for his admirers to fill his little atelier, since it was such a very tiny nook, so tiny, he would say jokingly, that his wife had had to do away with her crinoline. Some quite considerable painters bought his studies too. Among others, Troyon, whose condition worsened every day, asked Boudin to take him some pastel sketches to amuse him, and bought several of them.

In spite of these initial stages of success, he had no desire to settle in Paris for ever, and felt a persistent longing 'to struggle in front of the good Lord's adorable nature.' In his habitually precise and moderate way he wrote:

> The result of my stay will be to have, so to speak, fixed my style, cheered me up, and, above all, to have pushed me further ahead on the road I'm following and on which I have the satisfaction of being alone. (To Martin, 20 April 1864.)

And without pride, but with an exact idea of his value and of his place in the art of his time, he wrote to his brother:

> You have to push your wheelbarrow along despite the obstacles and the tiresome people who try to block your way. I can see that the courageous do gain ground, and that consoles me, but I can assure you I've got a long way to go before I can measure up to the strong painters, even to the second-rate ones. (To Louis, 1 February 1864.)

The summer of 1864 brought together on the Normandy coast three painters linked by an artistic affinity as well as by mutual friendship. While Boudin was continuing his beach scenes at Trouville, Jongkind was spending several weeks in Honfleur, and Monet too was in Honfleur, at Saint-Siméon where he was 'working furiously to improve a great deal before returning to Paris' (letter from Monet to Boudin).

During the next two years Boudin and Monet were to return at the same time as Courbet, who had been invited by the young Comte de Choiseul to stay in his house at Deauville. Courbet was then at the peak of his skill and his glory. His visits to Normandy, which were extremely productive, were of the greatest importance for him, for he absorbed himself in the contemplation of the sea he loved, and attracted the attention of the fashionable frequenters of the beach who paid honour to him either to annoy the government, or because his works had overcome their coldness, or for both reasons at the same time.

'I have received more than two thousand ladies in my studio', he said in 1866, 'all wanting to have their portraits done after seeing those of Princess Karoly and Mlle Aubé.... In one month I have painted thirty-five canvases, which astounded everybody, and bathed eighty times. Six days ago I was still bathing with the painter Whistler who is here with me. He is an Englishman and a pupil of mine.'

It was at this time, in 1866, that Courbet executed the admirable portrait of Whistler's pretty Irish mistress, known accordingly as *La Belle Irlandaise*, and now in the Nationalmuseet in Stockholm.

In 1864 Boudin did several preparatory sketches for etchings, but was able to carry out only a few of them. He had begun them the previous winter, before Troyon's departure for a mental home finally deprived Boudin of his financial support.

> I have had a distressing shock: poor Troyon who was so ill anyway has had an attack of madness. They had to take him to a mental home, and I have little hope of seing him again. Only last week I dined with him and his good old mother, who carries her age very gaily. He wanted then to see some of my pastel studies, and with a judgment that was still quite unimpaired chose some of them, which he paid for very generously. (To Louis, 22 April 1864.)

Boudin meeting with Courbet partly compensated for this loss. The frank and expansive friendship of the master of Ornans was of great help to those on whom it was bestowed. At Saint-Siméon or in Deauville, in the house of the Comte de Choiseul, or in the lovely countryside of the region, he held parties at which his exuberance communicated itself to all his guests, as did his creative energy to his fellow artists.

Crinolines on Trouville beach, 1865

Boudin returned to Paris towards the end of 1864, to settle in better conditions at 31 Rue Fontaine-Saint-Georges. His life became less of a struggle. His beach scenes continued to win him the approval of his admirers, who were also very impressed by his seascapes.

'Our little daubs are forging ahead very steadily,' he was to write to Martin in February 1865. He himself was well aware of his progress.

But this devil of a Paris is the only city where one can develop one's powers. At every step there are examples which spur one on to greater progress. In the course of several days I've been transforming myself and am becoming devilish energetic. (To Martin, 15 December 1864.)

He began seriously to establish his reputation, but as his success increased so did his scruples and his desire for perfection.

> I am tormented by the wish to give my painting the seal of perfection and expression so that I can display them in dealers' windows, without injuring my reputation too much, next to masterpieces by Corot, Jongkind, etc. (To Louis, 14 January 1865.)
>
> I am becoming more and more exacting, since they often hang my works between those of Corot, Daubigny or Jongkind and I have to cut an honest figure in such distinguished company. (To Louis, 25 March 1865.)

Boudin's contact widened, and his friendship with some of the masters became more intimate. Corot and Daubigny among others felt a great liking for him. Corot said to him: 'Boudin, you are the king of skies.' Daubigny could not help being interested in this painter of skies and lover of the open air, he whose shrewd judgment foresaw even at this date the importance of the efforts of Manet, Monet and Pissarro, and who was almost the only member of his generation to do so.

The loss of Troyon was a very great blow to Boudin. Not that Troyon's art could any longer be of much help to him in his own development, for Boudin was aware of his own nature and knew that he had to seek a quite different interpretation for themes that were often similar to Troyon's. But it was a grave financial loss for the improverished artist, for Troyon's commissions had now and then given him some financial security. It is true that the sums he received were never very great, for Troyon did not have a reputation for liberality; while recognizing his debt to him, Boudin could not hide the general feeling at the painter's death. As he put it to Martin:

> Did poor Troyon really need to work so furiously? He has been carried to his grave unlamented and unregretted. He could have been such a blessing to some people, without reducing his stack of money too much. Now it will all go to indifferent people who will be only too glad that his end was hastened since they receive his wealth. He never took time off to *live*. It is true that for the man who is productive, rest is hardly ever possible in the heat of work, but one should never allow that to degenerate into rapacity.

Other painters were to bring Boudin not only moral comfort, but also the support of dealers and private buyers. Among those who offered him unwavering friendship was Théodule Ribot, of whom Boudin wrote to his brother:

> One of the people who have been of most help and assistance to me is Ribot. He's a sensible fellow, which is rare, and makes no bones about giving me advice. Thanks to him I've persevered in following my own course of development in spite of warnings to the contrary by people who maintain that the things I wish to paint are unsuitable. (To Louis, April 1865.)

Boudin continued to benefit from the success of his 'little daubs,' as he called them, and sent two beach scenes to the Salon that year: *Concert in Deauville Casino* and *Trouville beach at bathing time.*

> I need a success at the Salon, but won't achieve it this year. I am not yet experienced enough in this manner of painting, since I only recently took it up, but next year I will no doubt make progress. (To Martin, 17 February 1865.)

In the meantime he was still amusing himself by engraving small views of Trouville. His output of watercolours was always limited, since it was not a particularly suitable medium for a painter concerned with impasto and surface, imbued with subtlety of tone, and watercolour was never more than an amusement for him, to be taken up from time to time.

All through the summer of 1865 he worked at Trouville in the company of Courbet and Whistler. Both of them were to be of great assistance to Boudin by virtue of their connections.

Whistler had been living in London since 1863, but it is likely that Boudin had known him since his arrival in Paris, for Whistler had known Courbet well since 1859, the year in which he was refused at the Salon.

When all three of them returned to Paris in the autumn, Courbet and Whistler continued to patronize

The Crinolines, *c.* 1865

Trouville pier, 1864

Bathing machines, 1866

On the beach, sunset, 1865

Boudin, and to find buyers for his little canvases. At that time he was considering larger-scale compositions, but was deterred by the expense involved.

I've seen how Courbet and the others dare to attack large canvases. How lucky they are. Young Monet has got one twenty feet long to cover. I am less ambitious, I'd just like to be able to undertake something larger than my tiny little canvases, but I have to consider bread, money and all the other unending little expenses. (To Louis, 20 December 1865.)

That winter the buyers' money was attracted to a sale which, as Boudin said, 'took half a million francs off the market': the sale of works from Troyon's studio. Nevertheless they all continued to scrape by. In his letters Boudin mentions Jongkind who was selling a little better, and Monet 'who is just finishing his enormous daub which is costing him every penny he has.' He himself continued his work patiently, lightening his style, and developing during these years towards the liberation he was to achieve in about 1871, when he perfected his first mature style and could at last be considered a really individual painter, although without his later subtlety of vision. Meanwhile, the insight that never failed him enabled him to recognize exactly what he lacked, to see his faults whilst still retaining his qualities of moral determination.

I must concentrate on eliminating a certain timidity which is still evident in my painting. (To Martin, 12 February 1866.)

They are beginning to recognize my work, thanks to the artists who are giving me disinterested support.... I am being asked to do a great number of seascapes, and although I would like to do other subjects I shall always be labelled as the painter of beaches. (To Louis, 29 November 1865.)

As far as my morale is concerned, I feel confident that it is quite high, the past has proved that. But if I had not been sustained by an intense love for the eternal nothings of the world – the sky, the water, the woods and the sight of this world in which so many have lived and in which they will continue for ever to live without ever really seeing it, then I think something would have cracked. (To Louis, 13 January 1866.)

Life continued monotonously, but more peacefully, for the painter. He had some bitter disappointments, like the use of an oil that ruined all the works he did in the winter of 1866, but they were compensated by the reception given to him by the dealers, who were opening their doors wider to him, thanks to his friends. Even the critics began to take some notice of him. Since Baudelaire's lines in 1859, no Salon reviewer had considered it necessary to devote even a paragraph to Boudin. The official critics were never concerned with anything other than official painting. It was not their business to discover genius or real talent, only to supply dogmatic justifications of the public's bad taste.

Ernest Chesneau, however, did take the trouble to go to Boudin's studio to see his studies. He devoted a few benevolent sentences to him in an article in *Le Constitutionnel* on the 1867 Exposition, and, by contrast with the silence of all the other critics, these do have a certain value.

Only Jules-Antoine Castagnary, whose name recurs continually in the course of French painting from 1860 to 1880, vouched for Boudin's real personality, in his habitually frank manner, and with his usual fighting spirit:

'M. Boudin is unique in his treatment of the marine, or to use Courbet's superior phrase, the seascape. He has made himself a charming little niche from which no one can dislodge him.'

This was the time when Fromentin and Courbet were at last commanding high prices, and when a pupil of Ribot, like Ferdinand Roybet, could already sell a canvas for 5,000 francs, when Meissonier and Alexandre Cabanel were triumphant. These were the days of the Second Empire, an age of splendour and insouciance, of an easy and improvident life that was to hasten the collapse of the régime. The peak of this was marked by the 1867 Exposition Universelle and even the painters were affected by this state of mind:

Painting seems to be going through a period of splendour because of the Universelle. The large dealers are monopolizing the big names in painting: painters like Courbet, Corot, Daubigny and others, so that those who can't affort to wave

Pavilion on Trouville beach, *c.* 1865

Groups of Breton peasants
Market scene in Brittany

thousand-franc notes around will be obliged to fall back on us, the pretenders to celebrity, who are content with hundred-franc notes. (To Louis, 8 December 1866.)

His reputation was growing, and that year the Société des Amis des Arts of Grenoble bought a picture from him, *Bathing time*.

The 1867 Exposition Universelle was a good measure of the insight of the juries, for a number of painters of merit were excluded, among them Monet, who had spent the winter in Honfleur, as this interesting letter (2 February 1867) from Dubourg in Honfleur to Boudin indicates:

'Monet is still here working on enormous canvases. They have remarkable qualities, but I find them inferior, or at any rate less happy, than the famous *Gown* which won him a success I can well understand, and which he deserved. He has one canvas three metres high and proportionally wide; the figures are slightly smaller than life-size, women, beautifully dressed, gathering flowers in a garden. He began it from nature in the open air. It has some good points, but the overall effect is rather obscured, no doubt through lack of contrast, for the colour is very vigorous. He has also started a large seascape, but it's still in its early stages and one can't judge it yet. He has done some quite successful snow scenes too. The poor fellow is very keen to know what's going on in the studios, and asks me every day if I have any news of you. It would give him great pleasure if you could let him have some information. He sends you his regards, and would like to know your news.'

Boudin was accepted at the Exposition, perhaps because the canvases he had submitted were not, in his own opinion, among his best works. The Exposition did not offer all they had hoped to some painters, the French section was shown in deplorable conditions, and, besides this, the rumours of war that were circulating limited the public demand for paintings. And so, in fact, Boudin had no news to give, except of his haste to leave Paris and see the sea again.

Every time we get a good strong gust of west wind, I think of the beautiful waves it whips up, and of the fine ships sailing full before the wind and carried into the harbour by it. This wind smells of the sea. (To Martin, 10 April 1867.)

Boudin's canvases were beginning to attract attention, and his name was even in the ballot for a medal, though he was not to receive one for many years. But there were no sales. The year which should have brought superb results for the painters, turned out to be one of the most disastrous. The excitement of the Exposition made Paris unbearable. Boudin made haste to finish off the work he had in hand, and left for Brittany on Monday 13 July 1867. He took a boat from Le Havre and left a documentation of this journey and visit, a little forty-two-page notebook, 13 × 10 cm, which he sent to his brother, and which provides a picturesque notation comparable with that of his painting.

That year he stayed in the manor of Kerhoan, near Le Faou in Finistère. The manor was in ruins and he found a huge room there, the only habitable one. He wrote:

Below is the farmer and above the storm which buffets the big fig trees planted perhaps by the Benedictines who built these granite walls. (To Louis, 21 July 1867.)

This visit was to reconcile him with Brittany, and this feeling is apparent in his canvases. He admired the countryside, and everything attracted him, the landscape, the picturesque cottages, the beaches and the rocks, the trees, the old interiors of the houses, the groups of people, the children playing in the doorways. 'What is lacking is the talent to make anything of it,' he remarked gloomily. The fact that Mme Boudin was herself a native of Brittany facilitated closer contact with the people, and with the countryside. They were invited to meals and to real peasant weddings. The pilgrimages renewed the impression he had felt on his first visit. He did sketch after sketch (see pp. 63-4, 69, 70), and wrote jokingly that he had almost as many aunts and uncles to visit as sketches to put in order.

E. Boudin

E. B

Harvest at Le Faou, *c.* 1871
Breton women at Plougastel, *c.* 1870

Whilst in Brittany he enjoyed above all a feeling of great calm and serenity, which put into perspective the effort and research he had done during his periods in Paris. Less disturbed, more sure of his means, and less obsessed by external agitations, he was at last to take full measure of himself, and achieve what will be referred to as his 'second mature style', which marks his first really personal expression. The following excerpt from a letter to his friend Martin illustrates his desire for a stronger synthesis, and his intention to eliminate the anecdotal to an even greater extent:

We finished our journey with a visit to Plougastel, where we stayed for a week. We saw some of the most marvellous pilgrimages imaginable.

I have a confession to make. When I came back to it the beach at Trouville, which I used to find so delightful, seemed nothing more than a frightful masquerade. One would have to be a near-genius to make anything of this troop of idle 'poseurs.' After spending a month among a breed of people doomed to the rough labour of the fields, to black bread and water, to see again this group of gilded parasites, with their haughty airs, makes me feel contempt and a degree of shame at painting such slothful idleness. Fortunately, dear friend, the Creator has spread a little of his splendid and warming light everywhere, and what I reproduce is not so much this world as the element that envelops it. But how much more beautiful Bihama is than these satin ladies, with her white calico skirt, her red and black bodice, and her long coif, as she wields her winnowing basket along the sea shore and the grain falls thick and pure on to the sail cloth. And those who thresh the rye and wheat, enveloped in a golden cloud of dust, and those who kneel in prayer on the granite flagstones of the church, stripped bare of chairs. (To Martin, 28 August 1867.)

This was not to be the last occasion he visited Trouville, but it was the last time he painted the groups of fashionable people on the beach. From now on he was to be concerned entirely with studies of the sky, of boats and of herds of animals. The infinite variety of light and air was to be his soul and endless theme. It was this study of changing light that from now on was to lead him from one coast to another, to Belgium, Holland, Brittany, to the Flemish or Picardy coasts, to Bordeaux, the South of France, or anywhere he could attempt to capture a new subtlety of the elusive sky. No matter how convinced he was of the truth of his own course of study, he observed, considered and listened not only to the works and advice of nature, but also the works and words of even the youngest of his contemporaries.

Rest assured that one can never arrive entirely by oneself, unless one's character is extremely strong, and even then.... One can't create completely alone, in some corner of the provinces, without criticism or the means of comparing one's progress, without resolute conviction. (To Louis, 20 April 1868.)

The moral and material support offered to him by some of his fellow painters at a sale of his works had confirmed the truth of this opinion. This first public sale in Paris took place on 25 March 1868, and this is how he described it:

They executed me yesterday, and now I am hastening to tell you of my quite considerable success, not in terms of money, as was foreseen by everyone, but a success of novelty and esteem among the painters and even the collectors. Three days ago Boudin did not exist, except for a few initiated individuals, now he has established himself and taken his place among those who have rights. The painters backed up the praise they expressed on the eve of the sale by pushing up the prices. Monet and his friends Jules Héreau, Amand Gautier, Charles Jacque, Veyrassat, Mouilleron, and several others whom I don't know so well, gave the signal and pushed along the collectors and dealers, the indifferent ones. Above all, the sale attracted a far larger attendance than I had expected.

In short, I hope that this will change my doubts into certitudes, and give me at last a firm footing on the slippery ground....

The little studies I did on the beach sold particularly well, much better relatively than the seascapes. The pastels, so rarely acceptable to the public, were nearly all carried off by the painters. (To Martin, 26 March 1868.)

I had thrown into the ring about a hundred drawings and varied studies, in front of one of the most surfeited and difficult to please of publics, and the artists. They all seemed to like it; they congratulated me heartily, and a few went so far as to cheer.

The collectors followed my friends' example, and even though the total profits were not vast, it is consoling to think that this represents a satisfactory beginning which establishes me in an unexpected, though rather tardy, way.

Another advantage of this confirmation of my painting will be to put an end to the hesitations that have beset me during the course of these long years of discouragement. A fortnight ago Martin sold one of my pictures in a public sale for forty-five francs, and he might now have got almost a hundred. It's true that Pereire has just let a Delacroix go for 76,000 francs that was sold by the painter many years ago for 1,500 francs. (To Louis, 28 March 1868.)

It was particularly just that from this time onwards he should have been appreciated by his fellow painters, since he himself showed a particularly judicious and shrewd mind concerning everyone else. Indeed, at this time, that is about 1868, it would be difficult to find such clear, courageous and penetrating judgments as those Boudin gave of Monet. It must be remembered that the earliest paintings by Monet which can be seen today date, with rare exceptions, from 1874. Seven or eight years later, in 1882, Monet was still exposed to all the lunacies of the critics, and he was termed an impressionist as an insult.

It was at the Salon of 1866 that Monet had exhibited the famous *Lady in green* which Edouard Manet's friends had mistaken for one of his works. In the 1867 Salon a canvas which Monet showed, entitled *Impression*, provoked many people to fury, and also brought about the invention of the word 'impressionism'. At that time Manet was thirty-five years old, and even he disapproved of the newcomer's efforts, and no less of Jongkind and Boudin. Manet's reputation, itself still an object of ridicule, dated from the uproar caused by his *Olympia* at the Salon of 1865, which had also drawn to him at the Café Guerbois the painters and writers who were ironically dubbed the School of Les Batignolles. This was the time, in 1867, that Manet, refused by the Salon, showed fifty of his works together in a shed on the Avenue de l'Alma. He was not to join with Monet and Renoir until about 1870.

This, too, was the time when Zola was obliged to leave the newspaper *L'Evénement*, in 1866, because in his Salon reviews he had had the audacity to defend Manet.

In 1866 Monet exhibited *Camille* and *The forest of Fontainebleau*; in 1868 *Ship leaving the quayside at Le Havre*. Daubigny had already recognized the young artist's qualities, but even painters like Corot cried out in horror in front of his revolutionary works.

Boudin, for his part, wrote:

Monet's two sketches interested me a great deal. I think your judgement was severe, my dear friend; only one thing upset me: the daring of the composition. (To Martin, 18 February 1868.)

I met Monet in the Salon. He has set an example to us all by his faith to his principles. One of his canvases has been exhibited, thus scandalizing a number of people; they are wrong, for this painting does display a praiseworthy research into *true tone* which everyone is beginning to value. (To Martin, 4 May 1868.)

Boudin was exaggerating when he added those last words, for more than twenty years were still to pass before the connoisseurs were prepared to recognize Monet as one of the leading painters of his time, and as one of the most inspired of French artists. Nevertheless, the incomprehension prevalent at the time makes Boudin's judgment all the more praiseworthy.

The painters whom he mentions in his letters at this time are not only Corot, Daubigny and Rousseau, who was soon to die, but also Courbet, Jongkind, Manet, Fantin-Latour, Monet and Puvis de Chavannes: in other words, all those who are most highly valued now. This seems quite logical nowadays, but the famous painters at that time were Alexandre Cabanel, Léon Gérôme and William Bouguereau; Roybet's tiresome glory was beginning, and Meissonier was triumphant.

Boudin persuaded Courbet, Manet and Monet to send canvases to the Exposition du Havre which took place in 1868.

Make sure that when the exhibition is mounted Courbet's pictures are not sacrificed to the idiotic contraptions they are sure to prefer. He would be furious with me if he had to suffer the same sort of surreptitious vexations in Le Havre as he had in Lille. I had to promise that he would be treated with a certain amount of deference. What can you expect? Whatever you say, he's an interesting figure. (To Martin, 15 June 1868.)

English ship at anchor, 1866

Gathering on the beach, 1865
Groups of strollers on the beach, 1869

Twenty-six silver medals were awarded at this Le Havre exhibition. Among those who received them were Amand Gautier, Yvon, Carolus-Duran and five others who really do credit to the jury's choice: Boudin, Courbet, Daubigny, Manet and Monet.

In the jury's report there is even this interesting appreciation:

'Another of the supplementary medals is allotted to Claude Monet. In his works some deliberate faults are redeemed by great precision of tone and undeniable sincerity of execution. It should be noted in passing that the feelings of the jury towards what, for the sake of convenience, is called the young school were very favourable. Their new aspirations and 'modern tendencies' have been amply rewarded in the realization of artistic problems. As well as this, the jury is openly in sympathy with a current that has made itself manifest in Le Havre in no uncertain manner, and therefore awards a silver medal to M. Courbet, whose *Horse by the sea* deserves a mention in this list of works.'

The work by Manet which received this distinction was the famous *Dead toreador*, that by Monet, *Fishing boats*, and that by Boudin *Trouville beach* (see p. 47).

Boudin paid another visit to Trouville that year, but the elegance of the summer visitors irritated him more and more, and he decided to go to Brittany for the summer.

> Trouville rather disgusted me and I am sick of circulating among those people. It's not that Brittany offers subjects for paintings of much greater interest, but I need a change from the sight of the population of Trouville, who really don't mean much to me. (To Martin, 15 June 1868.)

His work had been interrupted as a result of his wife's very delicate health, and he wrote about it in a very revealing passage:

> At the very moment I was about to set to work again I was held up by a latent worry which is going to cause me great pain. Keep this to yourself, for it does no good to expose one's weak points to the indifferent, or to people who have no need to know one's feelings. (To Martin, 11 May 1868.)

He left on 15 June, for a month in Brittany, first at L'Hôpital-Campoux near Daoulas in Finistère, then about four miles from there at Kerhoan, where he again took possession of the dilapidated little house he had stayed in the previous year. He wrote to his brother:

> I'm trying my hand near the church, where there's an old cross and all sorts of strange things of which seriously I hope to take advantage. (To Louis, 20 June 1868.)
>
> For two weeks I have been living like this under a burning sun, running to all the celebrations, weddings and pilgrimages I hear of. It's the only way to glean some good sketches. I've seen some marvellous things, feasts of colour that would bring on a fever. These pilgrimages, which do have a rather too religious side, are none the less dazzling reunions, the like of which one cannot see anywhere else. (To Martin, 7 July 1868.)

Unfortunately for Boudin, this stay could not be prolonged for more than a month. His meagre resources and the need to be near possible buyers brought him back to Trouville. The boredom he felt when in contact with the idle people of Trouville was well compensated for by the presence of Ribot. Twelve years had passed since the day when Ribot had first discovered Boudin in the little house on the Grand-Quai. Ribot had been awarded medals in the Salon in 1864 and 1865. He had done his series of *Cooks*, and of *Tinkers*, the portraits of *Cadart* and *Vollon*, his *St Sebastian*, *Christ and the doctors*, *Beggars on the corner* (now in the Musée de Rouen), *St Vincent*, and that year, in 1868, he exhibited *The Oyster and the litigants*. He was almost at the peak of his sincere, upright, and serious art, and after a lifetime of difficulties and struggles was at last achieving the true expression of his pure artistic conscience. The friendship which linked him to Boudin was to remain unbroken. Boudin was concerned with newer developments, and with the problems of painting in the open air, but all this did not lessen his admiration for the beautiful solemnity of Ribot's work, or for the nobility of his character.

This is only one of a thousand examples of Boudin's sound judgement. There is perhaps no better

E. Boudin
1865.

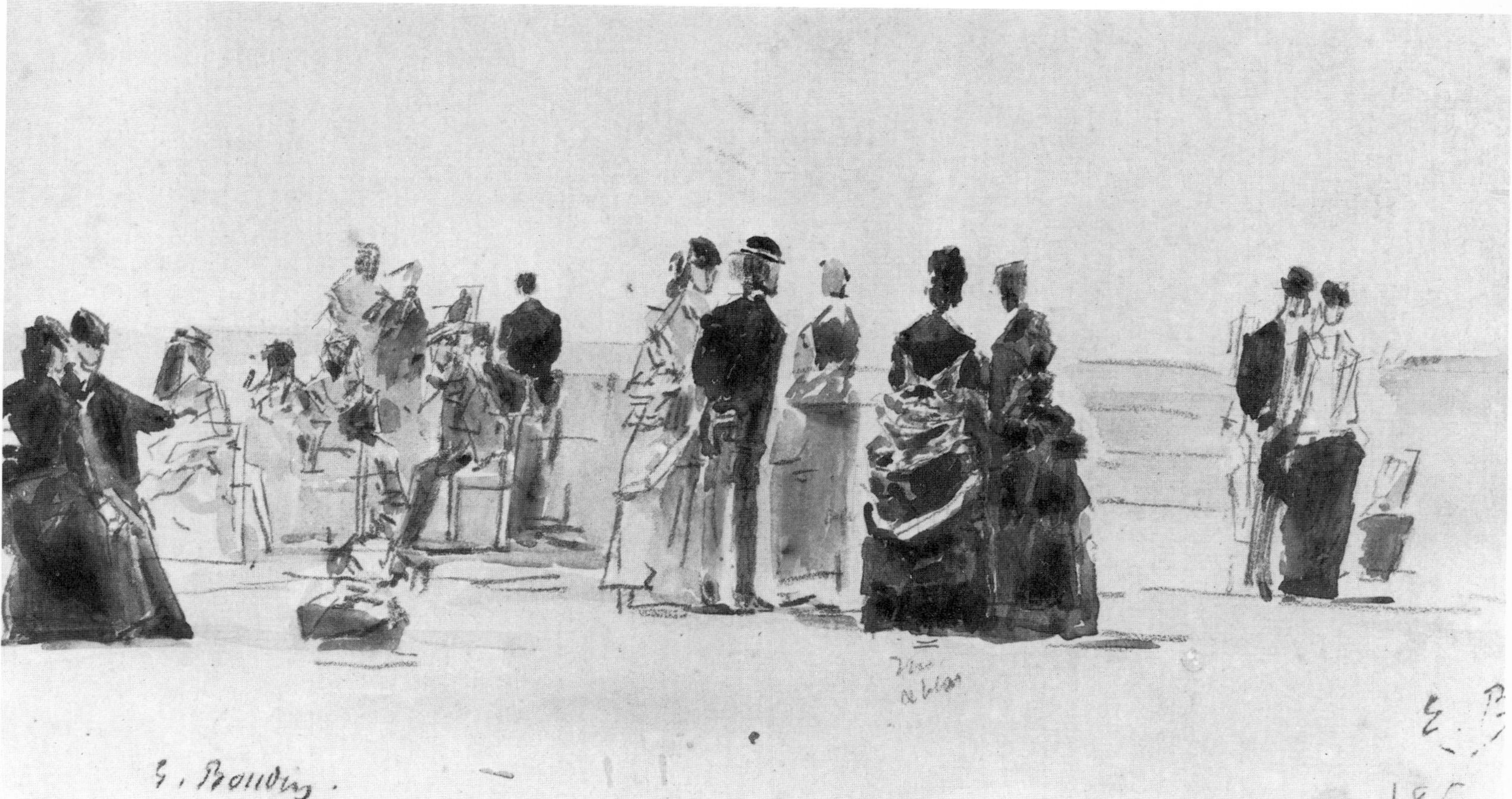
E. Boudin.

Pilgrimage in Brittany, *c.* 1867

Pilgrimage in Brittany, 1865

proof of it than this letter written at this very time, on the occasion of Ribot's visit:

Your letter arrived just when I was showing Ribot, Bureau and another person my little studies of the fashionable beaches. These gentlemen congratulated me for exactly that – for daring to depict in a painting the people and things of our times, for finding a way of making acceptable men in ulsters and women in waterproofs, thanks to the sauce and the garnish.

Yet these attempts are not new, for the Italian and Flemish painters achieved exactly the same thing, painting the people of their own time, whether in interior scenes or in vast architectural settings. The idea is catching on, and a number of young painters, led, I would say, by Monet, find that it is a genre greatly underrated up to now. The peasants have their painters, Millet, Jacque, Breton; and that is a good thing. These painters produce serious works, they are involved with God's creation, and they continue it by helping its manifestation in a fruitful way for mankind. Well and good: but, between you and me, the bourgeois, walking along the jetty towards the sunset, has just as much right to be caught on canvas, *to be brought to the light*. Between you and me, they too are often resting after a day's hard work, these people who come out from their offices and from behind their desks. If there are a few parasites among them, aren't there also people who have carried out their allotted labour? There's a serious and irrefutable argument.

I would hate to condemn myself to paint [no] costume pieces under any pretext, but isn't it pitiful to see serious people like Isabey, Meissonier, and so many others searching for the tinsel of carnivals, and using the pretext of the picturesque to rig up models who are often quite out of countenance in their borrowed trappings.

Le Poitevin has made his fortune with an old plumed felt hat and a pair of musketeer boots which he has painted over and over again at every pretext. I would very much like one of these gentlemen to explain to me the interest those canvases will have for the future, and if the picturesque character of these canvases will be very powerful for our grandchildren. I can't hide the fact that painting often earns its title and its right to be conserved by the perfection of its execution. Otherwise, why hang a jug by Chardin in a museum? If your committee sees it this way, let it hasten to buy a Monet, a Ribot or a Courbet; but it will have to give up one thing or the other. For, God knows, there's not a shadow of quality in their present choice.

I have permitted myself this little digression, my good friend, because your good friendship leads you astray: you are worried about me and feel I should take a retrograde step and make concessions to the public's taste. I have been a poor unfortunate for quite a long time, and therefore concerned enough ro rummage and ponder. I have sounded the others enough to know their resources and to compare them with my own. Well, my dear friend, I persist in following my own little path, however narrow it may be, my only desire being to walk with a firmer, more solid step, widening my path a little when necessary. One can find art in everything when one has the gift. Every man who wields a pen or brush must of necessity consider himself gifted. It's the public's business to judge, and the artist's to progress in his own way, and to embrace nature, whether he paints cabbages and cheeses, or, as our friend Lemarcis does (very badly), the supernatural and divine.

That is why I cannot accept your opinion on the bad choice of my subjects. On the contrary, it appeals to me more and more, and I hope to widen the scope of a genre which is still too limited. Ribot bought one of these studies, and so did his friend Bureau. (To Martin, 3 September 1868.)

Dubourg, Isabey and Rozier were in Honfleur, and Ziem paid a short visit to Le Havre. During this period Boudin worked even more eagerly. He had settled in at Trouville, near the Ferme du Cheval-Blanc, in a little house facing away from the sea, but overlooking a very beautiful stretch of country. He made some studies, and put the finishing touches to the sketches he had done in Brittany.

In short, I will bring back a hundred pictures, all in different stages, but all covered. I must try to work in a variety of genres, and this is an attempt. There is a little of everything in this pile: seascapes, beaches, pilgrimages, weddings, churches, interiors, markets, even ferry boats with animals. (To Martin, 11 November 1868.)

He returned to Paris for the winter, and, still disdainful of official support, saw hardly anyone except the more independent of his fellow painters. He searched continually for inspiration in their example; and this provides yet another proof of Boudin's wisdom, and of his accurate evaluation of himself:

I have just got back from seeing Daubigny's studio and those of some other gifted painters, where I saw some very beautiful things, which put me in a second class, it really has to be admitted. In these studies there was a daring and passion I would like to put into mine. We were speaking of Monet, and Daubigny told me that at the last Salon he had to fight to get one of his pictures admitted. They had already accepted the *Boat*, and when his other submission came up in its turn, Nieuwerkerke said to him: 'Oh no, that's enough of this sort of painting.' Daubigny, however, considered the *Jetty* far superior. A dealer in the Rue Lafayette here has a view of Paris which you may have seen and which would be a masterwork worthy of a great painter if the details matched up to the overall effect. That boy really has something solid. It's a shame you haven't seen the portraits of the Gaudiberts, especially that of Madame, which her husband tells me is remarkable as a burst of colour (To Martin, 18 January 1869.)

The taste for Boudin's work, which was still very limited, began to spread: he exhibited at Pau and Roubaix, and was asked to exhibit at Rouen. Space was too restricted in his lodgings to permit him to work on a dining-room decoration commissioned by

Boudin's palette, 1873

one Mme Rosenlecker for her Château de Bourdainville, so he moved to a more spacious and better-lit studio at 31 Rue Saint-Lazare. He wrote:

I am known as one of those rare painters who *sell*, after the ten or twelve established names. Here and there one sees many a Boudin, yet what does that produce in terms of actual cash received? A dozen canvases at prices from fifty to a hundred francs at the most. This price of a hundred francs is the most difficult thing imaginable to raise. If you accept it, you can never get out of that price range. If you refuse it, you never catch sight of the dealers again, and they take their revenge by indifference, and even worse, by biting criticisms.

And so it is that those who are termed the very young, or in other words the applicants for fame, generally have greying beards, furrowed brows, a disillusioned air, and have reached the age of military retirement. As for those who have managed to grab a field-marshal's baton, they are usually doddering ancients; apart from Corot and two or three others who survive, they are no longer anything but tired shadows of themselves. (To Martin, 25 April 1869.)

He saw the painters around him fighting material difficulties and the incomprehension and obstinacy of stupid people. This is how he wrote again of Monet:

You know that Monet has come back to us from Etretat, famished and with his tail between his legs. It seems that when your exhibition was closed all his canvases were seized and sold, for the profit of his rivals. Apparently the big seascapes were knocked down to Gaudibert, for the ridiculous sum of twenty-four francs, I think. He still claims that his aunt is very severe towards him, and witholds his pension from him. Anyway, this year They refused two of his canvases, but he took his revenge by exhibiting a study of Sainte-Adresse with one of our dealers, Latouche, which the entire artistic world rushed to see. There was a crowd outside the windows as long as the exhibition was on, and in the young people this unexpected and violent painting stirred up *fanaticism*. That's certainly some compensation for his Salon refusal. (To Martin, 25 April 1869.)

Boudin was working on his large-scale decoration for Mme Rosenlecker, which consisted of two large and two small panels. One was to evoke spring with flowers, the other autumn, and represented a wooded landscape with roedeer, for which he made studies in the Jardin des Plantes and asked Courbet's advice. Meanwhile, as relaxation from this work, he took up watercolour again, and even had several lessons from Harpignies. A few influential collectors were beginning to take Boudin's work into consideration, as he himself noted:

I have made some new conquests among the dealers and speculators, among them a rich Belgian of the latter category who greatly desires that I become a big name, and is encouraging me to produce strong works. (To Martin, 23 May 1869.)

As happened every year, when the first fine days arrived he was once again seized by longing for the coastal landscape.

I daren't think of the sundrenched beaches and the stormy skies, and of the joy of painting them in the sea breezes. (To Martin, 14 June 1869.)

As soon as he had finished the panels for Bourdainville he returned to Trouville to breathe in the sea air. He carried out on commission some more 'figures of ladies on the beach, which tormented him cruelly,' and once again fled to Brittany, to Plougastel, where he painted some more pilgrimage scenes. He returned to Trouville for the autumn, where he met the two Daubignys again.

During this time the Belgian 'speculator' he mentioned in his letter, a M. Gauchez, wrote to tell him that he had achieved a complete success in the art world with the canvases by Boudin he had taken home with him, and that he hoped that Brussels would in the future become an excellent market for the painter. This Belgian collector commissioned some seascapes from him, with the aid of which he hoped to do battle with the Belgian marine painters, whom he had already exposed to the competition of Jongkind. He was an extremely prudent man, and one who not only gave Boudin the means of working calmly during hard times but also procured him relative ease during the years to follow.

Boudin was at last to emerge from his period of poverty, repeated trials, discouragement and self-searching; by 1871 he had almost attained complete self-expression. He was nearly fifty years old.

Gathering on Trouville beach, 1868

Bathing costumes and short dresses for the beach. Designs by Mmes Maury and Le Riche, from La Mode illustrée, July 1878

Trouville: the promenade and the beach, 1860. Photo Dignemont collection

Conversation on Trouville beach, 1865

Dieppe or the Champs-Elysées-on-Sea. From L'Illustration, 1862

Brest: three-masters in the roadstead. Photo M. Sirot

Trouville: the beach at bathing time, 1880. Photo Neurdein

Antwerp: view from the Tête de Flandre, 1880. Photo M. Sirot

Visits Brussels and Antwerp · A Letter from Courbet
Visits Bordeaux · Death of Courbet and Millet
Sale in Le Havre · The State buys one of his works
A third-class medal · Exhibition in Paris · Dordrecht
The banquet in honour of Ribot · The Villa des Ajoncs

View of Antwerp, the Tête de Flandre, 1871

Chapter 3 1870-1884

The year has opened under more favourable auspices. I have only had three buyers so far, and here I am forced to finish off almost thirty canvases. Our friend Hagerman, the dealer of whom I spoke, fell upon my hoard of seascapes and wanted to buy them all on the spot. He wanted to take all of them, but I kept some in reserve for an old fellow called Martin. He's another dealer who also wants a pile of them. So you can see that the signs are good. Tomorrow I expect my Belgian, M. Gauchez, and another client who wants boats. Here I am, forced back into being a painter of seascapes. It really is funny. You can see the reason for all this: it's quite simply this: at the moment Jongkind is the object of unbridled speculation. His canvases fetch eight hundred or a thousand francs, so much that there is a need for less expensive pictures to fill the commercial gap, and they have fallen back on me as a last resource.... I am not complaining about it, for many other painters have no such luck, and envy me for it. In a word, people seem pleased with my new studies, which are an improvement on those of previous years....

Don't think that all this business is making me neglect serious art. On the contrary, I feel more than ever the necessity to be severe on myself, and to seek the perfection I pursue within the limits of my powers. That is why I exert myself to do better and better without worrying about the feeble prices my works fetch. It's just that I have to contend with talented fellows. (To Martin, 16 December 1869.)

In the very moment of mixing my palette I suddenly find it dull, when I think of the deafening colour of Delacroix or Rousseau. Dupré's powerful impasto makes my little canvas on the easel look flat and dry, and Goya, marvellous Goya, offers us garments painted with such magic that one wonders if he had not perhaps some secret that enabled him to do it so well.

Today there is great excitement among the gentlemen of the paintbrush: a deputation to the new minister for the suppression of official awards, and a counter-demonstration for the conservation of these playthings; loud protests from the crowd of painters who all want to be at the top, loud noises and perplexity on the part of the minister who can't decide which party is right. For my own part, I would perhaps be interested in it all if I did not have a great deal to do and much to paint, but I'm not joining in. (To Martin, 6 March 1870.)

Boudin was never to relinquish his wise disdain for these playthings, as he called them. He never considered them as anything more than a way of selling with less difficulty. He knew what a distance separates official rewards and the sincerity and independence of real painting. For the moment he felt only disdain for these idle distractions, all the more justifiably since the dealers assured him an easier existence. One or two of his canvases reached prices as high as 700 or 800 francs in the hands of dealers. But he was not the sort to lose his head because of the rising fashion for his work. Long accustomed to difficulties, imbued with the demands of his conscience and with the continual work that art requires of those who really honour it, he added:

They say I've made progress, but I don't feel I've got anywhere yet, and I try to inflate myself like the frog in the fable, though not to bursting point.

That year again, in spite of those who kept on repeating that he was sure to receive a medal at the Salon, Boudin was not awarded one. He wrote jokingly:

It seems that my skin is still too tough to be swallowed.

And he added, more indignantly:

Did you know they pitilessly refused Monet? One asks oneself with what right. (To Martin, 29 May 1870.)

Gauchez bought all the remaining beach scenes of Trouville, and commissioned forty or fifty canvases: 'no mention of the price, just a recommendation to make them good, and expensive if possible.'

After spending a month at Trouville, where he had arrived on 12 April, he left again for Brittany on Tuesday 13 September, and stayed at l'Hôpital-Campoux. Meanwhile, the war broke out. He wrote to his brother:

All over the place there are meetings of peasants lining up for exercise. I feel almost ashamed of any other activity than preparing to defend our homesteads. All this takes me back to long-forgotten times I never expected to see again.

Yesterday there was a pilgrimage not far from here. I went off merrily to sketch the women in front of the church, and undoubtedly caused alarm in the population's hearts: they took me for a spy. I've got no complaints about the temperature here. In striking contrast with the wicked passions of bestial man, it is wonderfully serene. You saw in Le Havre how people fled to England, but that is nothing compared with what we saw at Laval: the entire population of villages fleeing from the invasion, nuns, nurses, panic-stricken peasants rushing towards Brittany, all the wagons seized or stolen. All these people were carrying a few clothes and a little food tied up in bundles. Some were leaving their homes because the enemy had arrived, others were fleeing from the departments of Seine-et-Oise and Marne. It was heartrending to see, especially since they were all mixed up among thousands of soldiers, cavalry and volunteers coming and going in all directions, to such a degree that here in Landerneau there are fifteen hundred active troops, strong sons of Gard and Aveyron. (To Louis, 18 September 1870.)

A month later he moved to Plougastel, where he did some more studies, and thought of returning from Morlaix to Le Havre by the sea road, but unfortunately he decided to go via Le Mans. In the understandable panic that had taken possession of the railways his bundle of studies went astray. Their loss was reported at Nogent-le-Rotrou, but not even one of them was found. A whole season's work was lost, and his resources were almost exhausted. The only money he could count on immediately could not reach him, for his Belgian patron, whom he had asked for a payment, wrote in reply that it was impossible to send a registered letter because the post was unwilling to accept anything of value. 'Come yourself to collect it,' wrote Gauchez, 'and you will be welcome.'

That is why Boudin, who had already thought of leaving for England to join Daubigny and Pissarro so as not to die of hunger, went instead to Brussels. Since the money could not come to the painter, the painter had to go to the money.

Monet was in Trouville at that time, and wrote some discouraged letters to Boudin in Brittany. Soon after this he was to leave for Holland and then for London, attempting like Boudin to get by somehow. Vollon, who had been in Trouville for the autumn, had gone to Brussels to see what he was to return to; delighted with the welcome he had been given, he wrote to his wife telling her to join him, and to bring all the pictures he had left. Vollon had settled in Brussels, at 6 Rue du Persil. Boudin, who was very friendly with Vollon, knew, therefore, when he left for Belgium that he would find there not only the means of living, but also friends.

He left Le Havre on 7 December and travelled via Dunkirk, where he arrived on 9 December and spent three days in a friend's house. On 12 December he moved into 69 Rue de Mérode, in Saint-Gilles, a suburb of Brussels.

I have met my friend Vollon, and a whole crowd of Parisian picture dealers. I'm settled in quite comfortably. Vollon lives within a stone's throw, and I go to his place in the evenings for a few hours. Yesterday we went shopping for the first time. I'm already being asked for views of the canal, where there are a great number of very strange Dutch boats. I have also seen old Diaz who, like everyone else, laments the misfortune of our poor country. (To Louis, 17 December 1870.)

And two weeks later he wrote:

I feel happy to be able to work calmly in my little corner, instead of having stayed there, being of no use to anyone. (To Louis, 2 January 1871.)

The discomfort of his lodgings and the lack of light made him move. He took over a studio in the same quarter, 74 Rue de Hollande. He regained some enthusiasm and did a series of studies of Brussels market and the fisheries. During the bitterly cold winter of that year, using sketches and fragments of studies, he

Fish market, Rotterdam, 1876

tried to reconstruct the thirty canvases he had lost on the journey from Brest.

Vollon, who was very much in fashion, and overwhelmed with work, gave him very considerable support. He lost no time in carrying out the commission he received. But the only interest Brussels held for him was a financial one. He stayed there unwillingly, and now that his livelihood was assured for several months, this city without a port, or ships, held no attraction for him at all. He thought of spending a few months at Antwerp, and in the meantime visited Malines and did several studies of the Louvain canal (see p. 203).

His mother's illness recalled him briefly to Le Havre on 16 April. He had scarcely got back to Brussels, where he had left his wife ill, when he heard, at the beginning of June, of the death of his mother. He himself began at this time to suffer from the facial neuralgia that was to torment him until the end of his life. These illnesses, griefs and worries all combined to make his stay in Brussels unproductive, and convinced him even more that he should leave for Antwerp.

He arrived in Antwerp on 5 July, and was to leave on 20 August. During these six weeks he produced one of his most beautiful series, the first in date. In these pictures he really gives the full measure of his talent for the first time, and neither the beautiful, solid pictures painted in Dordrecht in 1884, nor the blond-toned series of Antibes, nor the subtle views of Deauville done during his last period, can perhaps quite surpass the quality of the Antwerp series (see pp. 78, 85, 99).

It is interesting to note the rather unfavourable impression he received at the beginning of his stay:

Here I am ready to paint seascapes for six weeks on the banks of the Scheldt. I have met up with my old friend Vollon, which makes my stay more bearable, for this is such a capricious country, alternately so hot and so cold, that one's health easily deteriorates. Life is expensive here, the beer bad, and to crown it all I am suffering terribly from my headaches, which at times even prevent me from feeling the beauty of things, and even affect my memory. In spite of everything one has to go on pulling one's cart like a poor old horse. And so I work on in this sort of torpor, in sun or wind. I have received some commissions. Antwerp is famous, and local views are sought after by collectors. From that it follows that there are many commissions and quite good prices to be got, which is the only consideration which keeps me working patiently, and prevents me losing courage.

People make a great fuss about these towns in the Low Countries. I find them interesting, undoubtedly, but I'm not mad about them, and the beautiful horizons of our France, not to speak of Brittany, mean just as much and even more to me. (To Martin, 17 July 1871.)

The quality of Boudin's work improved in proportion with his ease of execution, and the facility with which he modified his vision according to different atmospheres. In August he was in Antwerp, in September at Trouville, and in October and November he stayed at Plougastel, working eagerly. He did not return to Paris until December, and could only trust to fate during a time when the city was still in the throes of the aftermath of the war and the Commune. He wrote:

My foreign travels and the fuss that had been made about my studies had prepared a good business ground for me. All I had to do was to unpack my work to sell it, and since then my little business affairs are progressing very healthily. I hope to be able to reap the benefits of all my labours, since up till now they have been so poorly recompensed....

I have been seeing Monet frequently these days and we've been holding a housewarming at his place these last few days. He's settled in comfortably and seems to have a great desire to achieve a name. He has brought back some extremely beautiful studies from Holland, and I believe that his turn will come to take one of the most prominent positions in our school of painting. (To Martin, 2 January 1872.)

The picture dealers Boudin had met in Belgium were beginning to return to Paris, and the interest they had taken in his painting was maintained. He wrote:

I scarcely have a moment to think of myself, my little studio has become so busy, and has turned into a sort of boutique. There's a continual coming and going, which I really can't grumble about, since it's a sign of a growing reputation. (To Louis, 31 December 1871.)

Princess Metternich on Trouville beach, 1869

Finding himself at last in fashion did not sweep him off his feet. He retained the same calm, prudence and circumspection, even the touch of cunning inherent in a good citizen of Honfleur. Neither did it prevent him showing the frank sincerity of his nature and the solidity of his friendship, as he did to Courbet at this time. As mentioned before, Courbet was a prisoner on parole, ill, subject to the politicians' hostility, and abandoned by the majority of his fellow painters. Boudin sent this New Year's greeting to him on 2 January 1872:

My dear Courbet,

I can't let these days pass when one makes a point of visiting so many of one's friends, fortunate or unfortunate, without sending a reminder of my friendship to you in the depths of your prison. I would be happy to think that this feeble evidence of our friendship could, for a few minutes, bring you relief in your solitude.

I have just returned to Paris after a long absence, and hoped to be able to greet you, but they tell me that it is difficult to obtain the pleasure of seeing you. I speak for several of my friends, among them Monet and Gautier, who also send you their best wishes, and who would be just as eager as I would to spend a few minutes with you.

We console ourselves with the thought that you will soon be at the end of your term of imprisonment, and that in a short time you will be able to return to art, and to your friends who are so very concerned for your welfare. That is all the evidence I can give you here.

I would be happy if this reminder of those who have never stopped worrying about your fate for one moment were to reach you soon. With this hope, I send you my heartiest greetings.

Courbet's reply to Boudin's affectionate letter leaves no doubt as to what an exception it was for him:

'My dear Boudin, Neuilly, 6 January 1872

'I am all the more glad to have received your charming letter because these times are rife with cowards. Amand Gautier was courageous, but I was afraid of compromising him if I urged him to come to see me.

'I don't write to anyone because the police take copies and compile dossiers, and that must be avoided in these times.

'Now you have nothing more to fear. You can make a pilgrimage to see a man who has just completed seven months of solitary confinement, which is no laughing matter.

'That's all the reward I got for service rendered and for the good I wanted to do. I know that Gautier enjoyed those pleasures. You no longer have to go through any formality to see me, just present yourselves.

'After escaping the eager firing squads they intended for me, I have decided to undergo an operation by Dr Nélaton, which may achieve what the firing squads missed.... I can only continue to hope that I will escape, for I can't live like this. I suffer continually and cannot think of anything.

'So do come to see me one of these days, it would give me such very great pleasure. It does one good to see one's friends again.

'I am in Neuilly in Dr Duval's house, 34 Avenue du Roule.

'At last I have escaped from those ignoble prisons.

'I am painting fruit at the moment.

'Come with Gautier, Monet and even the ladies, if they can find it in their hearts. Best wishes to your wife and to everyone individually. *G. Courbet.*

'I am a prisoner on parole, my sentence is up on the 1 March.'

From this time onwards Boudin's life continued very peacefully. He always divided his time between Paris, Trouville and Brittany. In 1872, he was at Camaret, in 1873 on the Côtes-du-Nord, in 1874, at Portrieux, in 1875 at Le Faou. He continued to broaden his manner, examining with close attention not only nature, but also the works of painters of original talent. The avant-garde art world was already beginning to put him in his rightful place, as the foremost of the minor masters. Those who were fighting against the public showed him friendship and affection.

Manet has been to visit me several times, and seems satisfied with his lot, in spite of the struggle he has to get his painting accepted.

View of Antwerp harbour, 1871

Overleaf: Camaret harbour, 1873

Rotterdam: the Beursbrug, 1870

The Village of Le Faou, *c.* 1867

I have as much success as I could wish for. As soon as I unpack my work I sell it. I am fêted like a big-wig in the art world. What more could I hope for? Many a time one is undoubtedly weighed down by worries about one's progress, or about producing something worth while, so difficult in this profession. But all that would melt away if a fellow were firmly and steadily in a position like old Corot, who, at almost eighty, surpasses us all in courage. (To Martin, 12 December 1872.)

He was well aware, however, of the rank he was beginning to achieve. He ended a letter written at this time to Le Havre town hall, requesting certain information, with a mixture of pride and modesty:

I regret that I have so far been unable to offer any notable fame as a reward for the efforts made on my behalf by the administration that encouraged me, but I have at least the satisfaction of having held fast to my brush, and to the course I set for myself, despite the obstacles an artist encounters.

The facial neuralgia which tormented Boudin recurred continually, and from now on was hardly ever to leave him in peace. 'It is torture to put down my palette a hundred times until the attack has passed and I can take it up again.' Yet it was in this physical state that he was to accomplish all his works, with what one could justifiably call a growing courage, in spite of everything, and continually inspired by the desire to renew his vision and fortify his expression.

In the autumn of 1874, Boudin was in Bordeaux, where he painted a small series of canvases, one of which now hangs in the Musée du Jeu de Paume in Paris.

Bordeaux has held me for six weeks, and although as a town it's a pleasant place, I am beginning to feel ready to leave it. For my part, I'm not very fond of the quayside. It's filled with the hubbub of carts, parcels and casks, just like the quays at Le Havre, or rather Antwerp. The commotion is pleasant enough, no doubt, for those who calculate their profits according to the number of bales or casks lowered by the cranes, but it offers scant pleasure to the dreamer who prefers a little silence and solitude, and the voice of nature, more monotonous, perhaps, but also more poetic. These trading towns get on one's nerves; they are full of dust, and the pungent smell of hides, and above all guano, which are, after all, excellent things, but which cannot detract from the memory of the healthy smell of seaweed. Such cities can never replace the freshness of our salty, humid beaches. In short, my dear friend, this town is as disagreeable as Le Havre, as far as its quaysides are concerned, and that's saying quite a lot. (To Martin, 26 February 1875.)

Although the series of views of Bordeaux and of the Gironde (pp. 91, 204) are among the painter's most delicate works, they seem less serene than the views of Antwerp; at the same time they are animated with the sense of life, excitement and movement which is one of the caracteristics of Boudin's quick and subtle vision.

At this time he was suffering an inexplicable weariness, a sort of shrivelling up of his inner self, which he carefully recorded in one of his notebooks, proving that this persistent observer, this analyser of groups and movements, was equally capable of analysing the changes of his own mind and heart.

17 November 1874. Return from Bordeaux. Relative prosperity has come to me, but also illnesses, deaths, and afflictions of all sorts. And yet the times have changed. I now have a small amount of savings, and an almost certain knowledge of being able to live in comfort. How is it then that all this has not had the power to extinguish the germ of I know not what uneasiness and sadness? The further one advances into this dark future, the more one tries to lay hand on the flowers which border the precipice towards which we move. This is the madness of condemned men. Within myself I feel strangely detached from my feelings, and am drawn by the inexplicable without, the unknown. A sort of fatality is in motion within me and frightens me. My work is nervous and mechanical, but no longer brings me the calm and serenity that are so essential. Any trace of goodness and congeniality I had has been extinguished. I am surprised and frightened by my bad instincts and hard-heartedness. I feel a dislike and indifference for the things of this life that I never felt before. I don't know what I want, perhaps just to slide quietly downhill, down this dizzy decline. And yet something within me resists and prevents me from doing so.

That year Boudin took part in the first Impressionist Exhibition, which was held from 15 April to 15 May in Nadar's studio at 35 Boulevard des Capucines. His fellow exhibitors were, among others, Braquemard, Cals, Cézanne, Degas, Guillaumin, Monet, Berthe Morisot, Pissarro, Renoir and Sisley.

The year 1875 saw the extinction of two of the brightest flames of French painting, two painters who had been teachers and friends to Boudin for more than twenty years: Millet and Corot both died, with only a month's interval.

With great ceremony we accompanied Corot to his last abode. He had lived to such an age that we believed him to be eternal. A short time ago he was as valiant as any of us, more so perhaps. His mind was still as lively as when he was in his prime. We all loved him, for he was a good man, and an example to us all in our work.

Millet did not have long to enjoy his great reputation; if he had lived to papa Corot's eighty years he would have been able to bring up his large family: eight daughters. But he was sapped of strength; like many others, he had seen hard days, but those hard days had lasted twenty years or more. They were the two most strongly individual artists of our time, and although they had given the full measure of their talent, their death is a double loss of great extent for our art. (To Martin, 26 February 1875.)

To his great good fortune, Boudin had been able to put aside a small sum of money after his stay in Belgium, for the period 1875–80 was a lean one for painting. 'We are undergoing a crisis unprecedented in the annals of painting,' he wrote in a letter dated December 1876.

The big names in the art world are all closing in on Paris under the fallacious pretext of pleasing their wives. But in reality

View of Bordeaux harbour, 1874

Market in Brittany, 1869

Market in Brittany, 1869

Boudin's sketch for the catalogue cover for the exhibition and sale in Le Havre, 2–3 July 1879

it's because people no longer go out to them, to the Isle-Adam or elsewhere. I saw Daubigny a few days ago, he asked my advice about shipping works to America. One needs a large dose of courage to keep brush in hand in these times of neglect and indifference.

As for business, it's best not to talk of it. If Paris were besieged it would be easier to sell a canvas than it is this year. (To Martin, 17 March 1876.)

In despair for this reason, he left for Rotterdam for a period, but on his return he wrote:

Whether one returns from Asnières or from Rotterdam, the result is the same, the public seems to have no interest in anything. (To Louis, 26 March 1877.)

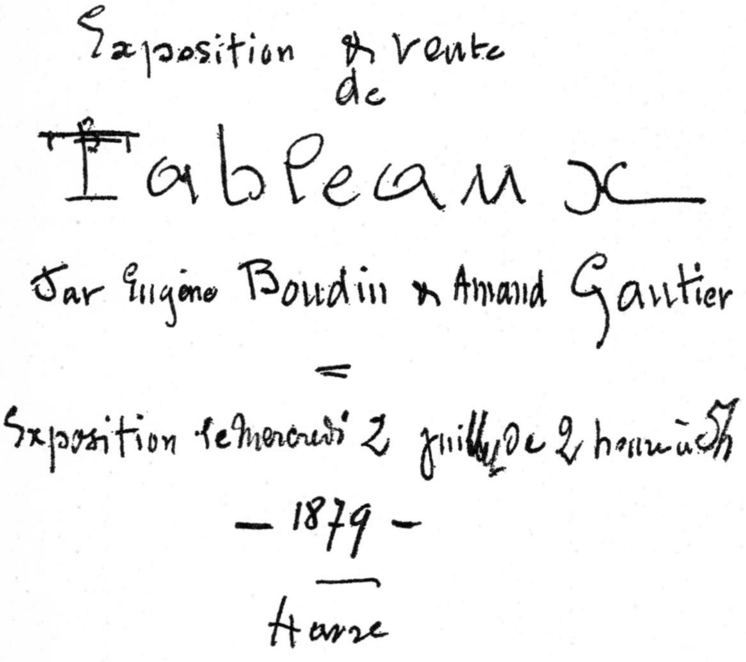

Eighteen months later the refrain was the same:

Today we see abandoned the talents who were most in fashion yesterday, witness Jongkind, Corot, and so many others who not long ago were considered current money, and who today are undergoing a slump just like ordinary painters. The very rich collectors run after artists like Fortuny, bringing the Spanish school into fashion, whilst serious French talents are neglected and no longer find any favour at all. (To Martin, 21 November 1878.)

And so he attempted several sales in the auction rooms. One was held in Paris in March 1879. It consisted of thirty-eight canvases, twenty watercolours and twelve sketches of beach scenes, and realized a net total of 6,000 francs, the canvases selling for prices between 200 and 400 francs, and the drawings for an average of 25 francs. 'The pictures in this sale which proved the most attractive were the markets, washerwomen, etc.'

Another sale, held in Le Havre, together with Gautier, on 3 July 1879, was – as even Boudin himself admitted – a complete failure. The manuscript of the catalogue, written in Boudin's own hand, shows that the sale consisted of twenty of his canvases, and fourteen of Amand Gautier's.

Boudin's pictures were: *The old fish market in Brussels*; *Fish market in Rotterdam*; *Fish market at Trouville*; *Jetty at Trouville (low tide)*; *Deauville harbour*; *Timber dock*; *Brick quay (Rotterdam)*; *Central harbour (Rotterdam)*; *View of Trouville*; two seascapes, *River Meuse at Rotterdam*; *Departure (Scheveningen)*; *Women of Berck*; *Women fishing (near Brest)*; *Stable interior*; *Dapple-grey horse*, etc.

Boudin sold four of his canvases for 210, 125, 105 and 85 francs. As for Gautier, he was unable to sell even one of his works. To safeguard their self respect and in the interest of Gautier, it was announced in Paris that the sale had not taken place.

It was a tremendous fiasco. We certainly don't deserve such indifference on the part of the collectors, but after all, there can't be more than four of them in this commercial town. (To Martin, 4 July 1879.)

To Boudin's credit, what saddened him most profoundly about this blow was the position of Gautier, for he had set great hopes on this sale.

In addition to the depression that had befallen painting, Boudin underwent physical suffering, and the successive loss of his teachers, who had also been his friends, for after Millet and Corot, Courbet died in exile, and Ribot and Cals were both at death's door. All this is evident in his work. Between the series of views of Rotterdam of 1876 and the first series of Berck of 1882, the subtlety of his vision underwent a perceptible decline, from which it was to recover in 1884 with the series of views of Dordrecht (see p. 142), in which it attains its most vigorous expression.

He himself was very much aware of this:

> As far as work is concerned, this year has been conspicuously bad for me. (To Martin, 3 November 1879.)

The weakening of his expression caused him extreme worry, although he noted:

> Several articles have been devoted to me which have surprised me. I am not accustomed to being spoilt by the writing public. (To Martin, 21 November 1879.)

The crisis in the art world continued; although dealers certainly began to send pictures by Troyon and Corot to America, and to profit from the considerable speculation, they aroused, the painters of the moment were at loggerheads with the indifference of the public. Even a man like Jongkind saw the collectors' interest in his work almost extinguished. Boudin wrote:

> They have made an attempt on Jongkind who no longer paints. He is resting in the country, but is certainly not dead enough. It's cruel to think that one only attains a value when one no longer needs it. (To Martin, 3 April 1880.)

Boudin himself was growing old:

> It's a distressing thought, but I who have been dabbling with colour for so many years, have become stupid and timid in comparison with the new generation of painters.
>
> If I had the time ahead of me, I could venture something, but I'm already one of the old men. Sometimes I long to cram all my odds and ends into a sale room, and to take my leave of everything without waiting until I have passed away entirely. Doesn't it seem absurd to you to pile up quantities of things over which one has worn oneself away, and which only our 'beloved descendants' will enjoy? (To Martin, 5 May 1880.)

And yet Boudin's reputation, even if it had not yet reached the general public, held a well-established position in the esteem of his fellow painters, as a passage from one of his letters proves.

> I have had a visit from some painters, Duez, Butin and another, and they absolutely insisted on buying a few of my rough sketches. You would have had a nervous fit if you had only seen how happy they were with them, and how they wanted to pay me just like good bourgeois. (To Martin, 1 November 1880.)

And even the esteem of the dealers was growing, for in December 1880 he managed to sell a *Trouville harbour* for the unhoped-for price of 900 francs (the *Journal des Arts* printed the price as 9,000, but he had still to wait to achieve such sums). At the beginning of 1881 Durand-Ruel, who had already had occasion to realize the painter's value, took an interest in his fortunes.

The history of art must take into account the insight, and even the disinterestedness, sometimes displayed by a few collectors or dealers. As one of these few, the name of Durand-Ruel is inseparable from the history of French painting. It was his obstinacy and his belief in their talent or genius that ensured the destiny of the impressionists against all opponents. We know today of the difficulties encountered by this man who, before all others, chose rightly. His daring brought some profit to Boudin.

> The year had scarcely begun when Durand-Ruel came one morning, and I showed him a few canvases. He said to me, 'I'll take those. And this one, and that one there.' 'Good,' I said, 'all of them?' 'All of them!' I had been worried about my stock of canvases, but you see that I was wrong. I took the dear man at his word.... He asked me to work exclusively for him, and I agreed very gladly, for I don't think much of the other dealers. Nevertheless, I made the condition that I should continue to supply my few private collectors, and to send some to my framer. (To Martin, 5 February 1881.)

And some time later he wrote:

> My protector is still eager and sends his boy to me every week in search of finished pictures. You can understand the dilemma of the poor painter who always has a few touches to add. They send the picture back... then they return to the attack, and one has finally to decide to hand over the canvas. Luckily I had a few bundles of studies, and let him take those – that satisfied the minotaur. (To Martin, 27 February 1881.)

The year 1881 marked the beginning of 'official' interest in Boudin. The painter was 56 years old, and had already painted his admirable series of views of Antwerp, Bordeaux, and the first set of Amsterdam. At last 'they' deigned to notice that as a painter of seascapes he had some talent. That year he received a state commission. The whole business of this commission was sufficiently edifying, in an ironic way, to be related here.

On 8 February 1881, Boudin sent this piece of news to his friend:

You will be astonished. Just imagine, I've got an official commission. Just that. Two views of Dieppe harbour, for the state. Yes, my dear friend, the under-secretary has requested them through Durand-Ruel, who had made him feel ashamed, and he gave me this commission. But he wants me to go to Dieppe in the depths of bitter winter; I have just written to him begging him to postpone it until the month of June. I hope he will agree, if he doesn't wish for the death of painters.

And in May he wrote as follows:

My official commission has gone overboard. I haven't got the ability to talk myself into success. My friend the secretary of the Beaux-Arts had already forgotten his protégé. Recently I reminded him of my existence by sending him a word, since I had no official commission. The ministry sent for me, the reason being that they wanted to know what it was all about. I accepted my fate philosophically; perhaps, deep down, I was content to be rid of the worry of a commission which would have become a tunic of Nessus, and I begged His Excellency's first secretary not to follow up the benevolent thought that had guided His Excellency.... That, my dear friend, is how I have profited from officialdom.... I am quite convinced that 1881 will not be the year in which I will figure in the state's account books, or have the honour of being decorated with even the meanest medal, even the paper one which designates the last category.

But let us be consoled. More than all these I love to abide in the fields, and on the Ocean shore, and other haunts of delight well verdured and sunlit, with good healthful airs, and to return from this country pastime and pleasure to find a cool and shuttered shade... good golden cider, cool and beaded at the brim of a twopenny can, and then a fine kid, and to bring from one's morning walk a good Pantagruelian appetite, both great and easily satisfied. All this is worth more than laurels, honours and other such childish toys. (To Martin, 25 May 1881.)

However, it was in precisely the year of this letter that he received the doubtful honour of being decorated with 'the paper medal which designates the last category.' His Salon exhibit, *The Meuse at Rotterdam*, won him a third-class medal, and two years later he was awarded a second-class one. At fifty-seven years of age Boudin was receiving honours that only a beginner could possibly welcome. It is understandable that he should have been rather indifferent to them at that age, even if he had not been so throughout his life. His opinion was the same as that of Paul-Louis Courier: 'What the state encourages languishes, and what it protects dies.'

At the moment when he was being granted these honorary distinctions, this is how he described his state of mind:

I am working like a madman, but am becoming ambitious, and if my life and health continue, I believe I shall emerge from my chrysalis, for I feel much more intensely serious than in previous years. I am more in control of myself, we shall see. (To Martin, 5 February 1881.)

I am so absorbed in painting that I no longer have time to breathe.... I would like to begin to put myself forward in a serious way. To do so, one must produce some important works, and there are days when one cannot manage that. It seems to me that the time has come to produce some works, at least I feel this need, but to do anything well I would have to look at nature again. I hasten to try once again to try hard to capture sky and sea with my newly-aquired boldness. (To Martin, 27 February 1881.)

Here I am, completely monopolized by Durand-Ruel. He has bought back all my works that were scattered among the dealers, and has forbidden me to keep any for private collectors, and above all for his fellow-dealers. In spite of myself, I attach great importance to this. Boudin is in demand. (To Martin, 10 December 1881.)

Believe it or not, I am exhausted, not because I work too much, but because work tires me. As one grows old one should take things at a leisurely pace, as you do, but in my case it's the reverse. The further one advances in one's career, the more difficult to please one becomes, and the better one wants to do, and this becomes a source of trouble and infinite disappointment for the painter. (To Martin, 27 February 1882.)

And yet one must continue, advancing shoulder to shoulder with the young, the eager. I would like to be already there on the battlefield, running after the boats, following the clouds,

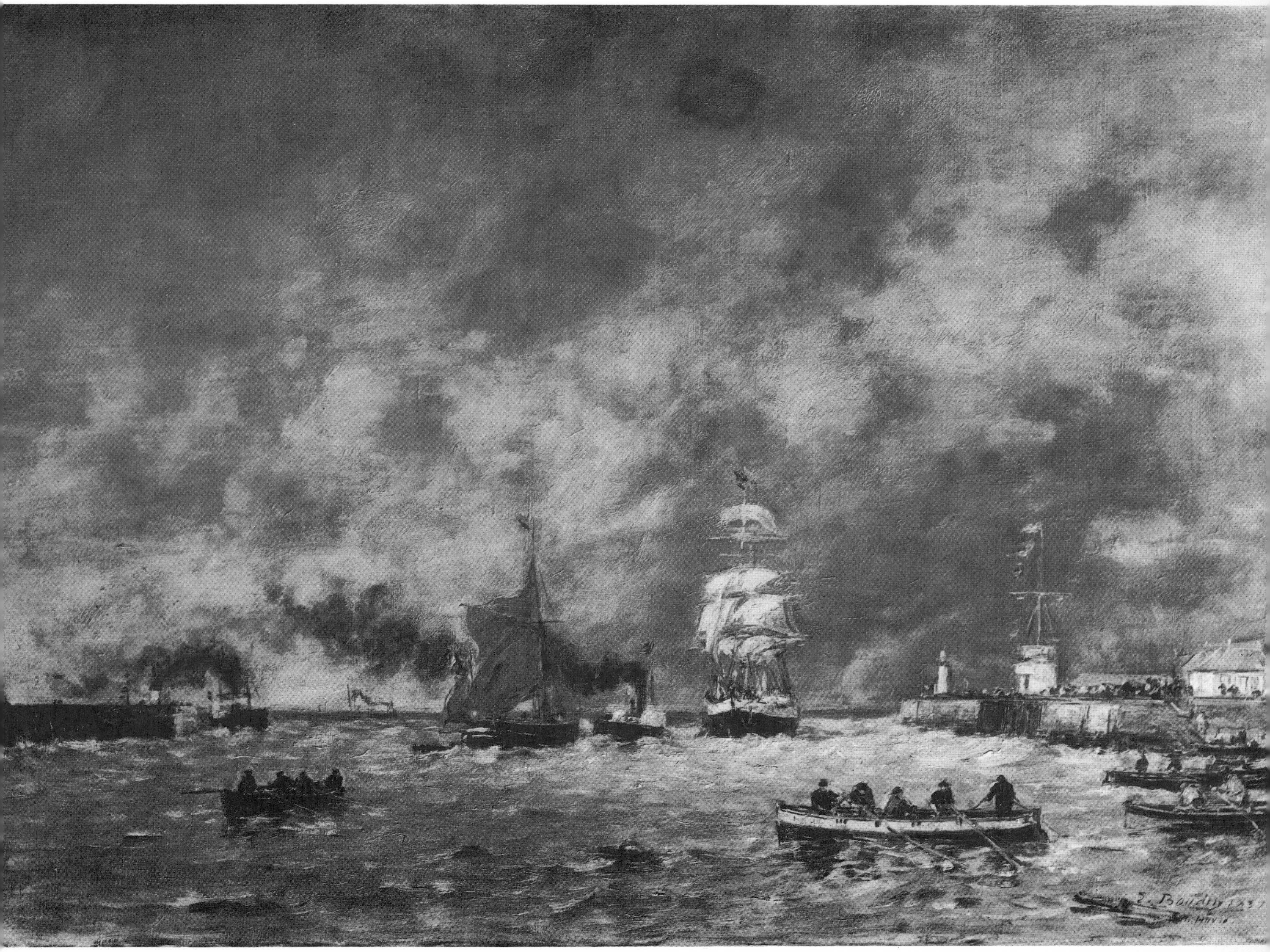

Entrance to Le Havre harbour, squall, west wind, 1887

Sailing ships at anchor in Deauville harbour, 1878

Estuary of the Scheldt, 1871

> brush in hand, savouring the good salt air of the beaches and seeing the tide rise... just to talk of it cheers me up. (To Martin, 16 June 1882.)

He spent part of the summer of 1881 working in Le Havre, and the rest in Trouville. In 1882 he undertook a short visit to the coast of Picardy, stayed in Berck for six weeks, and travelled as far as Boulogne, but the dreadful weather he encountered there did not permit him to work as he wished. 'My ideal,' he wrote, 'was to concentrate on large-scale skies, but the painter proposes and the weather opposes.'

He returned to Trouville, took up his work again, and began to feel a weariness caused by the monotony of his subjects. He felt an even more compelling desire to renew his subject matter, and awaited only the opportunity to search further afield for skies whose most delicate variety could be seized by his penetrating eye.

During this period, Durand-Ruel was expending considerable energy to establish 'his' painters: in March 1882 he had already held an impressionist exhibition. 'There are,' wrote Boudin, 'some beautiful Monets which Durand-Ruel is selling for between 2,000 and 2,500 francs... he is right.' (To Martin, 20 March 1882.)

In December 1882, Durand-Ruel decided to inaugurate his new gallery in the Boulevard de la Madeleine with a group of works by Boudin. The exhibition opened on 31 January 1883. It can be stated that it was this exhibition that definitively established Boudin's name, both for the art journalists and for the collectors.

He now received the justified fame that he should have known at least ten years earlier. His value was recognized even by unscrupulous admirers, as can be judged by this incident recorded in a letter of 17 December 1882:

> Martin has just bought two fake Boudins, for 300 francs apiece, and is vexed for his 600 francs and for having been taken in and exploited in this way, he who was the first to introduce me to the world of collectors.

Nearly all the Parisian newspapers devoted a few lines or long articles to this exhibition. Philippe Burty wrote a long and very judicious article in *La République*; *La Liberté* of 9 February contained an excellent article by Drumond; Gustave Geffroy, in *La Justice* of 15 February 1883, writing about Boudin, provided one of the first examples of the critical penetration and taste that were to make him one of the greatest aesthetes of our time. (See pp. 233-4 of this book.)

> Here we have our poor marine painter established; they call him master in numerous articles, declaring him to be a personality of our age, 'a man in love with the sea,' and a thousand things that would make me vain if it were a quirk I were capable of. What is surprising is that I have felt the effect of a revelation. I was swimming in the haze, and here I am out in the broad daylight.... It's a good exhibition: a hundred and fifty pictures and so many pastels, drawings, etc., all of which forms a very harmonious ensemble. (To Martin, 7 February 1883.)

By a fortunate chance, on the death of a mutual friend of Boudin and Jongkind, a certain M. Bascle, the question arose of putting up for sale a hundred works by Jongkind from Bascle's collection and of exhibiting them at the same time as the exhibition of Boudin's work:

'One would have received, at one and the same time two revelations, since, even though Jongkind is very well known, one would have had a real opportunity of measuring his talent, and it would have been the moment to make parallels and note similarities.'

The Bascle sale did not take place till April; an exhibition of Claude Monet's work followed that of Boudin at the gallery in the Boulevard de la Madeleine. Over a period of less than three months one could see one-man shows by these three painters, linked not only by mutual affection, but also by aesthetic affinities, comprising between them one step in the pictorial evolution of the period 1860–80.

During this time the papers continued to speak of the Boudin exhibition:

Kerhor bay, Finistère, 1872

I have reached my forty-eighth article, and there's even a cartoon. It shows an old woman coming out of church and seeing a poster saying 'Eugene Boudin Exhibition.' The caption: 'An exhibition of Boudin [*scilicet*, 'black pudding'] in mid-Lent, there's Republican morals for you!' (To Martin, 4 March 1883.)

Boudin spent the winter of 1883 in Trouville, apart from short visits to Etretat, Fécamp, Yport, and Saint-Valéry-en-Caux, where he did some studies.

He had not been dazzled by his success of the previous winter: he spent the following winter more secluded than ever, concentrating on improving his expression, continually feeling that he had not achieved that which he was seeking. Throughout this period Durand-Ruel was battling with financial difficulties, and for the painter life did not consist entirely of bright colours.

And to think that they are enlarging the schools to make painting flourish, a completely useless seed in these times. (To Martin, 31 January 1884.)

He was at last able to satisfy his desire to paint some more landscapes which had haunted him for several years. In June 1884 he left for Dordrecht. He was to bring back one of his most beautiful series, the most vigourous yet. He stayed in Dordrecht from 10 June to 12 July, working obsessively, even though he was not deeply attached to the region. On his arrival he wrote:

Otherwise, things are not altogether black for me.... I have found lodgings near the quay, and had the additional good luck to find several painters nearby, among others our friend Yon, the painter-engraver, and some others I didn't know... a real artist's colony. The countryside is very picturesque, and the river is superb. (To Martin, 23 June 1884.)

But a short time later he wrote:

We are not sorry to see the approaching end of our stay here. I resisted for love of art, and assure you that I shall leave with joy. I have worked like a mercenary for a month, not having had one day of rain since my arrival, but what difficulties I have had. (To Martin, 22 March 1884.)

He returned to Trouville to transform into finished works the sketches made in Dordrecht.

That summer the only person he had close to him was Ribot, the only friend that death had left him among his senior colleagues; the two painters had long discussions about their art. They were united by a profound friendship; and indeed Boudin was widely popular. He had been chosen to preside over the banquet arranged during the previous winter by a group of artists in honour of Ribot. All those who were considered to be artistically independent or original personalities, painters like Fantin-Latour, Monet and Raffaëlli, writers like Goncourt, musicians like César Franck and Lalo, came together to pay hommage to Ribot's obstinate integrity, scornful of easy success and official honours. Much moved, Ribot rose to reply: 'Gentlemen, I drink to art, but to the art I love, to the art of the emancipators, to the art of Millet, of Corot, of Daubigny, of Courbet, of Manet.' If he did not add the names of Jongkind, Boudin and Monet, it was because, motivated by extreme delicacy, he wanted to name only the dead.

In spite of his longing to travel, which he satisfied from time to time, Boudin was well aware that nothing could destroy his attachment to the Norman coast where he was born, the sight of which had been his perpetual companion for nearly sixty years, his beloved subject, and the instrument of his glory. From now on he desired an even more material attachment, and had built in Deauville 'a little Dutch birdcage', as he called it: the Villa des Ajoncs.

My wife claims that it resembles those Dutch birdcages which are made in the shape of a house, and that it lacks only the ring to hang it up by. She exaggerates a little. (To Martin, 20 November 1884.)

From now on, his health was almost the only thing that was to drag him away from those shores. His 'possession' of the skies and beaches became deeper, more demanding, and more irresistible, until the day when his eyes closed on the delicate, wind-brushed horizons of which his work remains the patient and passionate reflection.

Dordrecht: windmills beside the canal, 1885

Rotterdam: the Oosterkade, 1879. Photo M. Sirot

Le Havre: harbour entrance at high tide. Photo M. Sirot

Harbour mouth, Le Havre, *c.* 1891

View of Antibes, 1893

Antibes: view from the Château Salé, c. 1880. Photo M. Sirot

Weariness · The State buys *Russian Corvette*
Death of his wife · Exhibition in the Rue Le Peletier
The Legion d'honneur · Last journey to the south
Death on 8 August 1898 · Character

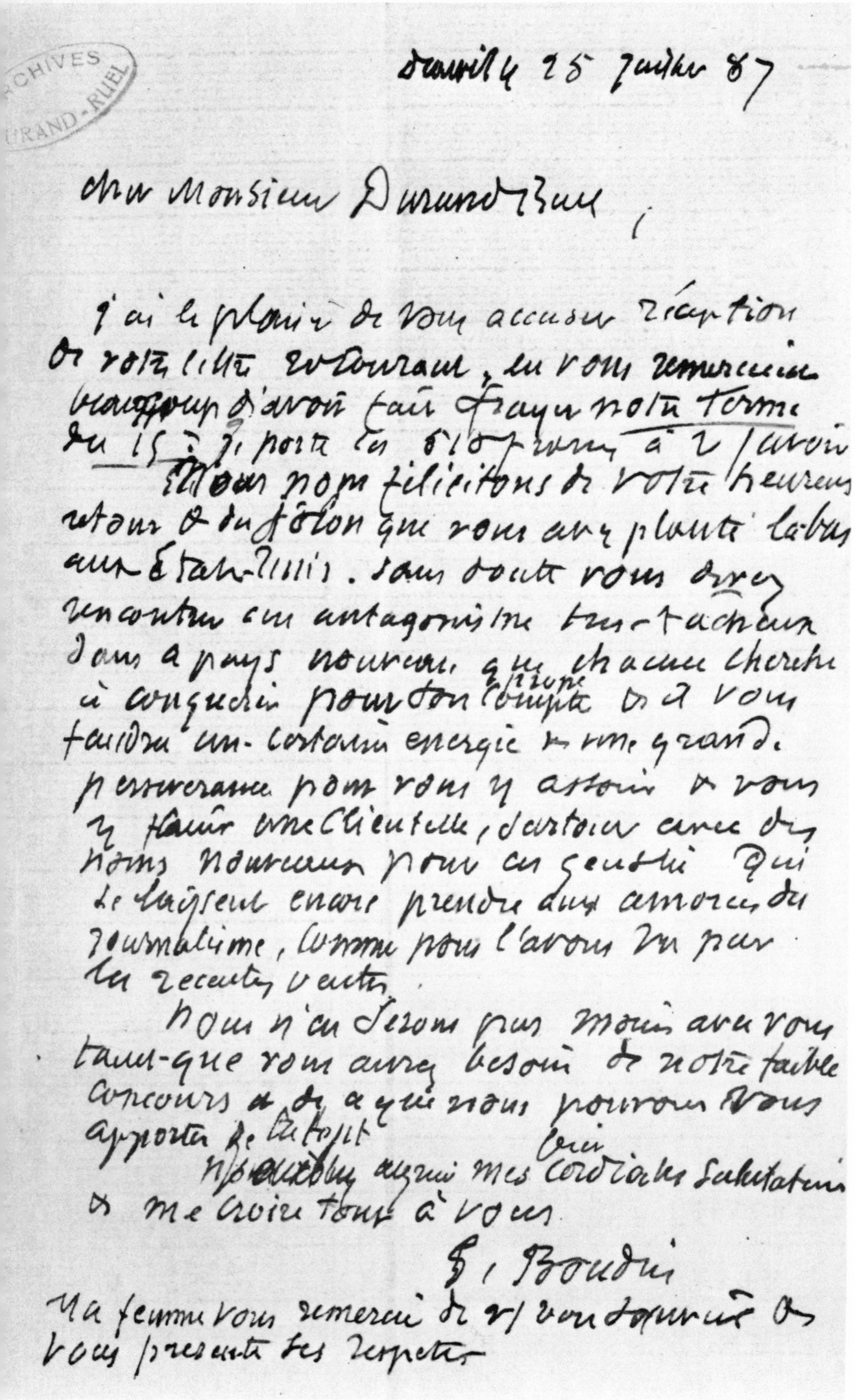

ARCHIVES DURAND-RUEL

Deauville 25 juillet 87

Cher Monsieur Durand-Ruel,

J'ai le plaisir de vous accuser réception de votre lettre et courant, en vous remerciant beaucoup d'avoir fait payer notre terme du 15, je porte les 510 francs à l'avoir.

Et nous vous félicitons de votre heureux retour et du jalon que vous avez planté là-bas aux Etats-Unis. Sans doute vous avez rencontré un antagonisme tracassier dans ce pays nouveau que chacun cherche à conquérir pour son compte et il vous faudra une certaine énergie et une grande persévérance pour vous y asseoir et vous y faire une clientèle, surtout avec des noms nouveaux pour ces gens-là qui se laissent encore prendre aux amorces du journalisme, comme nous l'avons vu par les récentes ventes.

Nous n'en serons pas moins avec vous tant que vous aurez besoin de notre faible concours et de ce que nous pourrons vous apporter de

Recevez aussi mes cordiales salutations et me croire tout à vous

E. Boudin

Ma femme vous remercie de votre bon souvenir et vous présente ses respects

Letter from Boudin to Charles Durand-Ruel after the latter's visit to New York. Archives of Galerie Durand-Ruel

Boudin at work. Photo inscribed: A Monsieur Durand-Ruel, souvenir d'amitié E. Boudin, 5.11.1896

Chapter 4 1884-1898

Life continued, monotonous in that it lacked adventure, but kept in perpetual movement for Boudin by his scruples and by his aspiration to gain greater control of himself.

> Perhaps I am getting rather slack: that is one of my preoccupations. In this profession one may growold, but to grow slack is forbidden. (To Martin, 30 September 1885.)

Neuralgic pains, difficulties with dealers, and inclement weather during his few short visits to Etaples and Berck all combined to render his task painful during the years 1885, 1886 and 1887.

> A lost year at my age has to be reckoned with; one grows tired, one's eyes grow faint, and enthusiasm grows cold. One of the tiresome aspects of old age is to lose one's eagerness and one's taste for the nothings that filled one with passion before. One continues because the machine is in motion, but how one grows cold. Then one feels a great need of rest, and one's only desire is to take things easy. But as far as work is concerned, I have to keep on forging ahead, for a whole crowd of young rascals push me in the rear and chase me; they travel fast, and if I arrive I will be out of breath and exhausted. (To Martin, 28 October 1885.)

And once again he bent over his easel, he withdrew into himself to find again in emotion all the subtlety of the sky, of which, in opinion, he had only been able to note in his sketches an all too vague memory. He sought to seize the intangible that fled from him, and in his studio in Paris he was constantly haunted by nostalgia for the horizons which for him were life itself.

Corot once said: 'For three weeks I have been seeking boughs in my studio.' Boudin wrote:

> Oh, how I miss a glimpse of horizon here, a corner of the sky marrying far away with the sea, the clouds, a little bit of sea and those nothings which I have so close in my little red-roofed cabin. Now I have all that only on my scraps of canvas, and that's a poor consolation. (To Martin, 29 December 1885.)

And he withdrew even more into himself, as if, in the Paris where he was forced to live, he wished only to see his inner dream of the places where his heart lived always. Nothing could distract him from his desire for the sky. Every year he was in exile, waiting for the first fine day which would bring back to the shore a sea-bird who only wintered in Paris.

He knew, however, that in some men's efforts he had to find ever-renewed counsel and inspiration. He did not remain immutably attached to the masters who had been his models during his formative period. He kept his eye on the crowd of 'young rascals', as he called them; but, to tell the truth, these young rascals were not numerous. Among them, and at their head: Monet, reviled, discussed and still derided, but almost in full possession of his genius.

> Yesterday I went to Petit's to see an exhibition in which Monet has caused a great stir. The damn fellow has become so daring in his tones that it is impossible to look at anything else after seeing one of his. He drives into the shade, and ages, everything around him. Painting has never been more vibrant, and more intense. If it were not for the handling, which terrifies the bourgeoisie, people would be falling over themselves to buy. But the husk is so hard that few people dare raise it to look beneath. (To Martin, 19 June 1886.)

But these were only brief oases in his solitude. Buyers were still rare, and dealers even rarer. Durand-Ruel attempted to open a branch in New York to compensate for the indifference of Paris; and this was the refrain of Boudin's letters:

> What do you expect me to do, in this Paris where I never see a soul any more? I am here, forgotten, or as if forgotten, in my little corner. (To Martin, 14 February 1887.)

I cannot see the necessity of prolonging my stay here where I am bored to death. (To Martin, 26 April 1887.)

However, at the Salon of 1886, the state bought *The Squall*, which is now in the Musée de Morlaix. Once again he returned with joy to the seashore, the little villa in Deauville, and all the great expanse of eternally renewed sky, the necessary nourishment for his eyes and his heart. He wrote to Martin on 26 October 1887: 'One must finish one's career valiantly, and show that one has not grown soft with age.'

And although it was a tiresome season, 'a thin year if ever there was one, poor in studies,' he strove to excel himself. He prolonged until the autumn the studies he had begun, 'of reflections in Deauville harbour', though at times this work became painful, and staying for three hours working in the mist made him conscious that his blood was no longer that of a twenty-year-old. And yet he was well aware that he had by no means exhausted the marvellous vitality of his nature. His lively sensibility still had some new impressions in store for him.

I do not lack courage, I've even made progress, which is consoling. It's so stupid to see oneself growing old. (To Martin, 17 October 1887.)

And then he was struck by discouragement at the indifference of the public:

The will leads us gradually to enquire the price of frame and stretcher. The hardest thing is that I am no longer a beginner, I have very few years ahead of me, without knowing what is reserved for me. My hand will grow heavy even if my intelligence remains lively. My eyes will tire too, and zest disappears like lightning. It would be the time to harvest what one has sown during the whole of one's life, but the contrary happens. (To Martin, 27 December 1887.)

But lasting discouragement was never to return. Absorbed in nature, indifferent to honours, anxious to study continually the themes dear to him because he knew them to be inexhaustible, he felt in his efforts how little his sixty years had weakened his vigour.

I assure you that I have never been in better possession of my palette, my understanding is greater, my goal more visible, and I feel that I would still have much to learn if I was elevated by success. (To Martin, 5 February 1888.)

The mocking, resilient philosophy of the old painter is revealed in these words, written without bitterness:

Instead of my retiring from business, business is retiring from me. (To Martin, 26 February 1888.)

Certainly philosophy, dreams, self-sufficiency as one would like to call it, are wonderful in theory, but the time of street philosophers has passed. Diogenes would be arrested as a beggar in our times; or he would be issued with meal-tickets in the street. (To Martin, 18 March 1888.)

A quite considerable sale which he held on 19 April 1888 at the Hôtel Drouot (sixty oils, thirty pastels, ten watercolours) renewed his courage:

The sale has taken place, and it went well: the exhibition was a very great success, although my colleagues showed themselves to be indifferent. But apart from that, I've had some unequivocal proofs of interest: the Prefect of the Seine, the Rothschilds, and some private buyers, new friends, came to the sale. Certainly, it is not great commercial business as far as profit is concerned, since the costs carry off a good part of the takings, but it is a little revival of attention and reputation, and in the present circumstances that is a great deal. They didn't expect to see me face this new day with a rejuvenated colour.... I already long to face the sea and to try myself out with the brush. The progress I have made in one direction is amazing, and so is my thirst for light. (To Martin, 21 April 1888.)

A short time after this, at the Salon of 1888, the State took a renewed interest in a painter who, by his quality as a marine painter at a time when they were rare, should have already drawn their attention. *Russian corvette in the Eure docks* was bought and placed in the Luxembourg.

Various collectors, delighted by his sketches of cows in meadows, declared them to be his most successful canvases, and this was the beginning of a series in which Boudin expressed with singular liveliness the attitudes and colours of the herds in the meadows which border the Touques, the little river at Deauville (see p. 145). He devoted almost the entire summer of 1889 to them, and was often to revert to this theme, which was constantly before his

Three-masted ship in Camaret bay, 1873

eyes during his visits to his villa. In these series of animals, as much and more than in the others, he gave his paintings the flavour of a sketch.

Do you really believe there are two ways to make high-priced pictures? Fashion makes them expensive, my good friend. Perhaps mine too will become precious, when I am no more. Didn't we long ago see, in Troyon's lumber-room of a studio where I worked, a sunset by Rousseau, rather knocked around and unframed? When I placed it on the easel to see it better Troyon said: 'It is pretty, but all the same I must make up my mind to give it a frame.'

Well, my good fellow, that scarcely sketched-in picture, as you did not fail to point out, has since been sold for 65,000 francs, then for 100,000, and it's still rising. You can see from this example, and a hundred others one could quote, that all this is nothing more than the passing of time. Look at the Daubignys which used to be called sketches, and which now fetch exorbitant prices. What it is, you see, is that you, and many provincial collectors, get into the habit of believing that excessive work constitutes good painting. I would really like to get that idea out of your head, even if I can't get it out of the others'. Far from bringing any perfection, labour and *'vidoursage,'* as they call painful painting in the studios, only make it insipid. I have made this detour to return to my own case. Contrary to the others, I do all within my power to conserve the appearance of a sketch in my painting. And already I am accused of overelaboration. Oh, if you could only see the exhibition of thirty-three at Petit's, there would certainly be some cries of horror there. (To Martin, 11 September 1888.)

Boudin set to work again with renewed courage. The state purchase, the success of his sale, the livelier attention of some of the critics, the passion, almost fanaticism, of a few collectors for his work, were all putting new heart into him. Then the illness and death of his wife threw his life, and his spirit, into a deep and sudden disorder.

All winter long he went to and fro between his studio, where he no longer had the heart to work, and the Dubois' house, where his wife seemed at times to be recovering from her operation, but made him feel more often an anguish which was very soon after to be justified.

I have before me the letters in which, almost day by day, he told his friend of the anguish, the renewed hope, and the despair that his wife's condition caused him. They reveal the sensitive nature of which he gave so many other proofs. This letter was written at his wife's deathbed:

Dear friend,

She died during the night: yesterday she still had a spark of hope. 'I feel I am getting better,' she said. 'Fetch the doctor, he will take care of me, and I will perhaps be saved.' She was clinging on to life by a feeble thread... it was a fleeting illusion.

My dear dead one is there, tranquil, in eternal peace on her bed... her face is calm, she is like one of those pale, medieval Virgins whose outlines are so thin and so suffering.

At a certain moment I felt myself to be alone, and heard what seemed to be the vibration of her voice in my ears.... I ran to her bed, she seemed to be alive again, but it was only an illusion.... It really is all over, they came to bring her flowers. Intruders arrived and dragged me away from my so sweet tête-à-tête with my dear dead one of whom I was making a sketch. Yesterday she bade me farewell, while still cherishing I know not what reserve of hope in the possibility of living.

She had heard someone coming into the studio.

'Who has come?' she asked.

'It's our friend L., he asked for news of you.'

'No, I know he came about the ground where you will place me,' she said, 'not too far away so that you can come to see me sometimes.'

'Well, yes, my dear, it will be at the Butte-Montmartre, it's a pretty place.'

'There will be two places.... for I want you to be with me, as you promised.'

My God, my God, I was crying like a child.

'Don't cry, I'd like to cry too, but I no longer can: I have suffered too much and am happy to die. Get yourself a good housekeeper. I did love you.'

Oh, my friend, my heart feels as if it were grasped in a vice, and I can no longer go near her bed without sobbing.

Work? Why, why? If I had ambitions or needs it would perhaps be a good thing. No, for me there remains nothing but the joy of seeing the great sky again and the air which I need so much. (To Martin, 24 March 1889.)

This letter is quoted, above all, for the conclusion. In such a painful circumstance the passion for nature which had always possessed Boudin haunted him even more. He knew that only there could he find peace:

Laundress on Trouville beach, *c.* 1873

I will soon feel, after this terrible shock, the need to go out and commune with nature, the great consoler. There I will no doubt find calm of hearth, and a little healt, since 'my hair grows white and my face is wrinkled.' You are right, dear friend, we who are maddened with work really do kill ourselves. When I am at the easel I can no longer tear myself away, and in the evening I am exhausted by a labour which requires so great an application. My body is broken and my brain cracks with the tension I maintain for days at a time. (To Martin, 28 March 1889.)

The numerous sympathizers Boudin had acquired, as much by the virtues of his work as by his own courteous nature, found the chance to show their feelings during his mourning. Monet, among others, who at the time was busy doing a series of the Creuse river, expressed his affectionate friendship and made it a pretext for once again affirming his debt to Boudin:

'I have many causes to reproach myself as far as you're concerned, and I very often do. Don't be angry with me for this, dear friend, I am always out in the fields, often travelling, and always passing through Paris. But do not let this make you less certain of the friendship I feel for you, nor of my gratitude for the advice you gave me, advice which made me what I am.'

Very fortunately, circumstances came to the old painter's aid to ease his sorrow, to help him take up his brush again, and to continue his work, which had not yet reached decadence, as indeed it never did.

By a cruel anomaly of fate, I am at the moment the object of a sort of unwanted vogue. I would have liked some peace, but they don't want me to have any. At Bordeaux, where I sent two small seascapes of Le Havre, they made a real success of me, and literally squabbled for ownership of them. (To Martin, 10 April 1889.)

I am overwhelmed with work, they literally tear it from me. (To Martin, 7 May 1889.)

Little by little he took up his work again, facing 'nature, the great consoler,' and he felt as if his great need to work was once more burning within him. His robust physique spent itself in these long periods of tension while he sought his own pictorial truth. His psychic balance was re-established, and to his friend Martin he wrote these lines which once again give insight into his good-natured and ironic spirit:

In spite of the yet undried tears which come to my eyes, I couldn't help smiling at your advice, to take a lady companion about fifty years old. Can't you see, I've conjured up a picture of Boudin accompanied by a lady of rigid morals, carrying a little dog under her arm and reading a volume of Legouvé: *The Merit of Women*, just like one I once knew at Saint-Siméon who unceremoniously burnt my Diderot. Oh no, dear friend, you see I really believe that the morals of a fifty-year-old Cato really wouldn't suit a lad of my temper.... Hem... what if she wanted to convert me, like that one once at Saint-Siméon, who used to preach sermons about eternal life, about religion, to an

GALERIES DURAND-RUEL

11, RUE LE PELETIER, ET 16, RUE LAFFITTE

EXPOSITION

DE

TABLEAUX, PASTELS

FUSAINS

PAR

E. BOUDIN

L'EXPOSITION

sera ouverte du 8 juillet au 14 août 1889

de 10 h. du matin à 6 h. du soir.

ENTRÉE: 11, RUE LE PELETIER

PARIS

Title page of catalogue of the 1889 exhibition

atheist like me? Oh no, you see, if I were to associate with a woman she would have a gay face, a good creature who would make me forget that I am old and already stooping. Oh no, no, rather a young servant than a Mrs Grundy. At my age one needs someone to give advice, not moralize. (To Martin, 10 April 1889.)

A friend dragged him off to Dunkirk, where he set to work in spite of the terrible wind. During this time Durand-Ruel organized a new and more complete exhibition of his work.

This exhibition took place in the Galerie Durand-Ruel, 11 Rue Le Pelletier, from 8 July to 14 August 1889. There were eighty-nine canvases, nine charcoal drawings, and a series of pastels (marines and landscapes). The eight-page catalogue preface, which was unsigned, was written by the engraver Félix Buhot, and said among other things:

'As a result of his recent and incessant research this exhibition will show, we believe, the painter's second style, which one could call the "luminous and sunlit style." His palette is enriched with new tones. His constant study of nature, his thirst for truth and improvement, have led him to the goal he sought: greater intensity of light, more powerful execution, deeper sonority in his fresh and lively colours.

'Certain pieces make his rare quality of harmony in brilliance shine with a particular energy, possessed this time by a superior mastery, not to mention the pastels, rapid notes, but composed from nature, comprising a real *liber studiorum*. We would like to single out the latest *Deauville beaches* flooded with morning sun, the seascapes under blue skies, like *English brig* and *Return of the fishing boats*; and last and above all, the picture of animals which he modestly calls *Study*, and which seems to me to be one of the most beautiful canvases in this genre ever signed by a master, including Paulus Potter, Cuyp or Troyon.'

This exhibition included views of Dunkirk, Etaples, Le Havre, Deauville, Trouville, Berck, Oisème and Antwerp; the charcoal drawings were all landscapes of the Côte de Grâce.

It was in a way the summation of all his work since the previous exhibition in 1883, though he had added a few earlier canvases, such as an 1871 view of Antwerp. One could have had no more complete and just impression of the painter's talent, conscientiousness and variety. Besides, the reviews of the exhibition were numerous and for the most part full of praise. Justice was beginning to be shown to the painter. He had waited a long time, for he was now sixty-four years old; he had known many difficulties and discouragements, and he felt his life to be empty and solitary, a life which for thirty years had been supported by the presence of his wife and the religion of his art. What then did the favours and distinctions, which he had disdained and which came much too late, matter to him now? At the Exposition Universelle of 1889 to which he had sent five canvases at the special invitation of Antonin Proust, he was allotted a gold medal. He did not even mention it in his letters. What could these distinctions, so envied by most people, do to relieve the sadness of feeling alone and old? What encouragement could they give to an artist who had never followed anything but his own conscience, and who had worked only to satisfy its demands?

I feel so isolated, so abandoned, that I sometimes fear for my sanity. A man who has lived for thirty years in a warm atmosphere maintained by a devoted wife finds isolation extremely hard, I assure you. (To Martin, 2 November 1889.)

Only relentless work could divert him from his sadness. Sadly, though, old age had come. He tired quickly, he could no longer allow himself to work as furiously as before, spending entire days in front of the easel. And yet his robust artistic temperament showed as yet no signs of old age, and the volume of work he turned out would easily have satisfied a younger man.

The enthusiasm of the collectors urged him on in spite of himself, and obliged him to work. Now, for the first time in his life, he felt the useful spur of demand, not that this could ever make him neglect,

On Trouville beach: sunshades, 1873

for the sake of quick profits, the demands of his artistic conscience. 'From now on', he wrote, 'I want to neglect nothing in my production.' (To Martin, 23 November 1889.) Had he ever had cause to reproach himself with neglect?

He took control of himself again. The year drew to a close, not so his labour.

I am finishing this year working like a Turk, so as not to think of all the sadness I have had in this fatal year. (To Martin, 28 December 1889.)

And work once again took possession of him; he was beginning to achieve what will be defined as his fourth style. In spite of his age, and the pain that frequently assailed him, his hand was still supple and light, and his eye, one would think, even more subtle. His eagerness to work had returned:

> I take up my yoke in the morning and do not put it down till evening, going out almost at daybreak so as not to lost precious time. I work like a slave, polishing and polishing.... I exhaust myself terribly to content the world, and never manage to content myself. (To Martin, 2 February 1890.)

He felt considerably the after-effects of a cold he had caught in Caudebec the previous September when coming back from painting under the driving rain, but the robustness of his sailor ancestry helped him overcome it.

That year, those who disagreed with the Salon founded the Société des Beaux-Arts, of which Ernest Meissonier was the president. Boudin could not help but join: his nature directed him towards independence. He found himself alongside his illustrious friends Puvis de Chavannes and Ribot; even one of the impressionists took part, Sisley, who showed six views of Moret. Boudin was represented at this Salon

On Trouville beach, 1874

by ten canvases, very different in type and subjects: a *Fog effect in the Eure docks*, two views of *Dunkirk harbour*, a *Scheveningen beach*, a *Departure of the boats*, and a *Return of the boats to Berck*, a *View of Caudebec*, two landscapes of *Outskirts of Dunkirk*, and a *Beach at Bénerville*.

His submissions were very widely noticed, although even at this time his works seemed to some contemporary critics to be too daring.

He once again felt the necessity of varying his choice of subjects, in spite of the attraction of his little villa at Deauville. He knew that if he went there right at the beginning of the summer he would not have the courage to tear himself away. He went instead to see again the beaches of the Pas-de-Calais and French Flanders, which he had not yet studied to his satisfaction, and at the same time visited some of the little towns inland.

He left on 7 June for Etaples, Berck, Saint-Valéry and Dunkirk, but, as on each of his visits to the north, he was crossed by bad weather, and since he was no longer at an age when he could without danger stay out painting for hours in the fine, penetrating rain, rheumatism brought him back to Deauville at the end of July. He had, however, been able to bring back from Etaples a few canvases which are among his most delicate. He had been unable to carry out his hope of making some studies of Dunkirk, and it was time to warm himself in the sun on the beach at Deauville.

> I have suffered so much from the cold in this calamitous month, that I really don't know how I managed to resist... for thirty-seven days I have received the most brutal gusts of wind on my back or my chest. Always in the whirlpool of wind which blows so strongly on the bridges and quays... what a torment, it almost made me deaf, and I felt pains that gave me much cause for worry. I thought I was really very ill, and only courage kept me going. (To Martin, 20 July 1890.)

In spite of everything he continued to work to resist the boredom that threatened him. He was pushed on by the collectors' commissions. For the first time all his submissions to the exhibition of the Société des Amis des Arts in his adoptive town, Le Havre, were bought: his fellow-citizens were beginning to realize that Boudin was one of the best of the many painters they had been able to see working on the quays or in the outskirts of the town.

And now he was sixty-six years old; age, after all, was beginning to sap his energy. At times he could no longer find warmth. Soon he was to have to leave Paris, and search in warmer climes for support for his body and the possibility of continuing work. But he was not yet overcome by decrepitude, and, in spite of one of the cruellest and most hopeless of illnesses, he was not to abandon his brush until the last moment. At an age when so many others can do nothing but repeat themselves, he was renewing himself.

> I become more and more demanding of myself.... My studio is becoming very much frequented even too much so. I'm not complaining about it, in my life I've had too many sterile years because I was not in vogue. Nevertheless, since my last exhibition I am completely launched and in fashion. (To Martin, Christmas 1890.)

'Launched' – what implicit irony there is in this word!

In December 1890 Boudin held a new exhibition in Durand-Ruel's gallery, and another in March 1891. Some time previously Durand-Ruel had organized an exhibition of works by Boudin in Boston.

Times had changed at last: the ostracism with which painters of the avant-garde had been met had at last been broken. The exhibition of Monet and Rodin at the Galerie Georges Petit in 1889 marks, historically, the end of the struggles of the impressionists. Certainly one could still read uncomprehending criticisms of Pissarro, Cézanne, Monet or Renoir, but the iron age of French painting was over and the golden age was beginning. The private collectors, dealers and salons were multiplying. Painters like Boudin found themselves pulled along in the

On Trouville beach, storm effect, 1894

wake of the new masters and could at last see their efforts crowned.

Some, alas, had not lived to see this new dawn, and among them was the painter who had played the most considerable and least noisy part in the liberation of landscape: Johann Barthold Jongkind died on 9 February 1891 at La Côte-Saint-André (Isère). His death was in Boudin's mind when he sent Monet, from Deauville, this touching letter:

With regard to your union, of which you sent me word, please allow me to send you a few lines of happy memories of time past... already so far away? And first of all to congratulate you on your marriage, and to congratulate Madame Monet whom I had the pleasure to see before, when she welcomed the artists so affably, and with such grace.

For many years the chances of existence and the necessities of life have separated us, but that has never lessened the interest I have taken in your efforts, and your success... I have followed with interest the bold, even daring endeavours which have brought you renown and reputation. How long it is since we set out to try ourselves out on the landscapes of the Rouelles valley or on the bank of Sainte-Adresse, or again at Trouville or Honfleur with the good, great, and regretted Jongkind... always followed by Mother Fesser. One evening recently I dined again in the little courtyard where we had such a good lunch with my poor Marianne, so soon departed, too early for me, and I was happy and sad at the same time to return to this memory and so many others.

But time marches on, we are still on our feet, you still full of health, and as for me, well, I'm beginning to totter and lose my aplomb. I still try to cut a brave figure, but I can feel it all draining away despite my resistance.

If I have one regret on seeing myself growing old, it's that among my souvenirs, which I keep religiously, I have not the tiniest little bit of a painting by you. I have Jongkind, Ribot, Vollon, Hamelin and so many other reminders of friendship and good comradeship... and I miss you, you who should be there on my wall to remind me of our years as beginners and, one has to say, years of struggle and hardship, and of discouragement, too.

I think this keepsake is no more than my due. I don't ask it of you for the commercial idea that your pictures are now valuable. I once had a very beautiful one which it has often pained me to see at Durand-Ruel's; that's the one I ask you to replace. When I say pain, I am not lying, for without a circumstance of which I don't have to remind you, it would still be on my wall at this hour.

Do as your conscience bids you, my dear Monet, but do believe that in remembering you would give me the greatest pleasure. You have regained possession of yourself. You are no longer in the times of struggle and difficulty. Be quick, for I am getting older every day.

My respects to Madame Monet and to you with all my heart.
The oldest of your friends in painting, *E. Boudin*. (28 July 1892.)

Justice is slow for true artists, and for some it is posthumous. Boudin at least lived to see his last years lightened with the favour that was his due. In 1892 at the instigation of Léon Bourgeois, minister of public education, the State bought *Villefranche roadstead* at the Salon. In October of the same year, Bourgeois appointed Puvis de Chavannes to invest Boudin with the cross of the Légion d'honneur. It was a thoughtful gesture, and added value to a decoration to which Boudin had alluded the previous year in a letter to Alfred Stevens:

For many years this promise has been made to me by a few friends like you who think I could deserve this recompense. I thank them from the depth of my heart, and am more vexed to see their wish thwarted than for myself, since I am not jealous of those who obtain the decoration. You know, my dear master, that after having struggled for material life for a number of years, I find that it is sufficient reward to have been able to live on my art, and have never desired any other, making little account of my merit and not believing myself justified in demanding more. Some time ago, when the question last arose of putting names forward for the decoration, I made a collective attempt with a certain number of admirers of that great talent who has left so many little masterpieces in France. I speak of Barthold Jongkind. It seemed to me that this master should come before me.

It would have been pleasant for me to see the last days of this great artist sweetened by giving him this great reward, which has so often been wasted on other foreigners who scarcely count in the art of our era. For my part, I have no pretension of equalling this great master, and consider myself sufficiently rewarded by the approval of the collectors.

He was forced to spend the winters in the South of France: in successive years he was seen at Villefranche, Antibes and Beaulieu. 'I feel pain whenever

Villefranche quay, 1892

Juan-les-Pins: view of roadstead, 1893

Gathering on Trouville beach, 1874

I like', he said. In 1895 he went as far as Venice, but once there he felt nostalgia for his Norman coast.

We have found lodgings on the quayside (Calle S. Zaccaria, 4688, Riva dei Schiavoni). Outside the boats are moored, the gondolas ply from morning till evening, but I must admit, the beastly great *vaporetti* are eyesores in front of the marble palaces... I wish I were twenty years younger, to be able to make this stay useful to myself and to art, but I am too exhausted for the rough labour of painting, and feel sure that it's too late to take advantage of it.... I would find it pleasant to feel a little breeze off our Channel. (To Louis, 26 May 1895.)

A letter to Charles Durand-Ruel reveals something of the impression Venice made on him:

In answer to your recent letter enquiring as to the price asked for my painting *Place Courbet, Abbeville*, I cannot give you any information, being unable to correspond from here with the owner of the work in question – which is in any case no more than a study.

I shall be able to let you know on my return. At the moment I am occupied in doing some views of Venice, a magnificent place, as I have no need to tell you, but somewhat disguised by the customary painters of the country, who have shown it under a blazing sun. In fact, Venice, like all luminous landscapes, is grey in colour, and its atmosphere is gentle and misty. And the sky is clothed in clouds like one of our Norman or Dutch skies, although the heat is intense at times. It is true that since I have been here it has been stormy all the time....

I regret that I no longer have ahead of me the years of youth which I would need to create a beautiful series of views of this place, which in any case is difficult to paint because of the historic monuments which demand a great deal of technique and long sessions in the city.... (To Charles Durand-Ruel, 20 June 1895: see p. 181.)

He returned with joy to Deauville, wishing to see again the shores where so many times he had attempted to capture the infinite variety of the sea and sky in all its aspects, and in which the slightest nuance could not escape his subtle eye. It seemed as if, by a secret warning, he wanted to see again, in a last visit, almost all the places he had painted. In 1896 he returned to Dieppe, to Fécamp and to Le Havre; in May 1897 he went to Pont-Aven, on to the roadstead at Brest, then Belle-Isle, Nantes and Saint-Nazaire; but these visits only augmented his passion for his own shores. From Pont-Aven he wrote:

I have grounded for a few days in Pont-Aven, very close to Quimper, and am sitting out a terrible squall adorned with rain, in a little hotel room. I visited the beaches of the villages, passing Nantes and Saint-Nazaire, villages which are rather insignificant as far as the picturesque is concerned, and which made me miss Le Havre. As for the other beaches, islands, etc., like Belle-Isle, Quiberon, Le Croisic and many other places, they're not up to our Norman coast, in spite of all the reports of visitors, and the rough crust of granite. (To Louis, 28 May 1897.)

He planned to return to Bordeaux, stopping at La Rochelle in memory of Corot, but exhaustion made him cut short his journey. It even seemed that the inexhaustible curiosity which had always animated him grew even more as death approached; not only for things concerned with his art, but also for the literary efforts of his time. He spoke to his brother of his taste for poets like Verlaine, and wrote:

I am going to send you some newspapers in which you will find extracts from [Zola's] *L'Œuvre*. This *Œuvre* seeks to acclimatize here the works of northern authors, of Norway, Sweden and England. You will see in it famous articles and very interesting discussions. I myself propose to go one evening to hear one of those plays. (To Louis, 17 December 1894.)

Death, however, grew closer; he felt its coming, in a thousand wearinesses which he fought against; but he could not hide his tiredness for much longer:

I am exhausted and feel a great need for rest, which I cannot, alas, grant myself. (To Louis, 30 November 1895.)

I have lost what I brought back from the sea, that energy of the lungs and even the suppleness of the knuckles which I absolutely lack. (To Louis, 29 December 1896.)

I am extremely tired, four months in the studio is hard to support, and I dream of being like the bats which flutter in the next door garden. I would love to be able to stretch my wings. (To Louis, 27 February 1897.)

One gets a little older every day and the day's work is hard to bear... but one has to go on, right up to the final tumble. (To Louis, 30 November 1897.)

He hid his weariness from his friends, as this letter to Monet shows:

My dear Monet, Deauville, 14 July 1897

On returning from a journey in Brittany I found your letter telling me of Jean's marriage with Mlle Hoschedé.

I have not the pleasure of knowing the bride, who they say is charming, but I can't resist the desire to return to a time so far away, on the occasion of your son's marriage.

He certainly doesn't remember me, and yet I carried him more than once on my shoulder, in the evenings when he came with his mother to see us in the Rue d'Isly.... How these memories carry me far back into a past that has not always been full of joy.... We have all had our moments of cruel anguish over money matters.... And I see you again with poor Camille in the Hôtel de Tivoli.

I have even kept from this time a drawing which shows you on the beach. There are three women in white, still young. Death has carried away two of them, my poor Marie-Anne and yours.... Only one of the three is still going strong. Little Jean is playing in the sand and his father is sitting with a piece of

Figures on beach, *c.* 1875

cardboard in his hand... and not working. It is a souvenir of those times which I have always piously conserved.

I could go even further into the past and see again for an instant the memories of our youth... our excursions into the Rouelles valley, on the banks of Sainte-Adresse. We have left a good many of these companions by the wayside: Bayeux, Courbet, Gautier, Jongkind and so many others. Do you remember a certain lunch we had at Villerville? All that is far away. Mother Fesser who was Jongkind's heiress, and who didn't live long enough even to pocket the 200,000 or 300,000 francs which passed straight to her boor of a son.

At that time we still had a sound foot and a sound eye, and hope in the future: you too have had your struggles, but you have been paid for your labour, it seems to me, since success has come to you, without officialdom playing any part whatever, thanks also to good old Durand-Ruel who has supported you with the faith of a believer.

For my part, I can't complain too much.... If I didn't feel old age coming on with the infirmities inherent in our profession, like the rheumatism which at this moment is nailing me to a chair, I should still be hale and hearty... but you, you have this good fortune, although our ages are not so far distant, for you were fifteen or sixteen years old when I sold you drawing pencils; I was twenty-two when I left the stationer's shop, but you are young in spite of yourself, and on my recent journey an American asked me if you were thirty years old, 'an impressionist without knowing it.' When I told him, he insisted that your son must be the creator of the canvases in question. The legend is made, you are young in spite of the years.

Do I have to congratulate you on your recent success? Why didn't you involve the officials in your game, you would have returned to Le Havre one day, like Harpignies, received to the sound of bells, or carried in triumph, perhaps. Or like Renouf you would see billboards on the street corners bearing your name in white letters.

Yours very cordially, *E. Boudin.*

He still struggled: in the autumn he painted in the streets of Honfleur; but he struggled in vain. At the end of the winter, in March 1898, he left again for Beaulieu. He had spent the entire winter in his studio in the Rue Vintimille in Paris, moving from his bed to his armchair, contemplating with sadness all his dear studies that he could not finish, in spite of the commissions that poured in. He attempted to work, but his hands and his courage failed him.

A moving and beautiful passion is still revealed in this passage of a letter to his brother, written shortly before his last journey to the south:

For two months I have been dragging from my bed to my armchair and from my armchair to my bed, ill, without courage, without strength, and above all without appetite, not having eaten two centimes' worth of bread for two months.

I am in a state of extreme weakness, every movement tires me.... Yet today I painted all day, and that seemed so good. I don't think I'll stay many more days in Paris. The doctor wants me to go towards the Midi to finish my convalescence beside the blue sea and the orange trees in blossom. My winter season is disrupted, and that at a moment when I am overwhelmed with commissions I cannot carry out. (27 February 1898.)

The cancer of the stomach with which he was afflicted made rapid advances; he could be fed only with difficulty. Already he could scarcely walk. He was taken once more to Beaulieu; he stayed at the Hôtel du Commerce, and then at the Hôtel Beaurivage, from 5 April to 20 May.

I am beginning to be able to drag myself along on my poor legs, which I couldn't do when I arrived, but if my legs are coming back to life, the same can't be said for my stomach. For months I have been unable to take any solid food, and at this moment I only sustain myself with two litres of milk a day.

Oh, my poor Louis, how we fade away quite quietly, how we slide towards the black hole! I who was formerly so brave no longer paint, I have neither the strength nor the desire to do so.... I warm my limbs in the sun when it shines strongly, for we don't have this resource every day, not even in this blessed country. (To Louis, 27 April 1898.)

The air was so good, and the sun which warmed him gave him some hope:

I hope to take out my brushes one of these days. (5 May 1898.)

But even for him these were no more than glimmers of hope; he knew himself stricken beyond remedy. He knew that he would never again be able to take up his palette. Already the sky no longer awakened in him a painter's curiosity. Then the great love which was life itself for him, rose up in him for the last time. He had now only one thought: to go to die on his

1883

Boats on Scheveningen beach, *c.* 1875
Boats on Scheveningen beach, 1876

native shore, to rest his last gaze on the horizon which at every period of his life he had painted, and so often with so much happiness.

He only stayed in Paris long enough to see to the classification of his canvases and his studies, and assure their distribution after his death. However, he was so weak that they despaired of being able to take him to Deauville. He concentrated all his remaining energy on this last wish. He did not want to die in the Paris that suffocated him, when in Normandy all that was life itself called him. He grew impatient with his weakness and despaired at moments of reaching his little cage in Deauville, and in one of his last letters, in which the still firm but jerky writing betrays his desperate will, he wrote to his brother:

We are waiting until I gain a little strength to leave for Deauville. When will that be? When? (To Louis, 28 May 1898.)

Roger Milès, who saw him at the beginning of that winter, retained a moving and just impression of his visit:

'He was sitting in front of the little cupboard where, in folders, his sketches and drawings had been classified in order, and, pulling them out one by one, he opened and leafed through them. All his life was passing in front of his eyes: fifty years' labour; the continual study of a delicate and prudent observer, witty when he sketched, with an expressive synthesis, townspeople scattered over the beaches, and full of emotion when he consecrated the same paper to seamen and boats, those shells which have a soul and those sails which are wings.

'There was everything that had been the passion of this man formed in the school of the masters of 1830; the fishermen, the fishing sloops, the gusts of wind and the hulls, the swarms of bathers on the fine sand, or the roughness of the shingle; human elegance tossed around by capricious fashion, and showing each year a new downfall and a new invention, in front of the immutable splendour of the sea, on the mirror of which the sun incessantly plays its enchantment of light in the fugitive setting of the clouds.

'And each page reminded the old painter of an incident, a picture long since dated and forgotten in his work: without weariness and without conceit he evoked a past that trembled with memories. His clear and lively memory spread out like an inexhaustible, untainted spring. It was a touching joy to hear him talk, he who is certainly one of the most distinguished of the minor masters of our French school, a 'minor master' in the sense one uses to describe the delectable seventeenth-century Flemish painters who are the pride of private collections and museums.

'I remember him saying to me, with a tear in his deep blue eye: "In Paris I am like an exile." The city did not suit either his temperament or his art. He needed the great horizons, the great disorder of nature, and its infinite tranquillity.'

In June, however, it was at last possible to take him to Deauville. Then he awaited death with serenity. Through the open window he saw the sky and the sea, his two great passions. The clouds which passed still diverted his blue eyes, which illness had not dimmed. He followed the capricious forms, measured the subtle colourings, he underwent, without bitterness, their lesson of inconstance and ephemeral beauty. The pain which gnawed at him could not reach the deep serenity of his soul, where the antique acceptance of his sailor blood continually tempered the ardent curiosity of the artist.

In spite of physical pain one could say of him that nothing troubled his end. Death came to him, on 8 August 1898, at the hour when the sun begins to gild the cliffs of La Hève across the estuary.

Such was the man, and such his life. Without adventures and without disorders, everything was measured by the fervour of a soul that was master of itself. Nothing hurried him. He awaited his hour, whether it was that of his precious friendships, that of glory, or that of death. There was in him a fatalism born of his race. He owed his entire character to them: with him ended a long line of sailors and fishermen, they are reflected in him as in a faithful mirror; all their dreams, their calm and their desires, left in his consciousness their lively and confused traces.

He was the product of a long, obscure past, humble and genuine, which each of his gestures recalled and eternalized. He did not hope to detach himself from it, or wish people to forget that he owed everything to it. His inheritance spoke through him quietly and without emphasis. He felt neither hate nor impatience, he knew how to keep silent and see, he could see things over and over again without wearying.

He was of Honfleur. For those who know this town, he epitomized the charm of its spirit, at once strange and measured. To tell the truth, one cannot see how he could have been born anywhere else, even in another little port along the Norman coast: for there are among those groups of fishermen, as there are even among their boats, differences which do not escape the patient gaze. Secret aspirations and different necessities have caused each of these ports to construct particular boats which, more effectively than by initials written on the sail or planking, betray their origin by their measurements and shape. One could pass close by Boudin, as one could by his work, without at first being struck, so little did he resemble those men, and those works of men, that are praised for their ostentation, their passion and their power. One might have said that Boudin dedicated himself to modesty, had that not been his natural inclination, not at all the self-effacement that is hesitation or diffidence, but that which conceals its own style and dimensions.

He was tall and slightly round-shouldered, with rather dangling arms, the posture of those whom the use of oars has at length bent, and whose hands are surprised to close on nothing. His gait was slow and balanced, that of a sailor whom nothing can hurry once he is on land. His voice was indistinct and his speech slow, with the monotonous intonation of those who speak little, and to whom what they say matters more than the way in which they express it.

But just to see his face made me think of the sea. He even had the face of a pilot, not only because of his fan-shaped beard and shaven cheeks, but also because of his blue eyes that were always on the watch, lively, inquisitive eyes, always moving in his calm face; his nostrils mobile, scenting the wind. His unforgettable eyes were of a singular blue in which the sky really seemed to have rested: two candid, yet shrewd eyes. Above them a wide forehead, huge and domed like a shell, from which his chestnut hair flowed down in soft waves to his nape.

In the course of these pages we have seen him continually forcing himself towards more complete, more delicate, and yet more economical expression. Nothing could lead him on except his own will and the secret virtue of circumstance. He was sure of his course, and held the rudder firmly, but for the rest he went with the wind.

Nothing blinded him, he knew his place and that of other men: he never encroached on others and while knowing some of their destinies to be greater, he did not undervalue his own.

Few men saw their own times clearer than he. Without support and without advice, he went directly towards the best, and, at a time when French painting was completely renewing itself, this was no mean achievement.

Nothing imposed upon him: success, honour, fortune, hostility or contempt. He weighed men up. He knew that the despised Jongkind was one of the greatest painters of the time, he knew that the derided Corot was the master of landscape; he knew that the abused Monet would one day be the glory of his age; nor did the fame of Isabey and Troyon conceal from him the weakness in their art.

View of Rotterdam roadstead, 1880

He bore no hatred for others: he despised them. It seemed that the Institut did not exist. He did not mention Cabanel or Gérôme any more than he did Bouguereau. He knew that such men had no place in art, but their success left him unperturbed. He knew too how to enjoy those whose vision was far removed from his: Ribot, Fantin-Latour or indeed Puvis de Chavannes.

In his work and spirit, as in his heart, there was a sure consistency and stability; he never took blind risks, and once attached he never withdrew. He lacked in his life the fantasy, the passionate violence and the marvellous contradictions that one loves in the lives of great artists. Boudin's virtue lay in moderation, though there was nothing petty about him. He stretched himself to his limit, and not without struggles.

Dejection is a bad guest, and, unhappily I give it lodging so often that it stops me short. There are, however, men as unfortunate as me who manage to get by. Those people have no more than I (Notebooks.)

His whole life is the proof of irresistible patience: In his art and in his life he carefully kept order. He was born practically in poverty; he had known arid days, but money did not dazzle him at the time when he became able to acquire it. He kept some of it back for difficult times, but he refused to bind himself to it, or to engineer manœuvres that would make his canvases suddenly rise in value. He ended his life almost rich, but his tastes had not changed because of that: he would not allow an increased income to make him forget his little home town and its way of life to which he still kept. He was more troubled by worries about his art than by the difficulties of his existence.

It cannot be denied that there are hard moments to be overcome. It's like that when all around one sees the impossibility of getting a little money, and needs surge up all around one. A poor old mother implores, the rent has to be paid, one needs things, even paints and a thousand things one has to do without. This petty economy kills slowly with the apprehensions that merge in with it and which tug at the brain like a saddening idea. In these moments of crisis all my courage disappears, and I find myself in the state of complete exhaustion that has too often paralysed me, for I see myself with faculties equal to many other people, and continual concentration, yet unable to do what they do. Praise therefore the graces of art. Art, it is true, is not there for nothing, and we owe it to ourselves to work according to our hearts, and do what we wish. You too, poor Jongkind, you pull the devil's tail and carry on your search while struggling in the meshes of a net, like a poor captive bird.

One must limit oneself to doing the little nothings that no one else produces. We ask so little of the public that in the end we must obtain it, with courage and a tiny bit of talent. (Notebooks.)

Everything merges in him, his sailor ancestry, the places which witnessed his birth, his works, and his life. There is no contradiction there, in whatever place one stands. The ancient curiosity of the captains of Honfleur in search of distant lands towards Africa or America was still alive in the soul of a painter searching for new means of expression. The adventurous coolness, the patient eagerness of those men were still alive in their descendant, who never tired of watching the incessant spectacle of the indolent or precipitate clouds, and who, with a soul full of love, was happy to contemplate the changing beauty of the great gateway which the estuary at Honfleur opened to the west.

Saint-Valéry-sur-Somme: moonrise over the canal, 1891

Venice: the Salute and the Piazzetta, 1893
Venice: the Dogana, the Salute and the Giudecca canal, 1893

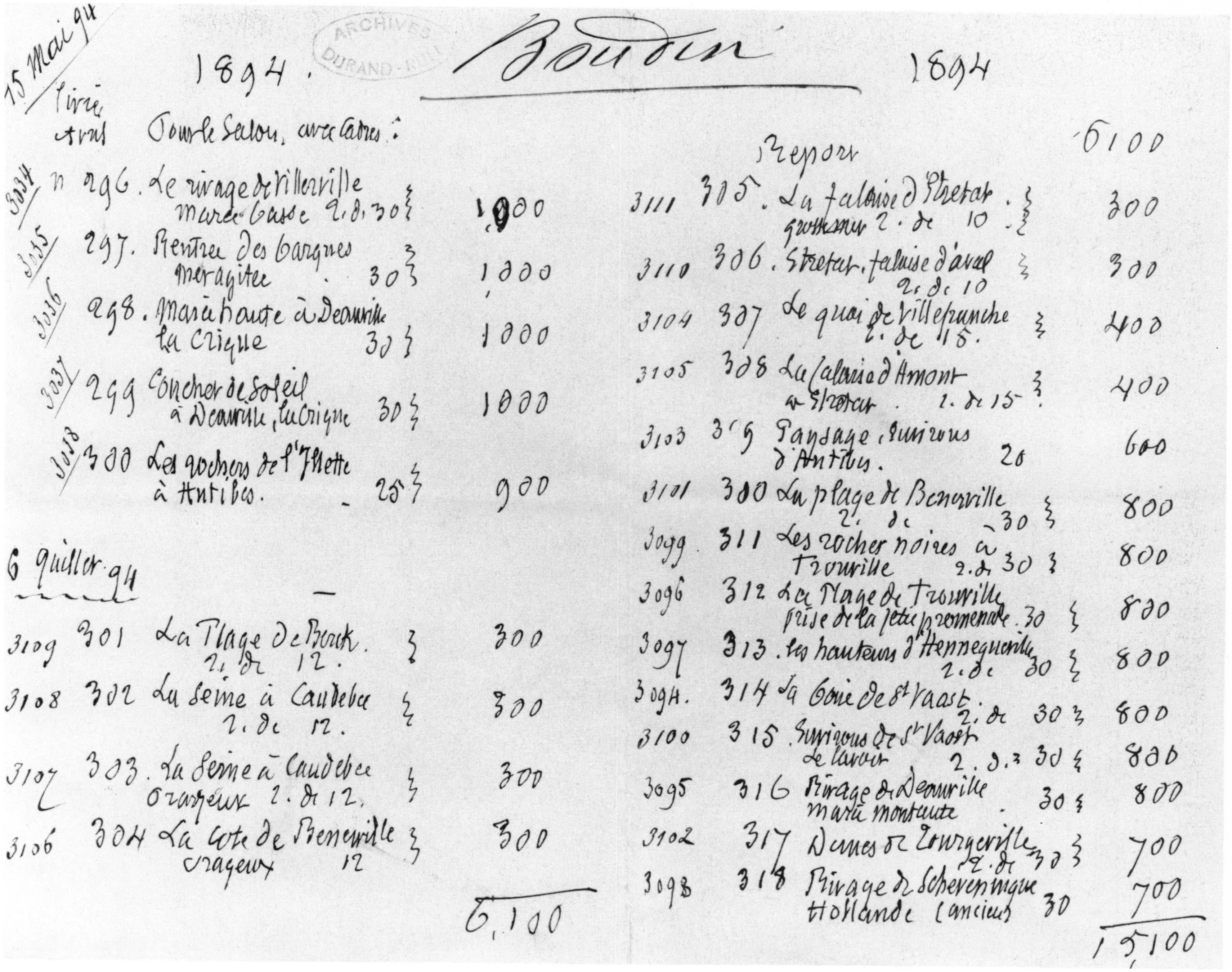

15 Mai 94
Livré avril

1894. Boudin 1894

Pour le Salon, avec cadres:

3034	n 296. Le rivage de Villerville marée basse 2.d.30		1000
3035	297. Rentrée des barques mer agitée	30	1000
3036	298. Marée haute à Deauville la crique	30	1000
3037	299 Coucher de soleil à Deauville, la crique	30	1000
3038	300 Les rochers de l'Ilette à Antibes.	25	900

6 Juillet 94

3109	301 La Plage de Berck. 2. de 12.	300
3108	302 La Seine à Caudebec 2. de 12.	300
3107	303. La Seine à Caudebec orageux 2. de 12.	300
3106	304 La côte de Benerville orageux 12	300
		6,100

Report 6100

3111	305. La falaise d'Etretat grosse mer 2. de	10	300
3110	306. Etretat, falaise d'aval 2. de	10	300
3104	307 Le quai de Villefranche 2. de	15.	400
3105	308 La falaise d'Amont à Etretat. 2. de	15	400
3103	309 Paysage, environs d'Antibes.	20	600
3101	310 La plage de Benerville 2. de	30	800
3099.	311 Les rochers noirs à Trouville 2. de	30	800
3096	312 La Plage de Trouville prise de la jetée promenade.	30	800
3097	313. Les hauteurs d'Hennequeville 2. de	30	800
3094.	314 La baie de St Vaast 2. de	30	800
3100	315 Environs de St Vaast le lavoir 2. d.	30	800
3095	316 Rivage de Deauville marée montante	30	800
3102	317 Dunes de Tourgéville 2. de	30	700
3098	318 Rivage de Scheveningue Hollande (ancien)	30	700
			15,100

Boudin's manuscript note of paintings delivered to Durand-Ruel, May and July 1894. Archives of Galerie Durand-Ruel

Eugène Boudin in 1890

Posthumous tributes · Commemorative exhibition
Bordeaux harbour bought for the Musée
du Luxembourg · Auction of his studio
Posthumous exhibitions

Ships at anchor in Camaret bay

Chapter 5 1898 and after

Marianne Boudin's wish that her husband should lie beside her in the grave deprives us of the melancholy pleasure of knowing that Boudin sleeps his last sleep in Norman earth. The ceremony took place on Friday 12 August 1898 at the Eglise de la Trinité, and his remains were interred in the cemetery of Saint-Vincent de Montmartre.

The ceremony was as simple as his life had been. There was no ostentation, pomp or ready-made words; just two speeches, and really the only just and necessary ones: one which paid respects to the painter's memory, and the other which was the grateful farewell of his native town.

Albert Kaempfen, the director of the Louvre, spoke on behalf of Léon Bourgeois, the minister of public education and fine arts.

'The sky and the sea: that is what he tried to paint when he escaped from the little paint merchant's shop he had opened to earn his living. And later on, encouraged and advised by a great artist who had crossed his path by a happy chance, when he had decided to leave commerce behind, that is what he painted continually, with passion and with his heart full of joy. And he continued to do so right up to the end.

'With what conscientious and patient ardour he sought the truth, all those who knew him will bear witness. He had the gift of life....'

The other speech was given by the delegate of the municipal council of Honfleur, M. Louveau, a collector fascinated by everything concerning the art of his town, and who had ties with the painter. With very just feeling and lively emotion he affirmed once again the indissoluble links which connected, and will never cease to unite the painter to the town of Honfleur.

On 20 October 1898, M. Gustave Cahen, Boudin's solicitor and executor, took the initiative in putting on an exhibition of the painter's work, and for this purpose asked for the use of the rooms of the Ecole des Beaux-Arts. On 20 December following a new request was sent, in the name of a committee presided over by Léon Bourgeois and which consisted of Albert Sorel, Vollon, Cormon, Harpignies, Carolus Duran, Fantin-Latour, Roll, Cazin, Gervex, Lhermitte, James Tissot, Eugène Carrière, Damoye, Guignard, Raffaëlli, Quost, Lebourg, Helleu, Kaempfen, Bénédite, Roger Marx, etc. The cooperation of many private collectors and several museums was assured to provide the pictures for this exhibition, the aim of which was to help the town of Honfleur raise the money for a statue bust of the painter. Among the collectors who had promised the works by Boudin that they possessed were Georges Feydeau, Constant Coquelin, Bourgès, the Comte de Kergorlay, Tavernier, Viau, Demeur, Decot, de Bériot, Abadie, the Comte de Sonneville, Brocq, Aurélien Scholl, de Saint-Albin, Van de Velde (of Le Havre), Fanyau (of Lille), Rouart, and the municipalities of Le Havre, Honfleur, Bordeaux, etc.

The request was granted; and the exhibition opened at the Beaux-Arts on 9 January 1899. It consisted of 364 paintings, 73 pastels and 20 watercolours, spanning the period 1857-97. It was the most complete collection one could have hoped for. It was above all the variety of the works which gave cause for astonishment and admiration, even to those who had been able to follow the development of Boudin's work from day to day.

It was at this exhibition that Georges Leygues, now minister of public education, and Henry Roujon, director of the Beaux-Arts, decided to buy one of Boudin's most important works, *Bordeaux harbour*, for which the State paid 3,000 francs.

The press was unanimous in its praise of the beauty of this collection, and among the articles that were devoted to him, above all Gustave Geffroy's article in *Le Journal* (cf. Appendix) and that of Fourcaud in *Le Gaulois* must be mentioned.

In February 1899, in accordance with Boudin's instructions, his executor sent three canvases to the Musée du Havre, and forty-three pictures to the Musée d'Honfleur.

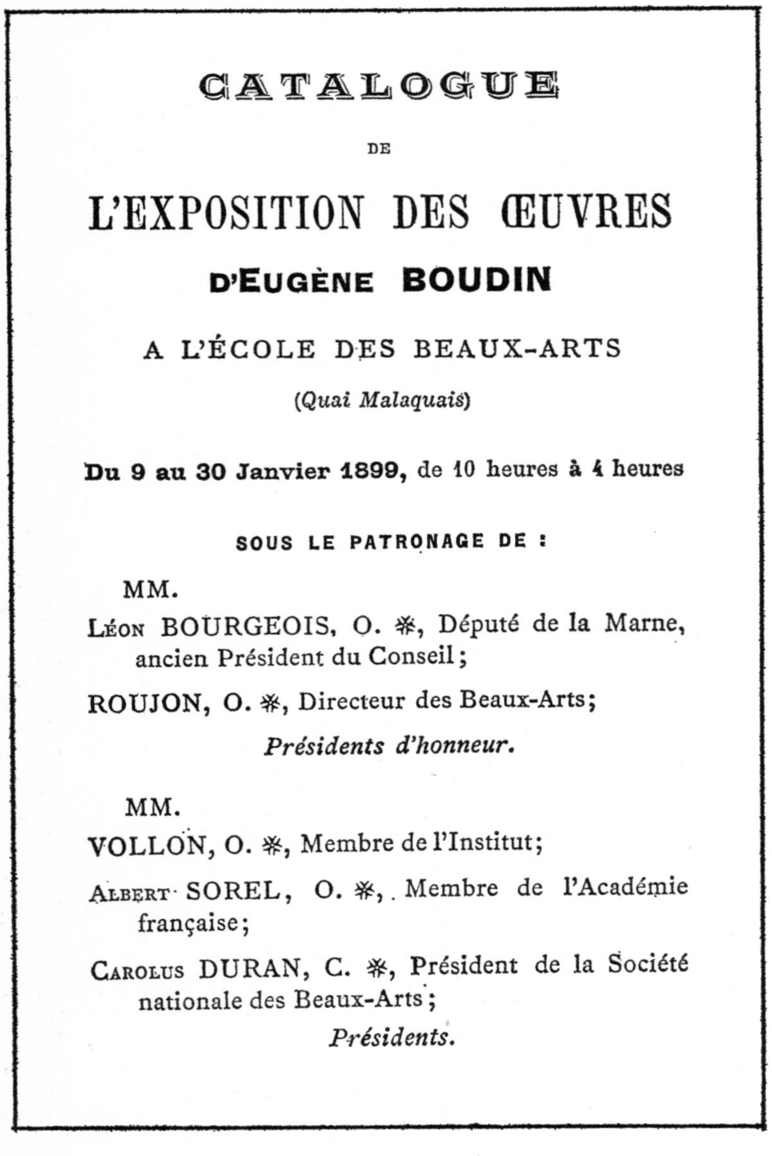

CATALOGUE

DE

L'EXPOSITION DES ŒUVRES

D'EUGÈNE BOUDIN

A L'ÉCOLE DES BEAUX-ARTS

(*Quai Malaquais*)

Du 9 au 30 Janvier 1899, de 10 heures à 4 heures

SOUS LE PATRONAGE DE :

MM.

Léon BOURGEOIS, O. ✻, Député de la Marne, ancien Président du Conseil;

ROUJON, O. ✻, Directeur des Beaux-Arts;

Présidents d'honneur.

MM.

VOLLON, O. ✻, Membre de l'Institut;

Albert SOREL, O. ✻, Membre de l'Académie française;

Carolus DURAN, C. ✻, Président de la Société nationale des Beaux-Arts;

Présidents.

Cover of the catalogue of the exhibition at the Ecole des Beaux-Arts, Paris, 9–30 January 1899

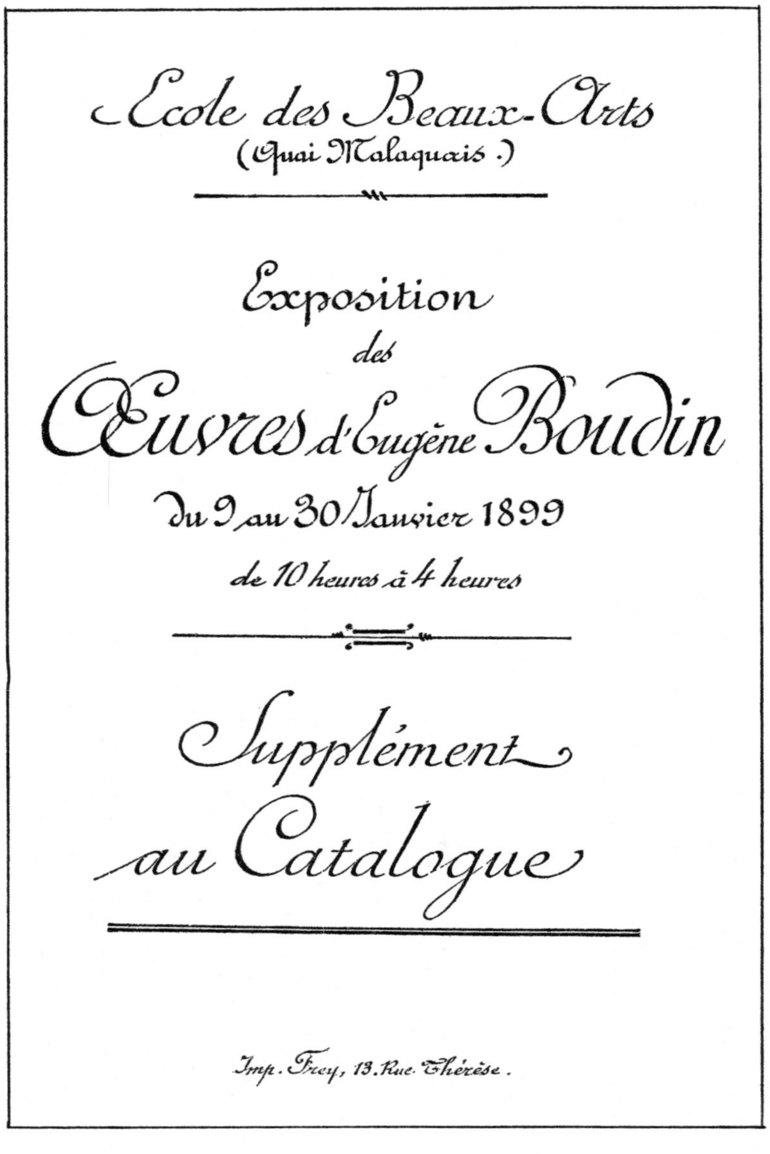

Ecole des Beaux-Arts

(Quai Malaquais.)

Exposition

des

Œuvres d'Eugène Boudin

du 9 au 30 Janvier 1899

de 10 heures à 4 heures

Supplément

au Catalogue

Imp. Frey, 13. Rue Thérèse.

Cover of the supplement to the catalogue of the 1899 Paris exhibition

Sailing boats off Deauville, *c.* 1882

On 20 and 21 March of the same year the sale of the contents of Boudin's studio took place in the Hôtel Drouot: 125 oil paintings, 99 watercolours, 56 pastels and drawings, and apart from those, a charcoal drawing by Corot, a watercolour by Jongkind, a drawing by Millet, and three drawings by Daumier.

The catalogue of the sale was preceded by an excellent study by Arsène Alexandre (see p. 235 of this book).

Atelier Eugène Boudin

CATALOGUE

DES

TABLEAUX

PASTELS

Aquarelles et Dessins

DONT LA VENTE APRÈS DÉCÈS AURA LIEU

HOTEL DROUOT, salles nos 5 et 6

Les Lundi 20 et Mardi 21 Mars 1899

A DEUX HEURES PRÉCISES

COMMISSAIRE-PRISEUR

Me LÉON TUAL, *56, Rue de la Victoire*

EXPERTS :

M. DURAND-RUEL	Me ALLARD	M. BONJEAN
16, Rue Laffitte, 16.	17, Rue Caumartin, 17	10, Rue Laffitte, 10

EXPOSITIONS :

PARTICULIÈRE	PUBLIQUE
le Samedi 18 Mars 1899	*le Dimanche 19 Mars 1899*

De une heure et demie à cinq heures et demie.

Title page of catalogue of sale of the contents of Boudin's studio, 20–21 March 1899

The care with which Boudin had classified his studies, and his custom of keeping carefully arranged jottings, sketches and often even finished canvases by way of documents, meant that this studio sale consisted not only of works in his last style, nor only of imperfect sketches, but also of many finished works, and some of his most beautiful, some of which he valued most highly. Number 96 of the Venetian series, which was almost complete, fetched 3,000 francs; a very beautiful canvas, a *Squall from the north-west*, of which there is a reproduction in the catalogue of the sale, reached 2,400 francs. A great number of works fetched more than 1,000 francs: considerable prices for that time. The pastels and drawings also reached very high prices.

On 13 August 1899 a museum of Norman ethnography and art was inaugurated in Honfleur in the ancient church of Saint-Etienne, and named the Musée du Vieux-Honfleur. It is an interesting collection illustrating the life and traditions of a little city justly proud of its past, and its glories. An exhibition of painting had been organized which gathered together the painters of the region. On the occasion of the inauguration an entire room was reserved for Boudin. It was decorated with a bust by the sculptor Guilbert, offered to the town of Honfleur by the painter's friends. On this occasion Albert Sorel, who was linked to Honfleur both by birth and by affection, made the speech which is reprinted in the Appendix, and which still forms one of the most complete and just studies ever dedicated to Boudin.

On his death Boudin had left a considerable number of studies, jottings and sketches. During the course of his life a large number of these had been scattered. The studio sale had spread many among the collectors, and besides these a whole collection of these sketches were left to the artist's brother, Louis Boudin. With great disinterestedness, Louis Boudin presented them to the Musée du Havre on 10 December 1899. These works, 60 studies on canvas, and 180 panels, are today the glory, and perhaps the greatest attraction, of this

Berck beach: setting sail, 1883

museum. One must go there if one wants to understand not only Boudin's finished expression, but also the tentative steps and the ready promptness with which in a few strokes he condensed life, movement, and shapes. It is a collection of studies whose equivalent one can find nowhere else.

On 8 August 1900 a bust of Boudin was unveiled in Honfleur. It was placed in the Boulevard Carnot, at the beginning of the jetty, at the point where, on leaving the town, one comes out into open country, and from which one can see the cliffs of Le Havre, and the estuary.

The works by Boudin belonging to the town of Honfleur were grouped together on this occasion, in the wedding room of the town hall, with works by other painters of Honfleur: Hamelin, Dubourg, Renouf and Marais. This was when Roger Marx, who for twenty years had never ceased to show affectionate interest in Boudin, as in all the best artists of his time, gave a moving speech, of which the conclusion must be quoted here:

'For those who knew him it will be a sweet feeling in the course of their walks to come across his effigy, not far from the port and the ocean, his favourite subjects. Later, embracing in the same glance both the image of the man and the themes that inspired his work, the passer-by will evoke the pangs of the artist, anxious to render the vibrations of the air, of the light, of the flight of the moving wave, and in their minds will be opposed the power of the elements, the fatal, irresponsible renewal of nature and the immanent beauty of art, the creative lustre of human genius.'

The work of Boudin was already preserved from oblivion. Several large sales at this period gave a measure of the eagerness with which the collectors sought to enrich their collections of the painter's work. Views of Trouville, Antwerp and Brittany fetched prices four times as great as those Boudin could have hoped for during his life.

After this there were other manifestations in honour of Boudin. In 1906, under the patronage of the municipality of Le Havre, the Cercle de l'Art moderne organized a retrospective exhibition of the work of Eugène Boudin, which took place in the town hall from 9 to 31 July. Almost exclusively composed of works lent by collectors of Le Havre, this exhibition, which consisted of fifty-six works, was at one and the same time the first homage paid by the town of Le Havre to its former pensioner, and a faithful representation of the painter: still-lifes, seascapes, herds, scenes of Brittany, washerwomen, each of the series was represented.

The fifth exhibition of the Salon of the French school which was held from 25 January to 26 February 1908 in the Grand-Palais on the Champs-Elysées, consisted of an exhibition of Boudin's work comprising about fifty pictures, thanks to the keen initiative of a few people, among them M. de Bériot, who had been one of the painter's first friends and one of the first collectors to discover Boudin in the already far distant days of the Antwerp series of 1871. During the course of this exhibition the author of this book was called upon, on 14 February, to speak of Boudin and his work.

Today the work of Boudin has entered history: one cannot talk of the evolution of nineteenth-century painting without paying homage to this painter who formed a delicate, indispensable link in the chain.

Part Two WORKS

Sailing ships on the Meuse at Dordrecht, 1884

Chapter 6 Historical background

No matter how much affection one feels for one's subject, whatever its charm and delicacy, nothing can excuse hyperbole. My intention is not to represent the work of Boudin as one of those which mark the great summits of art. He played a more modest role, and one which must be explained in its own way. Boudin will remain as one of the foremost among the minor masters of French nineteenth-century painting; that is why it is important that an account of him should be precise, truthful and measured.

In the history of art in France there is perhaps no period more remarkable than precisely that in which Boudin was born. Corrupted traditions were disintegrating, truth was returning to its fountainhead, windows were opening on life. A healthier air began to revive men's spirits.

The moment of Boudin's birth was also that of a great disturbance in pictorial art. History painting, the academic art that had been the delight of the Empire, was dying, in spite of Gros and Delaroche. David, exiled in Brussels, was at death's door (he died on 29 December 1825). In spite of his master Guérin, Delacroix had shown *Dante and Virgil* at the Salon of 1822, which had won him the sympathy of Gros, but the *Massacre of Chios* of 1824 was greeted with total incomprehension. This was the time when Rembrandt was outlawed in the studio of Guérin.

However, the wonderful example of the English landscape school was beginning to win over the younger French painters, and a movement was already beginning to take shape, though still in a confused way. Georges Michel, in fact, had already painted his moving and melancholy landscapes, which are still too little known today. But who was then concerned with this solitary, sensitive and unfortunate artist? For in France there were many rivals to those of whom Northcote, in a letter to Constable, said: 'They know nature as little as a cab-horse knows a meadow.'

Already Camille Flers, Louis Cabat, Roqueplan, Jules Dupré, and above all Paul Huet, were presenting the resources of landscape treated from nature and according to a vision stripped of all theatrical arrangement. Huet, by his effort alone, had freed French landscape from the excessive attention to order and style which, for more than a century, had impoverished pictorial conception, for since the sanguines of Watteau and certain works by Joseph Vernet, who had known how to render nature without conventions? As Philippe Burty so rightly said:

'Huet is the first of our lyrical landscapists. In him there was more of the precursor than of the revolutionary... but in his time he was daring and sincere. It must not be forgotten that the powerful foliage of Rousseau or of Jules Dupré has grown in the soil which Paul Huet cleared and tilled.'

In 1822, when Delacroix saw a watercolour by this painter, one of the watercolours done on the island of Séguin between 1820 and 1822, he understood all the artist's concern for independence, and embarked on a friendship with him that was never to be broken.

It was in Gros' studio, a short time before, that Huet had met Bonington, who had revealed to his French friends the still unsuspected richness of the English landscape school. In the very year of Boudin's birth the Salon offered several works by Constable, Bonington, Fielding and Reynolds which were to awaken in the young painters new perspectives rich in consequence. A short time before, Géricault had brought back from his visit to England, apart from his great Salon picture of 1821, *Epsom Races*, a deep admiration for Constable, the reformer of painting, which he communicated to many of his French colleagues. This was also the time when Huet was treated as a raving lunatic for having dared to affirm his admiration for the *Raft of the Medusa*. Delacroix was soon to leave for England, where he stayed from 24 May until August 1825. He was twenty-six years old, and Huet twenty-one.

Eugène Isabey had begun to exhibit at the Salon of 1824; in the Salon of 1827 one could see his *Storm off Dieppe* and the *Beach at Honfleur* which is today in the Musée de Versailles: the same Isabey who forty years later was still called by Charles Blanc, in his *Histoire des peintres* of 1863, 'a vivacious colourist.' In the Salon of 1827 Decamps was represented for the first time by his *Soldier of the Vizir's guard* and *Lapwing-shooting*.

This was the time when Théodore Rousseau, under the supervision of his uncle Pau de Saint-Martin,

Flock of sheep

Landscape: the river Touques, 1883

made his first studies from nature in the outskirts of Compiègne. He showed for the first time at the Salon of 1831, which was also the year in which he executed studies in Normandy, near Bayeux. A short time afterwards he had the double honour of being refused at the Salon, and, in 1834, of seeing his *Edge of a felled wood in the forest of Compiègne* bought by the Duke of Orléans at the instigation of Ary Scheffer.

It was in the very year of Boudin's birth that Corot, in the countryside round Rouen, was trying his hand at his first landscapes. A very short time after this he was to leave for the first of his visits to Italy, and to paint the views of the Colosseum and of the Farnese Gardens in which the trees, as in the *Bridge of Narni* of 1827, seem at times to bask in the pearly and delicate atmosphere that was later to eternalize the landscapes of Ville-d'Avray.

When the young Boudin, aged about six, played with his little friends on the edge of the harbour at Honfleur, he might have seen Corot painting the harbour-master's office. Huet, too, having gone to Normandy to meet Bonington, had grown attached to the province and stayed on after the latter's departure for London, to work among the landscapes which appealed to his Norman blood.

But neither Huet, nor Delacroix, nor Corot attracted benevolent attention. Twenty more years were to pass before, in 1849, Champfleury could write in all justice: 'The name of Corot is popular today, a fact which is even stranger because Corot is the only great French landscapist.'

And yet it was not until the year in which the pension from Le Havre permitted Boudin to go to Paris, that Corot, in the Salon of 1851 with *A morning*, inaugurated his immortal series of landscapes with nymphs, and evocations of misty trees.

Thus Boudin was born precisely at the moment when the various causes which were to determine the liberation of pictorial landscape were coinciding. He became aware of art at a time when the first honours were being accorded to those who, consciously or not, had directed this movement, and who opened to art a new, almost unlimited, field of action. He reached his full mastery at the time when they at last triumphed, and when a new school of landscape painters was straining towards new means of expression. This new school was to triumph, in its turn, at the time when Boudin died. His work is not only the mirror of his soul, but also that of the problems and artistic efforts of a half-century.

Although it is difficult to divide an evolution as continuous as Boudin's into periods, one can, without being too arbitrary, distinguish four periods which correspond exactly to the four divisions that have been made in the study of the life of the painter.

The first extends from the moment when he started to draw until about 1860. This will be called: *Preparation.*

The second lasts from 1860 to 1870 and will be titled *Influences.*

The third marks: *Mastery* (1870–84).

The fourth and last: *Renewal* (1884–97).

Three fishermen

Boats on Trouville beach, 1870

Chapter 7 Preparation 1852-1860

This artistic period really begins at the moment when the young pupil of the school in the Rue Saint-Jacques decorated the margins of his books with sketches. No examples of the child's beginnings survive, and one can hardly feel a deep regret on this account. All one need remember is the spontaneity of a gift which needed no outside aid to reveal itself. On the other hand, one must deplore the disappearance of a large number of pencil sketches, pastels, and small still-lifes in oils, which Boudin executed between the ages of fifteen and twenty-five.

With the exception of pencil or watercolour sketches, nothing remains of Boudin's work of a date earlier than the two little panels of 1852 in the Musée du Havre.

In 1852 Boudin was twenty-eight years old and a pensioner of the town of Le Havre. From the age of ten until that time he had set himself with constant patience and passionate humility to reproduce faithfully the views in front of him. He did this with no other guide but his instinct, with no other selective principle than the chance of his games or walks. He did his sketches during the rare moments of leisure left to him by his work as a clerk or as a stationer and framer. In the little shop in the Rue de la Communauté where Isabey, Troyon, Millet and others passed, the eager young man, his eyes ever alert, waited for his moment of liberty when he could wander along the quayside, or the beach, across the harbour, absorbing the arabesques of groups and clouds, the ephemeral fantasy which for a moment united the clouds with the sky, men with the ground.

At first it was a minute application, an exact analysis of the slightest objects, patient copying and impersonal imitation of things. He doggedly copied, again and again, the rigging of a ship, the shape of a group on the quayside. Then little by little he realized what was indispensable, and what could be suppressed without making the representation less evocative. Everything was simplified and enlarged, obeying the characteristic deformation which proves the artist's personal vision: then came a gradual and almost imperceptible process of adaptation: his hand became extraordinarily gifted in seizing the object in movement, realizing it, and evoking it as a living reality. Then the least of his drawings affirmed, as keenly as his paintings were to later, the 'presence' of Boudin.

One line was enough for him to evoke a human form, a few pencil strokes became three fishermen chatting on the quayside at Honfleur or Trouville, or boats at anchor in the Seine bay, or cows grouped together impassively in some meadow of the Auge valley where the lush Norman earth bathes in the sea air.

The rigging of fishing boats, the three-masters which brought the wood of the Scandinavian forests to Honfleur, all the subtle combinations of rope and canvas, were known to him. He expressed them, and it seemed as if they were all there, but before long his sketches revealed not minute detail, only the essential, the stroke of synthesis, the pencil line which could take the place of ten, with more truth and tone.

The number of sketches Boudin did at this time is incalculable, but only a few can be found. Negligence, the hazards of moving from place to place, and the action of time have destroyed nearly all of them, and yet these were the foundations of his talent, the eager expression of his vocation, and the index of his researches; all he did afterwards was to enlarge accordingly the subjects which, from childhood, he had chosen with a sureness of mind which schools and institutes could not supplement.

This fund of personal studies, these efforts, these tentative, unguided steps, were to form the essential part of his work as an artist. He submitted to various influences at an age when most people believe themselves to be independent, he submitted to them to attain the expression for which he hoped, but all these influences were to be gradually absorbed, and the artist's personality affirmed definitively the rare and delicate virtues which from now on were evident in the best of his sketches.

This is revealed distinctly if one can compare, as I have done, certain pencil sketches or pastels with certain painted studies, all dating from about 1855: the sketches already show a liberty and tone of which there is hardly a trace in the canvases.

One can feel that he already had a mastery of the pencil at a time when the brush still weighed heavy in his fingers. His sketches already have a real and charming personality, while in the painted studies he seems still to be chained to the material side of things, and scarcely concerned, one would think, with reaching the spirit of them. It seems that he dared not abandon himself to his real nature, that respect for the masters held him back, as far as painting was concerned; he dared be himself only when treating the sky, because there he knew what his pastel studies had taught him; apart from that he kept himself in check.

The first influence that appears in Boudin's painted work, or, at least, that which shows itself most clearly, is that of Isabey: this was an influence from which he did not really free himself until the end of the second period. Besides, this influence is not at all the sign of servile imitation, neither is it the obedience of a pupil to a master. The reasons which drew Boudin towards Isabey are the most evident proof of the direction the young painter of Honfleur was already taking.

We have already mentioned that Isabey began his work as a marine painter at the very moment of Boudin's birth. He inaugurated it, in fact, with studies made on the Norman coast, in Dieppe, and even Honfleur. Fifteen years later, at the time when Boudin was beginning to paint, Isabey took up his old themes again (*Dieppe harbour,* 1842, and *Beach at Villerville*; later *Varengeville wood*, *Meadow bordered by pines* and *Ango Manor at Varengeville*). He was one of the rare painters capable of rendering the sea without dramatizing it to excess. That could already have been one reason that drew Boudin to him, but another factor concerning feeling and technique attracted his sympathy even more: the candour, vigour and verve with which these first works of Isabey were run off. In them Boudin found indications of that which he was seeking, a quick way of placing a stroke, the art of making a warm note sing among sombre tones, a vision at once rapid and precise, a solid and exact construction, as well as a particular way of linking characters to the overall ensemble, a contained activity and a sense of mobility. He gradually sought a greater liberty, and while Isabey weakened his charming gifts of effervescence and verve into an official and dramatic way of painting (he was to find them again in his last watercolours), Boudin became more and more concerned to avoid all anecdote: more than the objects themselves it was the envelope, the vibrations of the atmosphere around them, that attracted him. 'The landscape painter who does not make of his skies a very positive part of his composition neglects one of his most important auxiliaries,' Constable wrote in a letter as early as 23 October 1821.

Boudin had already surpassed Isabey in his interpretation of the sky. In certain works of Boudin's early career one could sometimes really believe that the land and sky had been painted by two different artists; in the skies the touch is lighter, more eloquent and surer, one cannot see the limits of the brush strokes.

Deauville beach at low tide, *c.* 1885

All this early period of his pictorial life is remarkable for his patient analysis of the things around him. His spontaneity is constantly held in check, either by the timidity which results from his comparative newness as a member of his profession, or by the obstinate intensity revealed in his words and evident in his letters. He compelled himself to study the techniques of the masters. During this period he painted quite a considerable number of copies, particularly of the Dutch and Flemish schools; apart from the *Stream* by Ruysdael or the *Meadow* by Paulus Potter in the Musée du Havre, and the two copies of the Flemish school in the Musée d'Honfleur, I have seen copies of Teniers and Van de Velde done by Boudin at this time. Later he studied other masters, as proved by the copies of Watteau's *Embarkation for Cythera* and of the *Woman with goats* by Boucher in the Musée d'Honfleur.

During this period he accumulated the elements that were to serve him all his life. His sketches were to furnish the 'material,' the store of subjects and human figures, which he added to, renewed and enriched until his death. His studies of skies in pastel already constituted a unique 'repertoire.'

The little studies in the Musée d'Honfleur give an idea of just what the 'collection of skies,' which Boudin showed to Baudelaire in 1859, was like, and it is very much to be regretted that the fugitive and fragile nature of pastel has doomed these delightful sketches to almost complete disappearance. They were for the most part, little sketches of which the largest dimension was about four inches, and almost all consisted of studies of white clouds on a background of blue sky; but those who have lived on the shores of the Seine may know that such a subject offers inexhaustible variety, and is extremely difficult to render. No one had done it in such a way before him, and no one since then has surpassed him. One can easily understand Baudelaire's enthusiasm when he saw such proofs of an art so delicate and already so complete.

'From all these clouds of fantastic luminous shapes, these chaotic shadows, these green and pink immensities suspended and added one to another, these gaping furnaces, these firmaments of black or violet satin, crumpled, rolled or torn, these horizons in mourning, or streaming with molten metal, all these depths, all these splendours rose to my brain like a heady drink, or like the eloquence of opium' (see p. 232 of this book).

Sometimes these studies of the sky were augmented by the indication of a landscape, a simple line indicating the near or distant coast. Often the entire foreground of the sky was pure, of a spotless blue, and the clouds were as if held in reserve on the horizon, in the morning, as if they were preparing for their day-long procession.

Usually they are clouds of a peaceful melancholy with no hint of a sorm; sometimes one feels them melt into a damp dust whose transparence covers them with silver. Behind these clouds there dreams a sun which never shows itself completely, and which colours the light parts pale pink, in the passages where the white clouds merge imperceptibly with the blue of the sky.

The more one looks at these pastels, the more one asks oneself: 'How are they done?' They are done with nothing, and yet the fluidity and density of the sky and the clouds are translated with an unimaginable precision. This is what Boudin later forced himself to render with the aid of paint, and which he succeeded in doing, obtaining even from impasto a fluidity, lightness and transparence equalling both his earlier pastels and the watercolours of Jongkind.

Of all this early period only these pastels remain really unique and already personal, these and some pencil sketches which reveal the rapid subtlety of his vision. The painted works of this period, on the contrary, show little personality, and one can approve of Baudelaire's words when he said of the *Pilgrimage of Sainte-Anne-la-Palud*, of 1858 (in the Musée du Havre): 'A very good and very careful painting.'

Honfleur: sailing ships at the harbour mouth, *c.* 1860

Still-life: game, *c.* 1856

It is still certainly more careful than good: the painter seems ill at ease, the composition lacks balance, and similar blue values are abused; one can sense embarassment and a certain affectedness, especially if one compares with the large canvas the small sketch of the same subject, done most probably from the painting, since the details and arrangement of it are the same, although its execution undoubtedly indicates a later period. The small sketch reveals progress in the study of relationships, the grouping of figures, and the use of the tones of red in the women's bodies.

However, works like the *Still-life, game*, in the Musée du Havre, indicate a painter who already knew his job, and who, before seeking for fluidity and the enveloping atmosphere, had applied himself to acquiring a mastery of solid matter. Boudin also executed several portraits. He himself said:

> The portrait is in fashion, that was the genre in which I began. I would just about have made progress in it, no doubt, but apart from the fact that the bourgeois did not like my style, the daguerreotype had just been invented and because of this the painted portrait was stopped in its tracks, and was given up altogether.

The only known portrait by Boudin is a portrait of his father. It is much more reminiscent of the Dutch masters than of the school of Ingres, and must have been painted around 1850. It is, however, quite difficult, without exact references, definitely to attribute to Boudin some works which date from this time, for the influence of Isabey was not the only one to make itself felt: Boudin was still a painter hesitating between his own nature and the techniques of several masters.

He had, in fact, already met Millet, Couture and Troyon, who had given him canvases to frame and some advice. One cannot really find any traces of the influence of Millet. Despite the admiration and affection Boudin felt for him, their natures were too different. There was in Millet a sense of grandeur to which Boudin could not pretend, and the almost biblical feeling of the painter of peasants had little resemblance to the subtle preoccupations of the painter of Honfleur.

Such characters, like that of Courbet later, could inspire his sympathy, but not influence his course. At this time he was searching for himself, and advancing timidly in the study of his profession. His landscapes are reminiscent of Rousseau or of Dupré. His nature, in which anxiety and serenity were already mingled, was far removed from the element of grandeur and dramatic simplicity latent in Théodore Rousseau's soul, but he was attracted by the delicacy already apparent in the painter's work, of which the *Spring*, in the Louvre, was to be the most charming expression.

Boudin had not the leisure to choose his subjects in order to extract from them a character most in keeping with his own nature: he had set himself to learn his profession, and he applied himself to this with the same humility as had his ancestors to learn the movement of sails, the signs of the wind and of the sea.

Alone, without a guide, and without support, ignorant of all the movement of ideas which agitated painters in Paris, he went out to study nature on the spot. Even when he had the opportunity to contemplate the work of past masters in the museums, he soon went back to his eager study of nature, rather than men's masterpieces. Later, he wrote the following notes in his notebooks:

> Anything painted directly from nature and on the spot has always a force, power and vivacity of touch that one cannot find in the studio....
>
> Three brush strokes painted from nature are worth more than two days' work at the easel.

Right from the beginning his poverty protected him from teaching which would only have been troublesomely sterile, and which would only have made him lose time. On his own he accomplished the great achievement of restoring the flavour of reality to pictorial landscape.

Trouville beach: the nursemaid, 1885

At the same time, the very fact of living in front of strangely moving landscapes, of skies that were continually swept by wind and continually laden with clouds, the desire to capture this incessant mobility, to arrest it and to put on canvas its eternal wandering, were to lead him to search for a technique subtle, sure, and rapid enough to express nuances, detail, feeling and life. Working in oils, and faced by such changing sights, he could only be discouraged, or multiply his jottings and sketches, or else attempt the mad enterprise of keeping up with the speed of the clouds, a feat which, in his early pastels, he had already achieved. He had to strain himself for a long time to create paintings from the teaching of such sketches, and to achieve a more human rôle, a wider and more complete art than that which up till now, in spite of everything, had succeeded only in making him a 'chronicler of clouds.'

Chapter 8 Influences 1860-1870

Referring to the feelings with which he returned to Le Havre after the expiration of his bursary, Boudin himself later said:

> They had hoped that after three years I would return from Paris like a Phoenix of art. In fact I came back more confused than ever, perturbed by the famous painters of the day, from Rousseau, who enchanted me, to Corot who was opening up a new direction to me.

When, seven or eight years later he made the decision, not without great hesitation, to go to live in Paris, his perplexity was still as great on finding himself in the presence of the various techniques of the new masters, which could attract him and suggest to him the means of rendering his work more subtle and more supple, more obedient to the desires of his vision.

It was in vain that he said:

> If the provinces had provided me with more durable resources, I would certainly have stayed there, taking up teaching, like many of my fellow painters, but I hardly had the style that delights provincial collectors.

It was not the question of resources that made him go to Paris, or which prevented him from remaining in Honfleur or in Le Havre in 1860. The truth was that at that time he found himself in a perplexing situation of which he could not see the resolution. Certainly, he possessed not only an inner individuality, which made him refuse to make concessions to the public, but a personality that was already visible in his work, since, as we have seen, his studies could, as early as 1858, cause displeasure to the young Monet. What displeased the young man was certainly also what gave them their originality. His works of that period, however they may be considered today, were already sharply in contrast with the art produced in a provincial town. Boudin felt this, for all his life he had a remarkable degree of self-knowledge. At this moment he hesitated; one would think that he feared in going to Paris to feel himself even more perplexed and divided, to see himself even less clearly; one would say that he was apprehensive of coming too much under the influence of a painter greater than himself, since he wanted to be influenced by no one but himself. And at the same time he was well aware that a simple spark from outside would give all the flame necessary to the eagerness he possessed. It was the most critical moment of his life. This time he did not go first to the museums: he went to the auction rooms and the dealers' shops to examine the canvases of the artists who interested him, and comparing what he knew and said with what they expressed, he concluded: 'I know more than many who are in fashion, but my painting lacks a little of this and that, of breadth and boldness.'

As far as this was concerned, Troyon was useful to him, and his help was not only a material one, as we have seen. Troyon was at the peak of his career when Boudin went to Paris in 1861: one could even say that his decadence was beginning, caused both by his own declining physical state, and by the excessive orders which he attempted to satisfy, to such a pitch that even his almost unequalled virtuosity was soon exercising itself almost in a void. He no longer took the time to construct works solidly, and left everything to the brush and to slickness of hand. For some time he had already been accused of 'masonry' (piecemeal construction); Théophile Gautier had reproved him for this as early as the Salon of 1841.

His desire to cover the canvas in great haste was apparent, as it later was in Courbet's work, though with a passion that matched his nature and which made use of all his strength of age and freshness of vision.

However, in the case of a painter of Troyon's stature, there is something that lasts as long as the hand can guide itself, a technique that is often no more than technique, but which was the most Boudin could hope for at that time. Troyon's virtuosity, the ease with which he covered large canvases, led Boudin too to use larger ones, reversing his previous tendency towards an excessive minuteness, and to 'warm up his hand' as he put it. At the same time, Troyon gave him some very good advice. He lessened the young painter's timidity, both in matters of expression and of vision, thus reinforcing Isabey's example, but with greater strength. In addition, Boudin recognized in Troyon a mutual taste for painting flocks, a subject he had already tried and to which he was to return a little later; but whereas Troyon's interest was in the animals themselves, Boudin concentrates on problems of grouping and atmosphere.

Besides, little concrete evidence of Troyon's influence can be found in Boudin's work. It lies much more in the teaching of some useful 'methods' which Boudin transformed and used according to his own character, and in the moral encouragement of which Boudin has left a particularly engaging proof in his notebooks.

It was quite different in the case of Corot. He was one of the painters whom Boudin had certainly looked at the most and the hardest, whom he liked the most as people and as artists, and who affected him the most strongly.

Boudin and Corot had different merits, and it is Corot's that sometimes attain perfection, but they had delicacy and charm in common. Corot had certainly felt this when, at this time, he called Boudin 'the king of skies,' and bought some of his pastels.

Boudin could certainly not aspire to the poetry of Corot, to the expression of a Virgilian soul nourished on the grace of antiquity and the charm of France, that soul in which melancholy itself was calm, and which carried the tender love of nature to a higher level than anyone else. Boudin remained halfway between the serenity of Corot and the eager nervousness of a painter like Daubigny, whom he sometimes resembled. In London I saw a landscape of Brittany painted by Boudin which showed, strangely enough, the obvious influence of Corot in the right hand part (a group of flowers), whilst the middle distance to the left could have passed for a Daubigny.

He met both of them in 1861, at the beginning of his period in Paris, and was able to add to the example of their work the advantage of their words: by a strange chance that moment marked the end of an epoch in the work of both masters.

For Corot this was the moment when his apotheosis began, when at the age of sixty-five he harvested with serenity the fruits of his steadfast, peaceful, glory-disdaining labour. Ten years before he had undertaken the abundant series of *Landscapes with nymphs* which did more to render him immortal than his other works. Gradually the critics who had been relentlessly against him for a long time, or had ignored him, nearly all came to have more just feelings towards him: they stopped accusing him of not knowing how to paint a tree and of producing works in which smoke took the place of everything else. They began to cease contrasting his work with the solidity of Rousseau, Dupré and Troyon, of all those who perpetuated and developed the teaching of Constable, whom the public had taken twenty years to understand. They began to realize, though with difficulty, it is true, that Corot did not relate to these painters, that he was a case apart, and that he alone among the French painters of landscapes owed nothing to that great movement; he was not led by any concern for renewal, revolt or credit. He painted in this way, guided only by himself and imbued with the feeling that, in following his own nature, he was following the true tradition. It was for this same reason that

House and garden of the painter Braquaval, 1885

he was not very receptive towards the efforts made by those who came after; this is what prevented him, for example, from suspecting the potential of impressionism. It seems that the painter François-Louis Français must be held responsible for this estrangement. Français, a pupil of Corot, enjoyed a certain influence over his master, and used all his power to weaken Corot's interest in Courbet, through whom he would have been able to understand more easily what impressionism held in store.

As for Daubigny, he united with the qualities of great talents influenced by Constable, something of the fire of Delacroix. He was at the peak of his first period, when the ardent dissatisfaction that was later to devour and sustain him, and produce his most finished work, had not yet made itself felt; but he had already painted such admirable canvases as *Lock in the Optevoz Valley* of 1855 (in the Musée of Rouen), *The Spring* of 1857 (in the Louvre), and *Oysters by the sea, near Villerville* of 1859 (in the Musée de Marseille), which are perhaps his purest masterpieces.

Boudin met Daubigny at the time when the latter was developing towards a more staccato and violent expression, but one which was at the same time stronger and broader: it seemed that all his long-concentrated eagerness was at last blossoming out, that he had flung open new windows through which air had flooded, and that he wanted to capture nature with more immediacy. At the same time his palette became lighter, the impasto became deliciously creamy without weakening the strength of his expression. He was the first to paint large canvases in the presence of the actual landscapes; he was the first to attempt, and often very successfully, to grasp the fugitive impression. It is easy to understand that he alone among the older masters, right from the first, not only understood, but also supported the efforts of Boudin, then of Pissarro and Monet.

When Boudin arrived in Paris he had almost exhausted what was useful to him in the impulse given by the French followers of Constable. From them he learnt the patient study of landscape, and attention to exactitude, but he needed something else. Up until then he had followed one by one, whether consciously or unconsciously, mingling their influences, Rousseau, Dupré, Isabey and Troyon. But the rich earth of Constable slowed down the pace of a painter obsessed by the sky and by movement. Naturally he turned towards the two painters of his time who were the most supple, the most delicate and the least 'heavy.' Once again he was not mistaken, and from his words it is apparent that he felt he owed more to Corot and to Daubigny than to Troyon, although Troyon, and, later, Courbet, seem at first sight, to have played a greater part in his life.

What attracted him in Corot and Daubigny was their skill as colourists, as well as their attention to atmosphere, which after being marvellously displayed in Corot's *Ville d'Avray*, was to be revealed, with great beauty, in the misty *Thames* series which Daubigny brought back from his first journey in England in 1866.

Gradually, because of his study of these two masters, Boudin's palette became silvery, and more sensitive. He is less elusive than Corot, nor does his work resemble the passion of movement, reminiscent of Delacroix, which we find in Daubigny. Boudin's touch remained thinner and less free. There is more labouring of the brush in him, fewer of the beautiful deliberate strokes which enabled Daubigny, right to the end of his life, to produce paintings which are really superb sketches. Boudin always remained more curious, more picturesque, less lofty, and even in his most powerful period was rarely to aspire to the harshness of such works as *The Thames at Erith*.

It was almost at the time when Daubigny painted the *Thames* series that Boudin wrote:

> I must work to eliminate a certain timidity which still shows in my work and which is a long-cherished provincial habit. (To Louis, 29 November 1865.)

There is no better judge of Boudin than Boudin himself, and it was indeed an aid against his own

On the beach: the yellow sunshade, 1887

timidity that he had sought in the daring of Corot and Daubigny. However, if one examines the evolution of his mind, of his pictorial expression, it seems permissible to doubt whether he would have been able to conquer his diffidence, at least to the degree he did, or that he could have emancipated himself so completely, and attained such a perfect self-expression, as he did from 1871 onwards, if he had not met one man, born with the same gifts and the same curiosity as himself, and almost in the same circumstances, but blessed with more fire and genius: Johann Barthold Jongkind.

Jongkind was of about the same age as Boudin, being born in Latrop in 1822. After having worked for some time in Holland he went to France quite early, since he exhibited in the Salon of 1845. He worked with Isabey, whose fiery exuberance attracted him. In 1850 he had exhibited a *View of Saint-Valéry* and a *Memory of Le Havre*. It is therefore very probable that Boudin had seen works by Jongkind in Le Havre or Honfleur, or at least heard his name, long before meeting him in person. The circumstances of their meeting in 1862 have already been described, but even before this time Isabey, who gave advice to both painters, cannot fail to have spoken with praise to Boudin of such an interesting pupil.

Jongkind's odd character and nomadic habits made it difficult to understand him. At this time he was already very restless, subject to periods of misanthropy and dejection, at other times his lively natural sensitivity made him seek the company of his friends. He was always in search of documentation, jotting down on pieces of paper as big as his hand sketches which he used rather mysteriously for his canvases or his marvellous watercolours. He was then as he was always to be, throughout a life which was the most ardent, and perhaps the most wretched, of any painter in history, subject to spells of madness and extreme eccentricity, endowed with an excellent heart and a rare tenderness for the sights of nature, and for those whom he knew to feel the same love of it.

It is very much to be hoped that one day someone will set to work with pious patience to evoke this admirable figure of an artist, one of the greatest of his century; and to speak of Jongkind is necessary here, if only for the friendship that linked him to Boudin and for the influence he exercised on him: for Jongkind is Boudin with more genius.

Lively, robust and healthy, fired by a feverish poetry, capricious rather than fanciful or romantic, thirsty for landscapes: such was Jongkind. His eye was that of a man with sharp and lively air in his brain: his intelligence was even more ready than Boudin's, and his dream more elevated. At first his style was extremely tight and reminiscent of the old Dutch masters, 'bound together' with strength of will and an unshakable self-possession: he drew thinly, but his vision was already large, the contours were solid and his shadow transparent, and the air which bathed all his compositions revealed his later magical powers. But much sooner than Boudin, Jongkind had reached his full power. He had already shaken off the hesitations and scruples which still held back Boudin. He did not have the patient, curious, yet serene nature of Boudin: his was a restless, feverish, one could almost say, diabolical nature, and which concerned itself only with the essence of things, only with their soul. When he had analysed carefully the views that attracted him, when he had followed for long enough the teaching of his artistic forebears, such as Ruysdael, Van de Velde and Van Goyen, he then let the wind blow in his sails with all its force, and guide his boat with such freedom that it was sometimes to be doubted whether the man was still at the helm, or if a force of nature had been set free. Then his eye grasped everything, the sky, the sea, the reflections of the water, the nuances of the snow or the mysteries of the light of the moon, without ever copying anything with material exactness. There is no art further removed from realism than his, no vision more foreign to the 'slice of life,' and yet there is little in art that is more true, more real and more

Entrance to Trouville harbour, low tide, *c.* 1890

exact. In front of a landscape he did not concentrate on copying a moment with patient fidelity; he fragmented it, tore the life from it, the tone, the true reality, and recomposed it in his own way with a few strokes, with a few lines which at first seemed to be a sketch, but which soon revealed themselves to be all that was necessary to express a moment of life.

It is not without reason that the names of Bonington and Jongkind are linked: if their human destinies varied, in that one was short and brilliant, the other longer and above all more wretched, their pictorial destinies offer more than one tie. Both were foreigners, but it was in France that both became aware of their talent, in France that the purest examples of their art have remained, and in France that their influence made itself felt. The history of the French pictorial landscape of the school of 1830 could not be written without showing how great was the role of intermediary played by Bonington; while Jongkind's role was even more central. One cannot really consider as a foreign painter a spirit who, however closely linked to his Dutch antecedents, was tied to French art by his life, his friendships and his researches, and who must be considered as in some ways the point of departure for the impressionist school, and as the first in date of the painters of that movement.

For Jongkind, as for the majority of great painters, this was not accompanied by any theory: he simply followed his temperament, and found in it the indisputable reasons for his art. Boudin himself said with some justice:

> Jongkind began to make the public swallow a sort of painting whose rather tough skin hid an excellent and very tasty fruit. I took advantage of this to enter too the door he had forced open, and I began, though still timidly, to offer my seascapes. (*L'Art*, 1887.)

It must not be concluded that Boudin did nothing but follow Jongkind's footsteps; but their paths could not fail to meet, even if a thousand circumstances had not lent their aid. Jongkind's daring encouraged Boudin; the first successes of one painter were certainly of use to the other. Isabey's seascapes lacked the sense of truth inherent in the works of Jongkind and Boudin, and marine painters were rare; this alone would have been enough to ensure them a temporary place, if the merits of both of them had not won them a lasting fame. As a painter of seascapes, Bonington had been a precursor: one only has to see the charming and truthful *Seascape* in the Wallace Collection in London.

It must be seen with what precise modesty Boudin considered himself with regard to Jongkind:

> I am straining to give to my painting a seal of perfection and appearance that will permit me to exhibit them in the dealers' windows without too great a disadvantage, next to the masterpieces of Corot, Jongkind and others. (February 1865.)
>
> I become all the more difficult to please since they frequently put my works alongside a Corot, a Daubigny, or a Jongkind, and I have to cut an honest figure in such good company. (11 February 1865.)

Besides, Jongkind's fame at this time was only very relative, and material difficulties were not spared to either of the two painters. Independent of the artistic ties that united them, a very warm friendship was established between them. Only the circumstances of Jongkind's nomadic and unstable life could restrain its manifestation, but at this time they met frequently in Paris, Le Havre and Honfleur, the Honfleur of which Jongkind wrote to Boudin: 'I find Honfleur an admirable place, for living in as well,' and of which in 1864 he painted a canvas admirable for its truth and life, the *Entrance to the harbour*, of which the subject had inspired in Boudin his Salon picture of the previous year.

The great lesson in Jongkind's technique which attracted Boudin was his art of conserving in finished works the exact flavour of the rough sketch. Jongkind and Boudin have remained unsurpassed in the sureness of analysis which permits daring synthesis, and which, in the deliberately unfinished, gives a more intense sensation of life.

Berck beach, low tide, 1890

That is what Boudin had already achieved in his sketches and rough outlines, but in his canvases he did not dare to; he still laboured, corrected, and allowed himself to be possessed by concern for detail, for studio work, encouraged not only by his scruples, but also by the collectors' wishes, which he followed more often than he should have.

It is rather strange that it was not as a marine painter but as a painter of manners that Boudin first tackled this liberation, as if he wanted to arrive at the subjects closest to his heart by a roundabout way, and to try out a personal application of Jongkind's suggestions on subjects different from those chosen by Jongkind.

We know that in 1862 Boudin, on the advice of Isabey, moved to Trouville which was beginning to be a focal point of the fashionable world, and gave free rein to the study of this colourful and picturesque confusion.

On superficial examination of the work of Boudin, this series of studies, sketches and canvases, of which feminine society of the Second Empire forms the essential subject, seems to be an accident, a prelude, an anecdote, and, one could almost believe, a halt in Boudin's intimate expression, a choice imposed by material necessity.

It was certainly concern for his success that guided Isabey's advice to Boudin, and it was in the hope of attracting the attention of a public that he concentrated on the study of a social circle rather far removed from his usual preoccupations; but in fact such a subject was not contrary to his taste. It had already been shown that, in the course of his visits to Brittany, he showed a livelier taste for groups of peasants, meetings, peasant women gathering in church porches, and pilgrimages than for landscapes themselves; earlier he tirelessly sketched groups of fishermen and boats.

It is a characteristic that cannot fail to impress when his work is examined closely, and has already been noted in excellent terms by Arsène Alexandre, when he wrote in the catalogue of Boudin's studio sale that 'the beings with which he populates his landscapes are nearly always represented as groups of many people. Corot often places a solitary figure in his silver pictures: Boudin likes swarms.'

One by one he was to paint groups of fishermen, elegant socialites on the beach at Trouville, pilgrimages, markets, washerwomen, groups of boats in harbour or on the estuary, flocks and clouds: these series all reveal the same 'obsession with movement' which continually enlivened Boudin's research and which pursued him relentlessly. He examined his subjects, and transcribed their variations, with constant fidelity, but it was movement that delighted him, and movement that he wanted to paint: life in its different forms, the eternal exchange and the inexhaustible variations of images, line eternally moving in space. And it was to achieve this realization that, perpetually on the watch, he seized upon this or that moment of eternal evolution, and noted down the moments to combine them to his liking, he searched for groups of people to repeat what he had done for the clouds, and then there was the same profusion of sketches, rough outlines and documentations to be used in the history of moving objects.

It seems to me that the circumstance that probably played the greatest part in establishing Boudin's inclination has been insufficiently emphasized. He was born in a port, and not in one of those large, modern ports where there is movement everywhere, noisy, restless cities filled with the din of ships, cargoes and men. Boudin was born in a little port, and he spent his youth in Le Havre when Le Havre was still a little port, in extent if not in traffic. In both the towns in which he lived the course of daily life constantly led the men to meet on the quayside. In Honfleur this sight has scarcely changed, for the very configuration of the little town, which descends on all sides towards the harbour, inevitably encourages its inhabitants to meet there. At that time it was the same in Le Havre, in a more striking way than today. In such towns the

Bénerville beach, low tide, 1892

harbour itself is the meeting place not only of the fishermen and dock workers, but also of the idle strollers. Everything goes on there, as it does in a village square, or round a fountain. Men's activity or idleness are perpetually concentrated there.

Here Boudin differed from many of his colleagues. Millet, for example, had, since his childhood in the Norman countryside, seen a solitary peasant guiding his plough or harrow, or sowing grain in great lonely stretches of country: there the individual, or at least his particular shape and position, took on an absolute value and rose to the level of a symbol. On the other hand, what Boudin had seen since his eyes had opened was the anonymous swarm, and what had impressed him was not the particular character of such and such an individual unit, but the conditions of their meeting, of their exchange, and the way in which they unconsciously formed a new, more complex being, a group, through which life revealed itself. And one could say that the whole art of Boudin consisted in extracting life from this complex being, in gradually eliminating unnecessary elements through wise synthesis; the human being became reduced to a simple study. Equally, in his studies of herds, the cows, looked at closely, seem shapeless, just as do the strollers in Trouville or the peasants in the market. And yet, recomposed at the correct distance, and in contact with the other elements in the group, everything regains its order, its life, with a truth that could not be achieved in any other way.

Besides, one could apply to Boudin what Octave Mirbeau said of Monet in *La 628–E8*:

'An artist who is born in a seaport, who has passed his childhood and early youth amidst the variety, the unexpectedness, and the ever-renewed example of these sights, is naturally ahead of those who are born in the depths of the country, in a sleepy silent village, or in the stifling obscurity of the suburbs of a town. His imagination, greatly excited by all that happens around him, awakens earlier.... Unknown to him, and as if automatically, the movement of the boats on the sea, of the sea against the jetties, the rhythm of the swell, the entry of ships into the harbour, the fluctuation of the pent-up masts which relates to the loose curve of the ropes, the fleeing sails, which dance and fly, the spirals of smoke, all the silhouettes of the teeming quaysides, teach him better than a professor the elegance, the suppleness, the infinite variety of shapes....'

It was in this that Boudin surpassed the art of Isabey, for example, whose figures often seen to have been added one by one and do not form a unity; he rivalled Jongkind in the art of subordinating elements to the whole and of extracting the personality of the whole from the impersonality of the individual elements.

As a preparation for this series of painted works, there is a collection of drawings touched up from rough sketches (unfortunately lost), with the help of which, as has been mentioned before, one could recreate the fashions of a period seen by an artist who in this respect equalled the attraction and interest of Constantin Guys.

When one compares the large *Pilgrimage of Sainte-Anne-la-Palud* of 1858 with the *Trouville beach* of 1864 or some of the *Trouville Casino* series of 1868, one can judge Boudin's progress and to what extent his vision and technique have acquired more liberty and fluidity. The impasto is already applied with more relish, and it is a joy to see the subtlety with which the dazzle of costumes, materials and tents on the shore is rendered. They reveal more charm than solidity, and the artist has often made concessions to the picturesque and to amusement at the expense of penetration; but, even today, one cannot look at such works without appreciating why in their time they aroused a curiosity that has been renewed long after any mere interest for their actuality had disappeared.

With his increased daring the artist had also gained more freshness in his scale of tones. He began to give evidence of his refined sense of colour, he no longer

Fécamp docks, 1892

needed Troyon to add 'notes to the diapason' as he had before. He strove to conserve both the spontaneity and the freshness of his vision: 'Do not dirty the tones,' he wrote to his friend Martin, 'avoid dirty tones,' and he gave the same friend some advice for copying a picture (*Sheep*, by Troyon) which throws light on his technique:

> The simplest way of copying a picture is to firmly secure the drawing in chalk or charcoal; that done, one rubs in the shape with a rather warm tone in the shadows (which must be kept transparent) or with burnt siena, then one attacks the light parts with clear tones underneath the sketch. In finishing one stains it (this is called glazing) before laying on the highlights which one must be careful to arrange one next to the other, without exhausting them by the movement of the brush. (To Martin, 17 February 1866.)

A little later he added:

> One must use tones in their full freshness and try to make them shine. (To Martin, 3 April 1866.)

It can be seen from this that his ideas on this subject were not very different from those of his old pupil, Monet, against whom a coalition was beginning to form, and who was proscribed by the official Salon. It could be thought that in his turn the daring pupil had influenced his old master, and that the conversations and works of Boudin, Jongkind and Monet in and around Honfleur since 1862 had gathered together both their feelings of attachment and their pictorial ideas.

Possession of his true artistic identity was to be the reward of a long labour; after twenty years of tentative attempts, during which he was guided only by his instinct and his eagerness, he was to spend ten years considering the various tendencies, contrary and similar, of the best painters of his times. At times he understandably felt perplexed:

> I have got myself into a state that is impossible to describe, a sort of unreasonableness in my research, a too far-reaching search that has made me spoil everything that I touched. (To Louis, 20 February 1867.)

It was like a spirit-level fluctuating round its exact point of equilibrium before coming to rest. The painter's great patience was reaching its target. He could now exercise his knowledge, and was well aware that he had arrived at it; it was then that he wrote in his letter of 3 September 1868, already quoted:

> I have been a poor unfortunate for quite a long time, and therefore concerned enough to rummage, search and ponder. I have sounded the others enough to know what their resources are and compare them with my own.... I persist in following my own little path, however narrow it may be, my only desire being to walk with a firmer, more solid step, widening my path a little when necessary.

The de Beriot children on Trouville beach, 1892

Chapter 9 Mastery 1870-1884

However pleasant the series of views of Trouville and Deauville with which, from 1864 to 1869, Boudin gave scope to his quick, precise, and picturesque vision, and in which one can find, as he himself said, 'if not great art, at least a fairly sincere reproduction of the world of our time,' they still constituted an anecdotal element which limited his real range to a single epoch, and of which he must free himself if he was to achieve a broader, more lasting expression.

The reasons which, at the outbreak of war, led Boudin far from the places in which he was accustomed to work, were, as has been seen, quite unexpected and involuntary, but none the less the very distance from home seems to have liberated him to a greater extent than any example could have.

It has been seen from his letters how unenthusiastic he was about Brussels and Antwerp, and, a little later, about Bordeaux and Dordrecht, but the very impossibility of studying these places in great detail led him to a more deliberate attempt to express the overall effect. He became more daring, and he succeeded almost at the first attempt. In his studies of the markets in Brussels his style seems broader, the 'quibbling' disappeared and a more balanced concern for composition became apparent, but it was with the series of views of Antwerp of 1871 that he really came into his own. Some of the most beautiful canvases in this series were formerly in the Beriot collection: almost all of them represent the same place, with slight variations of position, but this does not lead to monotony; quite the contrary. In this series Boudin found the arrangement which he preferred to all others, and to which he was always to return right up to his last days, in the series of views of Antibes, Douarnenez or Venice. The landscape stretches out across the canvas; the river fills the foreground, and the sky alone occupies as much space as all the rest put together. That, briefly, was the extent to which Boudin's composition had been simplified, a simplification which enabled him to give free rein to the subtlety of his technique of evoking clouds and water. He invented nothing and arranged nothing, unlike Jongkind, who said that one must paint one's canvas looking around one, thus expressing a conception of a synthetic landscape. Boudin remained attached to the reality of places, and did not transpose them; for this reason his art does not achieve the moving generalization characteristic of the great landscape painters, nor the dream fantasy of Auguste Renoir's landscapes; but his achievements lie in the field of expressive truth, and authenticity without documentary precision.

Sometimes he concerned himself with a less simple composition; one could quote numerous other examples, but in place of others *Bordeaux harbour* (see p. 91) is sufficient: this balanced arrangement without a framework of dry bones, this section of landscape captured, one would think, by chance, yet evidently the object of an express purpose, the sort of negligence with which the groups and objects are arranged, interrupted in the foreground flush with the canvas, this is the composition which one finds almost continually in the work of Camille Pissarro. The essential and constant merit of Boudin's composition, however precisely detailed it may at times seem at first sight, is that nothing detracts from the overall view. In this *Bordeaux harbour* there is a great deal of detail – people, carts, ships, houses, carriages and so on – but the spectator's attention is held only by the picture as a whole, the glance is drawn towards the brilliant opening formed by the sky, from which a delicately distributed light spreads over everything.

One could certainly prefer more ample compositions in Boudin's work; but, given the painter's chosen limitations, few painters have succeeded as well as Boudin in expressing truth without falling into the poverty of anecdote.

In the series of views of Antwerp, as later with more asperity in those of Dordrecht, it is telling to note how, in the large canvases painted in the studio, he was able to preserve the power and vivacity of the studies done on the spot.

Often, above all later, the patient, precisely detailed work done in the studio is all too evident in Boudin's large-scale canvases, a concession to those of his clients who were too attached to overelaboration; coldness invades these canvases at the same time as a sense of the finished, and one returns with joy to the rough outlines and sketches, in which is evident the vital power which only strength of feeling can give to art. But in the series painted during his best period the large canvases have the spontaneity of the sketch, with all the benefit that longer reflection adds. This is what he expressed in one of his notebooks: 'Show extreme obstinacy in sticking to the first impression, which is the best.' No one could have displayed greater obstinacy; and it could not have borne better fruit. He tightened his grip to hold on to it, and one can estimate the force needed to preserve such spontaneity without betraying any constraint.

The further he advanced, the less he concerned himself with subject matter. He felt that light was the principal subject of landscape; and the factor which enhances a number of Boudin's works, of which the handling might otherwise diminish the range, is precisely that everything in them is subordinated to the light. Reflection in the water, the play of clouds and sky: the light is distributed with a delicate voluptuousness, without affectation or romanticism, without the restrained fury of certain works of Daubigny, without the dreamy sweetness of Corot, but with a discreet poetry which belongs only to Boudin.

And with what skill he preserves the bloom of the colour in his beautiful works! The *Antwerp* series (see pp. 78, 85) seems as if painted yesterday; in his frequently muted harmonies, with what skill he places a warm note to enliven a corner of the canvas! Boudin became a master of the art of colour sonorities, and if his range is narrow, it is correspondingly profound. In his work a single light stroke acquires its full value; it is obvious that he has weighed its resonance. In this he is supremely a painter.

It is not the undiscerning use of colour that makes a painter; the Dionysians of painting, a Rubens, Delacroix, Turner or Monet, sustained by their genius, and by the appetite of their joy, need a powerful flow of colour; it is like an orgy of which they are always masters. Others, like certain Dutch painters, or like Corot, love colour with an equally warm passion, but with greater economy. It seems that colour is a treat which they promise themselves, and which they do not grant themselves except with great precautions, and which they savour to the full. Boudin is one of these. The modest scale of grey had no secrets for him, he knew how to draw out of it new harmonies, and when to these discreet scales he suddenly added a warmer note, it took on such a value that the spectator could well ask whether all the other harmonies had not been established for that one note, to serve as its support, as atmosphere, and if everything else was not a tender approach towards it.

A little later the *Dordrecht* series of 1884 (see p. 142) reveals Boudin in a more austere mood: his painting achieved an extreme solidity. In it there reigns a weight more forceful than in any of the other series; the subject made an impression on the painter's style, to the extent of helping him to attain a force of expression worthy to rival the *Argenteuil* and *Holland* series by Monet, or Jongkind's views of Paris.

Le Havre: La Barre dock, 1892

However, his own nature did not push him in this direction, and the unease which his letters from Dordrecht betray shows sufficiently that he had to do violence to his nature to endow his work with the force which he felt he often lacked. He could accede to austerity only with an effort, and by nature was as far from this as from exuberant joy. His sphere was that of subtle melancholy; in that he found all the charm he hoped for in things, and his work embodies it with delicate abundance.

In the seascapes of Trouville (1880–85), in full possession of his painter's skill and his clear vision, he abandoned himself to the charm of the subjects he was intent on painting (see p. 156). In these, above all, the sureness and lightness of his hand reached a prodigious level: he knew the art of evoking, with a few strokes of the brush, the rigging of a ship and the gradated brilliance of sails. Only Jongkind could rival him in the art of evoking ships in movement, or at rest. There is no better proof of this than the evidence provided by unscrupulous imitators.

After Boudin's death, and even during his lifetime, sketches executed by the painter strayed into hands of people more interested than respectful, who ventured to add to these canvases a degree of finish which the painter had not had the time or the concern to give them. No matter how much skill their efforts contain, the betrayal is visible, however little is known of the way in which Boudin realized his works. Some of his 'finishers' were not at all lacking in skill; they were even able, at times, to win over the good faith of some of the private collectors, as long as they did not venture to attempt the sky or boats with their brushes; there the subterfuge became all too obvious. Corot alone was able to imitate Boudin's skies and Jongkind his boats. It required an intimate knowledge and an equally rare suppleness of hand.

In the works of this period the sureness of his hand never faltered, yet this was never at the expense of his vision. Boudin worked continually to perfect the simplification of his composition, which never seemed to him to be sufficiently strong or expressive; and in his smallest canvas with the magic of a deft brush, he captured life, as is the duty of every real painter, purely in order to extend, beyond mere subject matter, its tender or agonized pulse.

Chapter 10 Renewal 1884-1897

One might have thought that at this point he would have been satisfied and, on the strength of an impeccable technique, do no more than recopy his own work, like so many others, obstinate in his own truth, and wishing it to be immutable. He was sixty years old: there are few painters who at this age are really prepared to admit the perpetual necessity of renewing their technique, and the inevitable diversity of human vision. Success had begun to come to him after more than forty years of effort; he could have sat down and satisfied the taste of a public more easily bewildered by changes than likely to grow weary of a habit. He could have adopted, for once and for all, a style and a subject, and have taken from this formula as many copies as he needed to 'satisfy the demand.' He could at last have rested, and tended gently towards a stability of expression that would have been justified by his age and the success he had won so painfully. But, and this is perhaps where the old obstinate blood of Honfleur guided him again, he maintained his hope of going even further, his perpetual adaptation to new desires; age could not lessen his enthusiasm or his appetite for greater knowledge and greater understanding.

He did not want to grow old, and knew that the best proof he could give himself was not to resist, but to advance still further, not to maintain his position, but to renew himself, not to profit from his own experience alone, but also from the efforts of the younger generation. He continually kept an eye on their tendencies and their conquests; his former pupil, Monet, was at that time providing the first proofs of his maturity, as were Pissarro, Sisley and Renoir.

They are right, all the same. Exaggeration in the blue tinged with violet. There is progress to be made in this field....

One can still grow old in this profession, but to grow slack is forbidden.

With his penetrating awareness, he understood entirely the element of rejuvenation that the efforts of the impressionists were bringing to painting. He made no attempt to hide this when, referring to an exhibition of Monet's work, he said of him: 'he puts in the shade all those around him, and puts years on their age,' and again in the charming letter that has already been quoted, and in which he speaks of 'the crowd of young rascals' who pursue him.

When the series of works painted during this period are examined a little closer, the tenacity with which the old man refused to let himself go into decline becomes evident, as does the subtlety of his vision which seemed to have increased even more. When one compares the works done between 1890 and 1895, for example, with the previous series of Antwerp, Bordeaux and Dordrecht this renewal becomes obvious: although his taste had always drawn him to paint skies and to envelop them in atmosphere, he now took care to incorporate more charm, delicacy and even warmth. At times his palette became creamy, with a grace reminiscent of Sisley's most delicate works.

And yet this was far from being a sudden renewal, it even seems to have been preceded by a sort of momentary decadence. The works done in 1887 and 1888 at times reveal dryness and hesitations: often the balance of luminous variation, which Boudin usually understood so well, leaves something to be desired, and one feels, in certain canvases, that he was no

Fisherwomen on Berck beach, low tide, 1894

Landing-stage and jetty, Deauville, 1895

longer able to reconcile the solidity of his former way of seeing with the new sensations he was trying to express.

The success that had come to him, and the insistence of the buyers who drove him to over-elaborate against his will, combined to delay for a time the possession of his goal. At the same time the death of his wife disorientated him, and his series of views of Caudebec, painted in 1889, shows Boudin's art at its weakest. Practically the entire series gives the impression that his hand and eye worked mechanically, with none, or almost none, of the soul, fervour, and love of sky and air that usually lend his works their power of feeling.

But this was a weakness that was quite soon to be dispelled: from 1890 onwards he felt the need to see new places. It has already been seen on several occasions how profitable these changes of place were to Boudin. They became even more numerous in the last phase of his life, and if it is true that the demands of his health and his increased resources contributed to a certain extent to his travels, he was guided also by an artistic motive, as he admitted, and not only by the necessity of varying his subjects, but also by the search for new images, for a new expression.

It is indeed wonderful to see the delicacy, the even more intimate poetry, and the increased simplicity with which he transcribes the perceptions which nature evoked in him.

Some admirers of Boudin prefer the work he did in the last years of his life: and this is not surprising since the views of Abbeville of 1894 (see p. 225), so handsome and exquisite with their masses of dark foliage rising up against white clouds, are just as delicate and as true as the pastels of 1859, as are the series of views of the south, the various versions of the *Fort of Antibes* and *Roadstead at Villefranche*, bathed in gold, and sun and joy, the shores masked in morning mist.

Following the example of a few journalists, the habit has arisen of saying that Boudin was incapable of painting Venice. But it is unlikely that, with his rare critical sense and penetration, which was just as acute in valuing his own work as that of others, he should have made a mistake so manifest as to feel, without any justification, such particular affection for a certain number of his views of Venice that he was unwilling to part with them. Once again it must be admitted that Boudin was right; for example, the eight views of Venice which were shown in the Salon of 1895 and later put into the sale of works in his studio, are in fact extremely good. Worthy to be considered as among his best works is the *Venice at Sunset*, which shows the entrance to the Grand Canal, the church of the Salute and the corner of the Piazzetta, with a few gondolas laden with people, a smoking steamer, and above all this a great, fiery sky, with blazing clouds spread across it, sinking away around the dome of the Salute, in a pure sunset as golden as a dawn.

When one considers that he painted the *View of Douarnenez, Tristan island, morning* when he was seventy-three years old, in 1897, the year before his death, one cannot help but admire, with feeling, the miraculous energy, the irreducible tenderness which helped the old painter to overcome the suffering caused by his illness, to express again exquisitely his love of sky and sea. This canvas is like a testament; it is one of the last, perhaps the last, which Boudin finished and signed; in it he was still able to show the full extent to which he was able to capture flowing water and fleeing cloud. The bay of Douarnenez, with its houses and church, Tristan island and the white stroke of its lighthouse reflected far away in the calm, blue water form the composition stretched out in the centre of the canvas; below this, the sea, reaching to the foreground, which is accentuated by the crest of a rock; above, one of his great blue skies with white clouds, those he loved most and portrayed best.

One should also reconsider the small studies of Honfleur, painted during the last autumn of his life,

Venice: the Dogana, the Salute, the entrance to the Grand Canal, 1895

the views of the harbour, the harbour offices, street corners, an old house, the entrance to the harbour at morning tide, on misty days, the corners of the old harbour, all these little, often unfinished canvases, humble views of his native town, which he evoked with a spirit as eager as it had been when he first attempted to paint them fifty years earlier, at the beginning of his career.

If only one could have seen him painting these works, with the little board he used as a palette propped against the easel, the brushes passing from one sensitive hand to the other, seeking the stroke and placing it suddenly, just as seagulls skim over the water. At times he would lean back, a brush between his teeth, his hands continually fidgeting with the handles of other brushes, his blue eyes half-closed, and would stay like that for a few seconds, gazing first at his canvas and then at the landscape, and the brush strokes followed, in a controlled fever. He was perpetually on the alert, nothing escaped him, his nerves were tensed, his eye always ready to note the ceaseless changes of a view or of the sky, in a country where neither trees nor waters are ever seen in repose.

Or, leaning against the granite of a jetty, he would look out down the estuary of the river, where boats sail noislessly away, balancing their delicate masts and a far-off patch of bright light makes the tiny reflection of a sail sparkle. Clouds approach from the horizon, dissolving and gradually taking shape again, lending to the infinite variations of grey a beauty of which it is impossible to weary. A man lived in these places: he loved them and contemplated the sky and water from this shore; and this man felt such a deep affection for these places that we can no longer look at the horizon of the sea without thinking of him.

Chronological Table

1824 12 July: Birth of a son, Louis-Eugène, to Léonard-Sébastien Boudin, a seaman, and his wife Marie-Félicité, née Buffet, in the Rue Bourdet, Honfleur.

1834 Sails as cabin boy on board his father's ship, the *Polichinelle*.

1835 The family moves to 51 Grand Quai, Le Havre. Eugène goes to the Ecole des Frères, Rue Saint-Jacques.

1836 Leaves school and is engaged as a clerk by the printer and publisher Joseph Morlent; he later goes to work for Alphonse Lemasle, a stationer.

1840 Birth of Claude Monet.

1844 Boudin and Jean Acher open a stationer's shop. Several painters exhibit their work there, and Boudin meets Eugène Isabey, Constant Troyon, François Millet and Thomas Couture.

1847 He decides to be a painter. He sells out his share in the stationery business to buy himself free from military service.

1848 Visits Belgium with the sculptor Rochet to raise funds to support needy artists and writers, and studies the work of the Flemish masters.

1851 June: settles in Paris on a study grant from the municipality of Le Havre, which is to last three years. He divides his time between Paris, Le Havre, Honfleur, Rouen and Caen. In return for his grant he sends three paintings to the Musée du Havre: copies of Ruysdael's *Brook* and Paulus Potter's *Meadow*, and an original still-life of game.

1852 Boudin sends eleven paintings to the six-monthly Le Havre painting exhibition.

1854 Spends some time in Honfleur, staying at the Ferme Saint-Siméon, the home of Mme Toutain. His Saint-Siméon notebook dates from this time.

1855 First stay in Brittany: Douarnenez, Quimper.

1857 Second stay at Quimper. Thanks to his friend, the poet Gustave Mathieu, Boudin is able to show some of his work in Paris, at the Concert Musard, Rue Basse-du-Rempart. Alexandre Dumas the younger buys two Boudins.

1858 Boudin shows two paintings at the exhibition of the Société des Amis des Arts in Le Havre. He meets the youthful Claude Monet and takes him painting in the open air at Rouelles.

1859 Moves to a temporary address in Le Havre, 10 Rue de la Halle. Meets Gustave Courbet and Alexandre Schanne. The three friends go to stay at Honfleur, where they meet Baudelaire. For the first time one of his canvases is hung at the Salon des Artistes français in Paris; this is the *Pilgrimage of Sainte-Anne-la-Palud*. Urged by his friends, he decides to move to Paris, where he finds a studio at 8 Boulevard Montmartre.

1860 Visits to Honfleur, Trouville and Quimper.

1861 Boudin leaves the Boulevard Montmartre and moves to 66 Rue Pigalle, where he lives with a Breton girl, Marie-Anne (Marianne) Guédès. From 1861 onwards, he is to spend the winter in Paris and the rest of the year in Brittany and Normandy. From April 1861 onwards, he works as an assistant to Constant Troyon, laying out large compositions and often painting in the skies. He meets Jean-Baptiste Camille Corot and Charles Daubigny.

1862 Visits Trouville and meets there Johan Barthold Jongkind, a former pupil of Isabey and a friend of Monet. On Isabey's advice, Boudin paints beach scenes.

1863 January: marries Marie-Anne Guédès. February: moves to 27 Avenue Trudaine, Paris. June: death of his father, Léonard-Sébastien Boudin. During the summer he works at Le Havre, Trouville and Deauville. Sends a *Honfleur harbour* to the Salon.

1864 Summer visits to Trouville, Deauville and Veules. Paris address changes to 15 Rue Durantin. One painting at the Salon.

1865 Moves house again, to 31 Rue Fontaine-Saint-Georges. Strikes up a friendship with Corot and Daubigny. Spends the summer at Trouville with Courbet and Whistler. Three paintings at the Salon.
Death of Constant Troyon.

1866 Visits to Trouville and Villerville. Three paintings at the Salon.

1867 Boudin stays at Trouville, later in Brittany (Kerhoan, Le Faou, Landerneau). Two paintings at the Salon.
Death of Théodore Rousseau.

1868 25 March: successful public sale of Boudin's works in Paris. Exhibits in Le Havre with Courbet, Daubigny, Manet and Monet. Works at Dieppe, Trouville, Portrieux, Doualas, Kerhoan and Landerneau. Two paintings at the Salon.

1869 Is commissioned to paint four decorative panels for the dining-room of the Château de Bourdainville. Finds a bigger Paris studio at last, at 31 Rue Saint-Lazare. Visits Le Havre, Trouville, Doualas, Landerneau, Plougastel, L'Hôpital-Camfrout and Portrieux. Two paintings at the Salon.

1870 Visits Fervaques, Trouville, Portrieux, Brest, Kerhor, Landerneau, Plougastel, Camaret, Berck, Etaples and Dunkirk. Two paintings at the Salon. War breaks out. In December he moves to Brussels, where he finds Virgile

Diaz and Antoine Vollon in residence. Courbet refuses the Légion d'honneur.

1871 Brussels and Antwerp, where he paints some of his best pictures. September: returns to France and revisits his favourite spots in Normandy and Brittany. Courbet found guilty of instigating the destruction of the column in the Place Vendôme, and sentenced to six months in prison and 10,000 francs compensation.

1872 Visits Antwerp, then Normandy (Trouville, Deauville, Touques) and Brittany (Landerneau, Kerhor, Camaret, Portrieux and Le Faou). Two paintings at the Salon.

1873 Visits Brittany and Normandy, also Antwerp, Rotterdam and Bordeaux. Two paintings at the Salon.

1874 Takes part in the first impressionist exhibition, at Nadar's gallery in the Boulevard des Capucines. Visits Trouville, Brest, Plougastel, Le Faou, Portrieux, Bordeaux and Antwerp. Two paintings at the Salon.

1875 20 January: death of Jean-François Millet. 22 February: death of Camille Corot.
Boudin visits Belgium and Holland. Summer visits to Brittany and Normandy. Two paintings at the Salon.

1876 Visits to Bordeaux, Trouville and Holland. Two paintings at the Salon.
18 November: death of Virgile Diaz.

1877 Death of Gustave Courbet, in exile in Switzerland since 1873. Boudin visits Trouville. One painting at the Salon.

1878 19 February: death of Charles Daubigny.
Boudin visits Berck, Trouville, Deauville and Camaret. One painting at the Salon. He returns to Paris and takes a studio at 54 Rue Lamartine.

1879 Death of Manet's teacher Thomas Couture.
Boudin visits Trouville, Brest, Portrieux, Bordeaux, Berck and Rotterdam. One painting at the Salon.

1880 Visits Holland, Normandy and Brittany. One painting at the Salon.

1881 The dealer Paul Durand-Ruel visits Boudin's studio and acquires sole rights to handle Boudin's output. Boudin shows *The Meuse at Rotterdam* at the Salon and is awarded a third-class medal.
Visits Trouville, Deauville, Le Havre, Pont-l'Evêque, Berck and Dordrecht.

1882 Visits Berck, Boulogne, Le Havre, Trouville, Deauville and Dieppe. Moves to new Paris studio at 11 Place Vintimille. One painting at the Salon.

1883 31 January: Paul Durand-Ruel opens his new gallery in the Boulevard de la Madeleine with his first Boudin exhibition, which is a marked success.

1884 Boudin has a house built at Trouville, the Villa des Ajoncs. Spends the summer there after a brief stay at Dordrecht. Two paintings at the Salon.

1885 Visits Holland and Normandy. His first trip to the South of France, where he is to return frequently, especially to Antibes, Beaulieu, Juan-les-Pins, Nice and above all Villefranche. Two paintings at the Salon.

1886 Visits to Normandy and Holland. Two paintings at the Salon, one of which, *Squall*, is bought by the state.
Death of Eugène Isabey.

1887 Visits to Normandy and Brittany. Two paintings at the Salon.

1888 19 April: highly successful sale of Boudin's work at the Hôtel Drouot (60 oil paintings, 30 pastels and 10 watercolours). The state buys *Russian corvette in the Eure docks*, at the Salon.

1889 24 March: death of Marie-Anne Boudin. 8 July: opening of a second exhibition at the Galerie Durand-Ruel, 11 Rue Le Peletier. The catalogue lists 89 oil paintings, nine charcoal drawings and an unspecified number of pastels, described as 'seascapes and landscapes.' Boudin shows five paintings at the Exposition Universelle, and is awarded the gold medal. He becomes a member of the Société des Beaux-Arts, of which Meissonier is president.
6 October: death of Jules Dupré.

1890 Visits to Normandy, Holland and the south of France. December: opening of Boudin's third Durand-Ruel exhibition in Paris. Durand-Ruel also arranges a Boudin exhibition at Chase's Gallery, Boston, Mass. Boudin sends two paintings to the Salon de la Société nationale des Beaux-Arts.

1891 9 February: death of Johan Barthold Jongkind. March: opening of fourth exhibition at Galerie Durand-Ruel. Boudin visits the south, Normandy and Brittany. Six paintings at the Salon. Death of Théodule Ribot.

1892 Boudin's first visit to Italy: Venice. Eight paintings at the Salon. The state buys *Villefranche roadstead*. October: Boudin receives the cross of the Légion d'honneur from the hands of Puvis de Chavannes.

1893 Visits the south of France, Normandy and Brittany. Seven paintings at the Salon.

1894 June: second visit to Venice. Eight paintings at the Salon.

1895 Third and last visit to Venice, then Normandy and the south of France. Six paintings at the Salon.

1896 Visits Normandy. For the first time since 1863 Boudin sends nothing to the Salon. His health begins to cause him anxiety.

1897 Boudin's last Salon submission: four paintings, plus eight studies in one frame.

1898 Spends a miserable winter in Paris and goes south to Beaulieu in March. Weak and exhausted, he is brought back to his house in the Rue Olliffe in Deauville, where he dies, his face to the sea, on 8 August. Friday 12 August: funeral at the Eglise de la Trinité, Paris; burial at the Cimetière Saint-Vincent de Montmartre, Paris.

1899 9 January: opening of commemorative exhibition at the Ecole des Beaux-Arts in Paris. The catalogue lists 337 oil paintings, 72 pastels, including 16 framed in groups of four, and 17 watercolours. A supplement listing 27 paintings, 1 pastel and 3 watercolours mentions a projected bust of Boudin, by Ernest Guilbert, which is to be set up at Honfleur. 20 and 21 March: public auction of the contents of Boudin's studio, at the Hotel Drouot, Paris. The catalogue lists 125 oil paintings, 98 watercolours and 56 pastels and drawings. 13 August: opening of the Musée Saint-Etienne at Honfleur.

1900 8 August: unveiling of the bust of Boudin at Honfleur. Death of Antoine Vollon.

Exhibitions

IN THE ARTIST'S LIFETIME

1850 Le Havre, Société des Amis des Arts.
1852 Le Havre, Exposition Bisannuelle (11 paintings by Boudin).
1857 Paris, Concert Musard, Rue Basse-du-Rempart.
1858 Le Havre, Société des Amis des Arts.
1859 From this date onwards, Boudin exhibits regularly at the Salon des Artistes français.
1862 Caen, exhibition of works by Boudin, Dubourg and Hamelin, 22–3 June; sale, 24 June.
1874 Paris, Société anonyme coopérative d'artistes peintres, sculpteurs, graveurs, etc., at the gallery of the photographer Paul Nadar (the first impressionist exhibition).
1879 Le Havre, Hôtel des Ventes, exhibition of works by Boudin and Amand Gautier, 2 July; sale, 3 July.
1879 Le Havre, Société des Amis des Arts.
1880 Le Havre, Société des Amis des Arts.
1883 *Boudin*, Paris, Galerie Durand-Ruel.
1885 Le Havre, Société des Amis des Arts.
1887 Le Havre, Société des Amis des Arts.
1889 Paris, Exposition Universelle.
1889 *Boudin*, Paris, Galerie Durand-Ruel.
1890 Boston, Mass., Chase's Gallery.
1890 *Boudin*, Paris, Galerie Durand-Ruel.
1890 From this date onwards, Boudin exhibits regularly at the Salon de la Société nationale des Beaux-Arts.
1890 Le Havre, Société des Amis des Arts.
1891 *Boudin*, Paris, Galerie Durand-Ruel.
1891 *Boudin*, Boston, Mass., Chase's Gallery.
1896 Le Havre, Société des Amis des Arts.
1898 *Tableaux de Boudin*, New York, Galerie Durand-Ruel.

ONE-MAN EXHIBITIONS SINCE 1898

1899 *Œuvres de Boudin*, Honfleur, Musée Saint-Etienne.
1899 *Exposition des Œuvres d'Eugène Boudin*, Paris, Ecole des Beaux-Arts.
1900 *Eugène Boudin*, Paris, Galerie Bernheim.
1906 *Rétrospective Eugène Boudin*, Le Havre, Hôtel de Ville. Preface by G. Jean-Aubry.
1908 *Rétrospective Boudin*, Paris, Grand-Palais, Salon de l'Ecole française.
1913 *Tableaux par Eugène Boudin*, Paris, Galerie Chaine et Simonon.
1926 *Tableaux d'Eugène Boudin provenant de la collection P.*, Paris, Galerie Fiquet.
1927 *Tableaux de Boudin*, Paris, Galerie Durand-Ruel.
1929 *Rétrospective Boudin*, New York, Galerie Durand-Ruel.
1931 *Rétrospective Boudin*, Paris, Salon d'Automne.
1933 *Eugène Boudin*, New York, Galerie Durand-Ruel.
1935 *Paintings by E. Boudin*, Chicago, Art Institute.
1936 *Boudin*, New York, Galerie Durand-Ruel.
1937 *Rétrospective Boudin*, Paris, Galerie Raphaël Gérard. Preface by Claude Roger-Marx.
1941 *Les décorations de Boudin pour le château de Bourdainville*, Paris, Galerie de l'Elysée. Preface by André Villebœuf.
1945 *Rétrospective Boudin*, Paris, Galerie Charpentier.

1947 *Boudin*, Paris, Galerie Michel.
1947 *Eugène Boudin*, Paris, Galerie Michalon.
1953 *Les Boudin du Musée du Havre*, Dieppe, Musée des Beaux-Arts.
1954 *Eugène Boudin*, Nice, Musée Masséna. Preface by Jean Cassou.
1956 *Les Boudin du Musée municipal d'Honfleur*, Paris, Galerie Katia Granoff. Preface by André Warnod. Foreword by Jean Dries.
1956 *Eugène Boudin. Peintures, pastels, aquarelles*, Paris, Galerie Brame. Preface by Claude Roger-Marx.
1958 *Trésors du Musée de Caen. Cent tableaux d'Eugène Boudin*, Paris, Galerie Charpentier.
1958 *Eugène Boudin*, Paris, Galerie Brame.
1958 *Rétrospective Boudin*, London, Marlborough Fine Arts.
1959 *Soixante tableaux par Eugène Boudin*, Le Havre, Palais de la Bourse.
1962 *Eugène Boudin*, New York, Thaw Gallery.
1964 *Eugène Boudin en Bretagne*, Rennes, Musée des Beaux-Arts. Preface by Marie Berhaut.
1965 *Eugène Boudin*, Paris, Galerie Schmit. Preface by Robert Schmit.

COLLECTIVE EXHIBITIONS SINCE 1898

1903 *Boudin, Jongkind, Lépine, Sisley*, Paris, Galerie Petit.
1905 *A Selection from pictures by Boudin, Cézanne, Degas, Manet, Monet, Berthe Morisot, Pissarro, Renoir, Sisley, exhibited by M. Durand-Ruel of Paris*, London, Grafton Galleries.
1906 *E. Boudin et A. Lebourg*, London, Leicester Gallery.
1912 *Eugène Boudin et Janine Aghion*, Paris, Galerie Bernheim. Preface by G. Jean-Aubry.
1930 *Paysagistes et peintres de genre. De Devéria à Boudin*, Paris, Galerie Cambacérès.
1931 *Boudin, Jongkind, Pissarro*, Mulhouse, Maison d'art alsacienne.
1934 *Honfleur et ses peintres*, Honfleur, Musée municipal.
1936 *Eugène Boudin and Some Contemporaries*, Londres, Alex Reid & Lefevre Ltd.
1937 *Naissance de l'Impressionnisme*, Paris, Galerie des Beaux-Arts. Preface by André Joubin.
1948 *Les peintres normands de Jouvenet à Lebourg*, Rouen.
1951 *Jongkind, Boudin, marines et paysages*, Paris, Galerie Alfred Daber, Preface by Alfred Daber.
1952 *La mer vue par les peintres de Jongkind à nos jours*, Saint-Brieuc, Rennes.
1953 *Boudin, Jongkind, Dubourg*, Honfleur, Société des Artistes honfleurais. Preface by M. Drucker.
1953 *Nature et peinture. Paysages de Corot, Guigou, Boudin, Jongkind, Lépine*, Paris, Galerie Alfred Daber. Preface by Alfred Daber.
1953 *De Corot à nos jours au Musée du Havre*, Paris, Musée d'Art moderne. Preface by Bernard Dorival.
1958 *Jongkind, Boudin*, Aix-en-Provence, Galerie Louis Blanc. Preface by Claude Roger-Marx and Jean Dries.
1958 *Le Havre et les Havrais au XIXe siècle*, Le Havre, Musée des Beaux-Arts.
1960 *Les peintres à Nice et sur la côte d'Azur, 1860–1960*, Nice.
1961 *Les bains de mer*, Dieppe, Musée des Beaux-Arts. Preface by Jean Lapeyre.
1966 *French Paintings from the Collections of Mr and Mrs Paul Mellon and Mrs Mellon Bruce*, Washington D.C., National Gallery of Art. Preface by John Rewald.

SALON SUBMISSIONS

Salon des Artistes français, 1859–89

1859 *Pilgrimage of Saint-Anne-la-Palud.*
1863 *Honfleur harbour.*
1864 *Beach near Trouville.*
1865 *Concert in Deauville casino. Trouville beach at bathing time.*
1866 *Trouville beach. Gathering on the beach (Trouville).*
1867 *The Pier. The Beach.*
1868 *Le Havre pier. Leaving for the pilgrimage.*
1869 *Beach at low tide. Beach with tide coming in.*
1870 *Brest roadstead. Fisherwomen of Kerhor (Finistère).*
1871 No salon.
1872 *On the shore. Roadstead.*
1873 *Camaret harbour. Camaret roadstead.*
1874 *Portrieux quay. Seashore at Portrieux.*
1875 *Bordeaux harbour.*
Bordeaux harbour from the Quai des Chartrons.
1876 *Berck beach. The Scheldt at Antwerp.*
1877 *Rotterdam.*
1878 *Portrieux.*
1879 *Beach.*
1880 *Fishing.*
1881 *The Meuse at Rotterdam.*
1882 *On the Meuse (near Rotterdam).*
1883 *Entering harbour (Le Havre). Leaving harbour (Le Havre).*
1884 *Low tide. Hightide.*
1885 *Setting sail. The Meuse at Dordrecht.*
1886 *Squall. Low tide.*
1887 *Etaples, low tide. A shore.*
1888 *The pilot boat. Russian corvette in the Eure docks.*
1889 *Return of the fishing boats. Entrance to Le Havre harbour.*

Sailing barges off Trouville, *c.* 1892

Salon de la Société nationale des Beaux-Arts, 1890–7

1890 *Eure Docks, Le Havre (mist effect).*
Scheveningen beach (Holland).

1891 *Etretat, cliffs from upstream. Etretat, cliffs from downstream.*
Tide coming in (Deauville). Low tide (Trouville).
Saint-Valéry-sur-Somme. Old harbour, Touques.
Le Crotoy quayside. Berck beach.
Etaples church (Pas-de-Calais). Seashore at Etretat (mist).

1892 *Beaulieu bay, morning effect. Beaulieu, Baie des Fourmis.*
Beaulieu, Baie de Saint-Jean. Villefranche roadstead.
Villefranche, the Lazaret. Villefranche quay.
Villefranche, view of the town. Villefranche fort.

1893 *View of Antibes. Juan-les-Pins (Alpes-Maritimes).*
Golfe-Juan. Antibes harbour. Reefs at Antibes.
Villefranche quay. View of the sea at Saint-Vaast (Manche).

1894 *Seashore at Deauville. The boats come in (Trouville).*
High tide, Deauville. Sunset. Ilette rocks, Antibes.
Fortifications, Antibes. Mistral at Antibes.
Seashore, Juan-les-Pins.

1895 *Fortifications, Antibes. The Fort Carré, Antibes.*
Le Havre: La Barre dock. Old town, Touques.
Place Courbet, Abbeville. Tide coming in, Deauville.

1896 No submissions.

1897 *Seashore at Deauville (October). Marsh, Deauville.*
Gust of wind off Frascati (Le Havre).
North-westerly squall. Venice (8 studies in 1 frame).

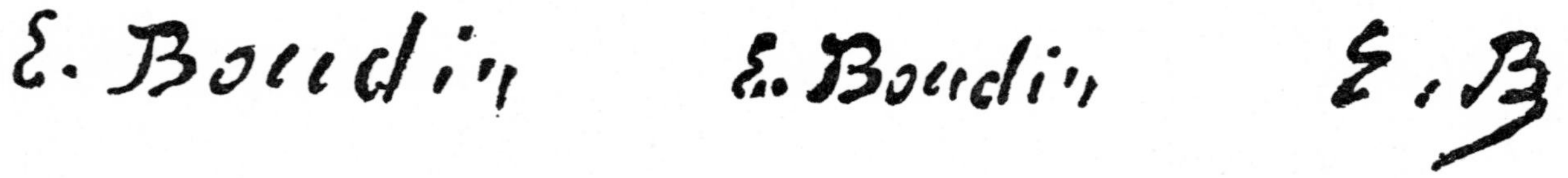

Stamps used for unsigned paintings in the Hotel Drouot sale, March 1899.

Still-life: flowers and basket of fruit, 1869

Gleaners returning
from the fields, 1850

Hunters returning
from the chase, 1850

Fisherwomen near Honfleur, *c.* 1852

Women sieving grain, *c.* 1858

Pear tree by a pool, Normandy, *c.* 1856

Norman meadow, *c.* 1858

Seashore at Honfleur, *c.* 1860

Near Honfleur, *c.* 1860

Still-life with oysters, *c.* 1862

Still-life with mushrooms, *c.* 1862

Meadow near Honfleur, 1864

The farm of Saint-Siméon, Honfleur, 1860

Gathering on the beach, 1864

Crinolines
on Trouville beach, 1865

Le Havre docks, *c.* 1867

Beach scene, 1868

Fish market,
Trouville, 1868

Old fish market,
Trouville, 1871

Landscape in Brittany, 1870

Le Havre harbour, 1870

On Trouville beach, 1871

Groups of figures on Trouville beach, 1871

Market, Le Faou, 1870

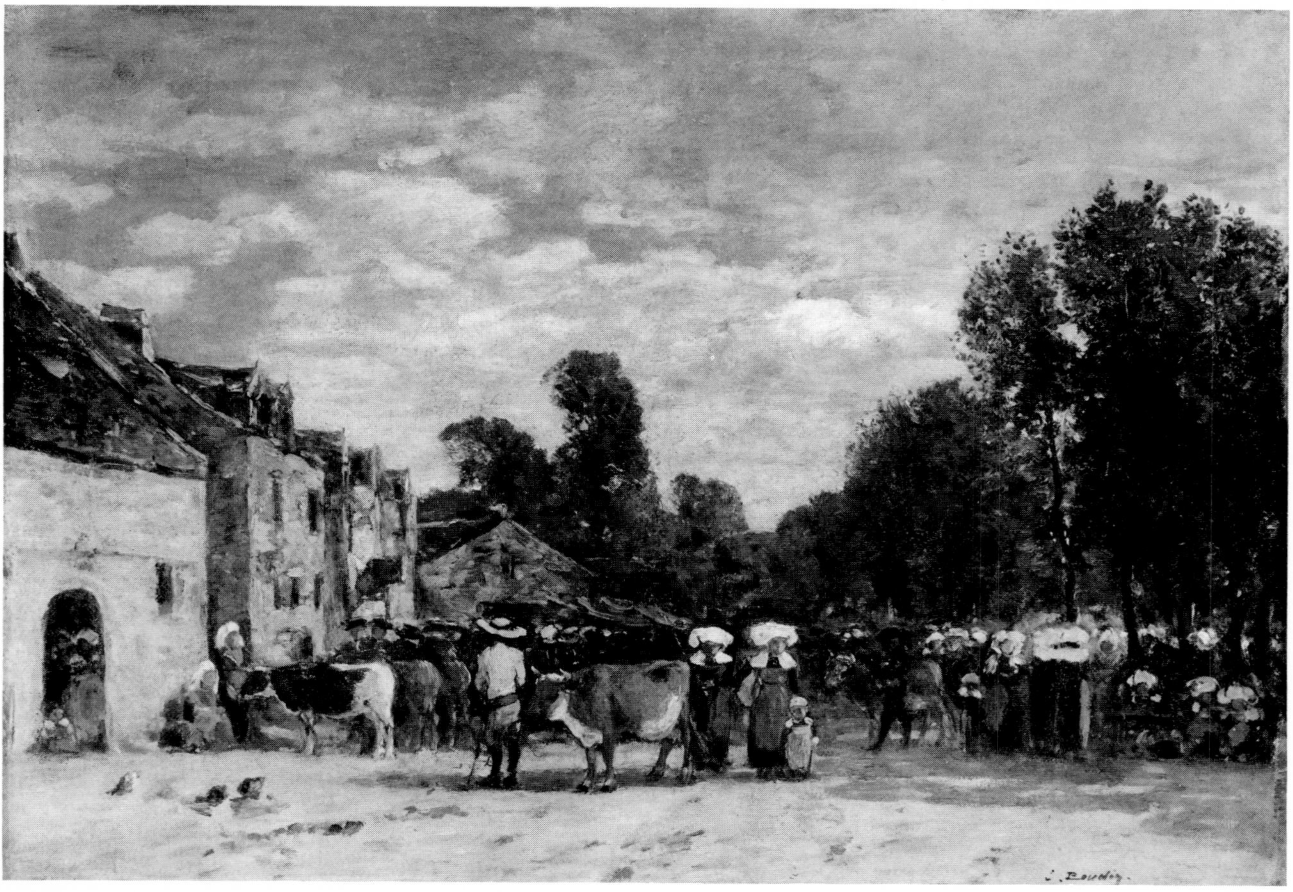

Market in Brittany,
c. 1870

The Canal de Louvain, Brussels, 1871

Brussels dock, 1871

Boats at Portrieux, 1873

Fishwives at Berck, 1874

Bordeaux harbour, 1874

Crinolines on Trouville beach, 1874

Scheveningen beach, 1875

Near Bordeaux, 1876

Seashore at Berck, 1877

Boats beached at low tide, 1879

Deauville harbour, *c.* 1880

Deauville docks, 1881

Meadow by the river
Touques, 1880

Meadow by the river
Touques, 1886

Etaples: La Canche, low tide, 1883

Inner harbour, Trouville, 1884

Gathering on Trouville beach, 1862

Sunshades on the beach, *c.* 1882–4

Berck beach, *c.* 1885

The Chemin des Bœufs, 1884

The garden of the Mareile residence, Oisième, near Chartres, 1888

Deauville races, 1885

Fisherwomen on Berck beach, *c.* 1888–90

Street at Caudebec, 1884

Street at Dordrecht, 1889

Sailing ships in Dunkirk harbour, 1889

The Seine at Caudebec, morning effect, 1889

Deauville pier, 1890

Capstans at Etretat, 1890

Canal at Saint-Valéry, 1891

Canal at Saint-Valéry, 1891

Entrance to Saint-Valéry harbour, 1891

Saint-Valéry-sur-Somme, 1893

Road to the Citadel,
Villefranche, 1892

Old Road,
Villefranche, 1892

Landscape, Oisème, near Chartres, 1894

Oisème valley, 1891

Nice harbour, 1892

Juan-les-Pins, 1893

View of Antibes, 1893

Antibes harbour, 1893

Abbeville square, 1894

High street, Abbeville, 1894

Old town, Touques, 1893

Bordeaux harbour, 1894

Venice: Isola di San Giorgio, 1895

Venice: The Mole and the Salute, 1895

Venice: the Mole, the Piazzetta, the Salute, the Dogana, 1895

Venice: the Mole, the Dodges' Palace and the Tower, seen from San Giorgio, 1895

The Côte Sainte-Catherine, Rouen, morning mist, 1895

Piers in Trouville harbour, 1896

Beaulieu bay, 1897

Regatta in Deauville harbour, 1897

Boudin and the critics

CHARLES BAUDELAIRE

Yes indeed, it is imagination that makes landscape. I can understand that a mind trained to take notes cannot abandon itself to the prodigious dreams inherent in the spectacles of nature: but why does imagination flee the landscape painter's studio? Perhaps the artists who cultivate this genre mistrust their memories far too much and adopt a method of direct copying that conforms perfectly with the idleness of their minds. If they had seen, as I did recently in the studio of M. Boudin who, let it be said in passing, has exhibited one very good and very careful painting *(The pilgrimage of Sainte-Anne-la-Palud)* and several hundred pastel studies improvised in the presence of sea and sky, they would then understand what they do not seem to understand, namely the difference between a sketch and a picture. But M. Boudin, who has cause for pride in his devotion to his art, shows his curious collection with the greatest modesty. He well knows that all this must be made into a picture by applying poetic impression recalled at will: he is not pretentious enough to claim that his sketches are finished pictures. In time to come, no doubt he will display before us the prodigious magic of air and water in finished paintings. These studies, jotted down so rapidly and so faithfully sketched from the elements that are the most inconstant and the least tangible in their strength and their colour, from the waves and the clouds, always have written in the margin the date, the time of day, the wind: for example, '8 October, midday, north-west wind.' If you have ever had the leisure to become acquainted with these meteorological beauties, you will be able to verify from memory the accuracy of M. Boudin's observations. Hiding the description with your hand, you will guess the season, the time of day, and the wind. I am not exaggerating at all. I have seen for myself. Eventually, all these fantastically shaped and luminous clouds, these chaotic shadows, these immense green and pink forms suspended and merging with each other, these gaping furnaces, these firmaments of black or violet satin, crumpled, rolled or torn, these horizons in mourning, or streaming with molten metal, all these depths and all these splendours rose to my brain like a heady drink, or like the eloquence of opium. Rather strangely, in front of this liquid or aerial magic I did not once regret the absence of man. But I know better than to extract from the plenitude of my enjoyment a word of advice for anyone whatever, any more than for Boudin. Advice would be too dangerous. Let him remember that man (as was remarked by Robespierre, who had studied his humanities carefully), never sees man without pleasure: and if he wants to gain a little popularity, let him be careful not to believe that the public has achieved an equal love of solitude. (*Curiosités Esthétiques: Salon de 1859*, VII.)

JULES-ANTOINE CASTAGNARY

Perhaps you find the seascapes of M. Boudin, the *Le Havre jetty*, or the *Departure for the pilgrimage*, insufficiently finished, and the drawing a trifle slack? Yes, if you put your nose right up to them to see them; no, if you look at them from an optical position. How delicate and accurate in tone they are, how all these little characters live and move in the air around them. These are effects such as you can see continually on our Norman coast. Nothing is felt more warmly, or rendered in a more picturesque way; and then, it is original. M. Boudin is alone in his treatment of the marine, or to use Courbet's superior expression, the seascape, he has made himself a charming little niche from which no one will dislodge him. (*Salons (1857–70)*, Paris 1892, vol. I, p. 309.)

M. Boudin has made the Norman coast his speciality. He has even invented a genre of marine that belongs only to him and which consists of painting, as well as the beach, all the beautiful, exotic society that foregathers in the summer in our seaside towns. It is seen from far away, but what delicacy and vivacity there is in these tiny figures. How well they look in their picturesque milieu, and how this, gathered together, forms a picture: the sky rolls its clouds, the swell rumbles as it rises, the breeze that blows teases the frills and skirts, this is the sea, and one can almost breathe the salty air. (Ibid., p. 375.)

M. Boudin's pictures go slightly beyond the limits of landscape. He used to favour those fashionable beaches which are covered with idle people every summer season, and he rendered the picturesque effects of them with inexhaustible humour and verve. This year he has given more character and fullness to his compositions. His *Brest roadstead*, with its sailors, ships, overcast sky and subtly varying sea, is perhaps a little less black in the shadows, but has a sincerity of appearance verging singularly closely on reality. M. Dubourg follows M. Boudin closely, he treats the same subjects, and almost in the same way, but M. Boudin is superior in that he invented the genre. (Ibid., p. 429.)

Should not a medal be awarded to the *Beach* of M. Boudin, this artist of such delicacy and such distinction, who has suffered a chilly reception in our Salons for fifteen years without obtaining anything? What are they awaiting to render to this man the justice that is his due? What are they awaiting to give him the medal he has deserved ten times over: the moment when his zest is exhausted and his hand grows heavy? Oh, sometimes I am overcome with rage at the blindness or frivolity of this jury, which thinks only of the favours it dispenses and not of the despair it causes. (Ibid., p. 259.)

EDMOND DURANTY

The little villages induce me to think how interesting it would be to write the history of a place, an earthly entity, as a monograph of its existence throughout the changing seasons, the days, epochs and hours, an intimate and, so to speak, biographical notation of all the variations of the sky and the vegetation around a little house and garden, of a hamlet, of its fields and its stream. This notation, in a word, is what M. Boudin has applied to the sea and its little ports. But why should one do it? For who would be tempted by the fate of M. Boudin?

This artist's impulsive intelligence and initiative has never, since he began to exhibit, won him any recompense: this is a glaring unjustice that one must never cease to publicize. They will let this painter grow old, they will let illness weaken him, and they will make his decline their pretext for abandoning him to his death, uncaring of his great value. (*Gazette des Beaux-Arts*, vol. XVI, 2nd year, p. 55.)

PHILIPPE BURTY

M. Eugène Boudin, without imitating M. Jongkind, had his eyes opened by M. Jongkind's works. He in turn had a pupil who, boldly abandoning himself to his own impressions, extended the method even further and simplified the palette. This is M. Monet, whose landscapes painted in the open air, when they have not been brushed in too hastily, evoke a feeling of charmed astonishment in the sensitive spectator. Other less sincere or less extremist hands have at times compromised the cause, but that is the usual course of human affairs.

The seventeenth-century Dutch painters, with a sureness of method and a perfect, intimate charm, have documented the pattern of waves, the movement of clouds, the noble aspect of a well-rigged ship, the character of rivers flowing level with their banks, towns built of brick, the dunes, the meadows dappled with virgin cobwebs whitened by the dew, the castles surrounded by moats from which a heron rises, and the water mills which chatter under the massy trees. They are classics. The English painters at the beginning of this century, our romantics, and Courbet, all sang a different, more moving and more peasantlike song. We are free to place them on a different shelf of the library. Would we dare to consign them to the flames?

In their turn the impressionists tried their hand at seizing more rapid sensations, and lines that were closer to the absolute appearance of the outer skin of objects. Their poetry has grounds for its existence.

M. Boudin is one of the least revolutionary in this group, though not one of the least determined. He is not an unprepared impressionist. He has arrived at his conclusions by reasoning, comparing and attempting. Also, reviewing the 150 canvases and the 50 or so watercolours and pastels which he has gathered together in the four rooms which we urge the public to visit, it is apparent that his conviction is a sincere one. Only the study of the special conditions in which nature presented herself has concerned him, and only that has guided him. No trace of a school. If the state of his mind and the will of his hand had been any different from this, when he sat down on his folding stool, and attacked his canvas in the midst of a Breton beach, or in the centre of a Dutch town, on the quayside in Le Havre or the beach at Trouville, if he had arrived with a preconceived idea of a certain picture in which the bald rocks, the painted houses, a three-master in dock with its fascinating sails, the bathers in their multicoloured slips had done no more than provide him with incidentals, then the artist would not have been able to assemble, picture by picture, such a consecutive number of large or small fragments. His exhibition would have been killed by monotony. The repetition of effects would have rendered him inferior. On the contrary, these paintings and studies evoke precise, accentuated memories of walks we could have taken in this country, on these coasts, on grey or calm days, overwhelmingly luminous, in green or dying seasons.

I do not want to single out any one of his pictures in particular. The painter's procedure varies according to the appearance of places, or perhaps even to the unconscious state of his personality. In general, his painting is light, indicative of the coloured transparence of air and of the substance of objects. At times it is more lofty, and then has some resemblance to the beautiful fragments painted by Daubigny in his youth.

The sketches are firm, and interconnect well. The people who animate the landscape, if there is room for them, are indicated with all their inherent movement and the characteristics of their costume. Charenton is clearly distinguished from Bordeaux or from Le Havre.

I would like to dwell on some watercolour sketches done in Brittany, pilgrimages and markets, in which the faded black of the women's dresses is delicately combined with the white of their coifs. The studies of skies in pastel or wash are reminiscent, by virtue of their charm and the warm accuracy of their tone, of the skies for which the admirers of Eugène Delacroix contended at the posthumous sale of his portfolios. (*La République Française*, 3 February 1883.)

GUSTAVE GEFFROY

Those who visit the exhibitions of circles, invaded by the attempts of amateurs, with the hope of at times finding sincerity of impression and fidelity of execution, have always been stopped in their tracks by canvases in which the science of observation and feeling for nature are affirmed with a pleasant tranquillity that surprises, seen in the midst of placards done to old formulas and full of homemade, facile effects. These canvases (seascapes for the most part), signed Boudin, reproduce the changing states of atmosphere, the play of light on beaches and wet rocks, hovering mists, cloudy skies, the indecision of marine horizons, as well as the movement of ports and fishing villages, the picturesque effect of jetties, masts and spars, the work of dockyards, the departure and arrival of boats.

The accuracy of these notes, the smell of this salt air, is generally admitted, but to see these seascapes at long intervals, without being able to imagine the ensemble they form, one sometimes goes so far as to accuse the artist of monotony, of knowing only how to paint the same picture. It is fortunate that a considerable part of the work of M. Eugène Boudin has been gathered in an exhibition room in the Boulevard de la Madeleine; reproaches fade on the lips, everything falls into place, all these notes form, on the contrary, an ensemble of rare variety.

Passing in front of these 150 paintings one has the impression of a journey taken along the north coast of France. Eugène Boudin has done this journey over and over again, from Finistère to Pas-de-Calais. The appearance of sky, water and earth changes continually; a catalogue is useless in front of these works in which nothing lies, in which greenery answers the clouds perfectly, the waves attack the rocks, the undulating swell that dies on the sand of the beach, the thatch and tiles of a cabin and the indication of a costume, all tell us unmistakably exactly where we are on the coastline....

No aspect of sea life is foreign to him. He sees and reproduces on canvas the hamlet crouching between two rocks, he watches the solid, round-flanked boats leaving to fish, with their brown, patched sails stiff with tar: he sees them sailing out of the narrow passage, filing out one behind the other like a shoal of fish; and then scattering far off on the rough sea. He is there when they return at dawn, laden with fish, and dancing joyfully on the waves. On his walks he stops to sketch with feeling a wrecked boat, torn to pieces by the rocks, bleached by the rain, aground on the sand, its carcass evocative of the trellis of a skeleton's ribs. He washes in a watercolour at a Breton pilgrimage, where the red caps of the Plougastel boys flash in the midst of the lace coifs and nun-like robes of the women. He records in pastel the state of the sky and of the sea.

Then he arrives with his painter's apparatus, the apparatus of a marine and landscape painter, at a beach where all Paris is on holiday. He calmly sets up his easel in this high-society atmosphere, and reproduces the latest dress fashions, sweeping in with lively strokes the profile of a Parisian on a crumbling headland, against a grey sky and a blue green sea.

Where is the monotony in this? Is it not the supreme condition of an art of this kind that the artist should have an intimate knowledge of the beings and things of which he wants to speak, and of the environment whose life he wants to catch and express? The close and continual study of one race and one nature is worth more than ethnographical anecdotes collected at random all over the world. Let us leave aside genius and its divination. The comings and goings of inhabitants, work and customs, the shop, the studio and the place of pleasure, the garden and the field, have to be penetrated in foreign countries like the syntax and common phrases of a language. A lengthy initiation, a long stay, and the force of habit are needed. Only then can one know and explain one's surroundings, understand the language and translate it. Boudin knows the surface of objects in this way, and brings out their meaning; he establishes a perfect harmony between them, assigns them to their true place in the whole, and prevents their colours forming a dissonant note in the orchestration of his pictures. He is obsessed by the sea, by its enchantments and its rages, he is interested in the existence of sluices, stones, chains on a quayside, ships, rudders, sails and anchors, and he is becoming the sincere and knowledgeable painter of the Atlantic and Channel coasts.

I cannot judge the journey he made to Flanders; I can see clearly that he found the skies there greyer and paler, the sun blonder, like the light of a lantern, and that the more humid air made the grass greener, the tile roofs and brick pavements shinier. But there Boudin was struggling with lines and a play of light that were new to him, he did not always achieve freedom of tone, and his skies are often opaque. Anxiety in face of the unknown took the place of certitude.

To sum up, Eugène Boudin is one of the immediate precursors of impressionism, together with Corot and Jongkind. He has perceived that opaque black does not exist, and that air is transparent. He observes the value that objects acquire when exposed to light, and how planes fall into place and lead to the horizon. He varies the infinite and delightful scale of grey, from grey mixed with dark violet to a silver grey like a fish's underside, and he triumphs in using them; he captures the movement of objects at the same time as their shape and their colours: the cloud that rises, the water that flashes, the sail sparkling in the sunlight, the passing boat, and records the synthesis of elements and beings in action. However much other people dispute his summary technique, the results are there to impose themselves. I will add a few lines of biographical detail. Eugène Boudin was born in Honfleur, has been poor for a long time, has kept a stationer's and a paint shop in Le Havre, where his humble trade helped him make the acquaintance of a few painters. He came to Paris with Troyon, and helped him lay out his large-scale canvases, whilst working unremittingly for himself. For twenty-five years he has been exhibiting the little masterpieces that will one day be the glory of collections and museums, and for which, in 1881, his fellow-painters awarded him a second-class medal. (15 February 1883.)

ARSÈNE ALEXANDRE

One experiment suffices to assess the value of the work of Boudin. In no matter which gallery, next to no matter which master, hang one of his pictures, however small. He will always hold his own, and will lose none of his qualities of delicacy, transparency and grace.

In the same way, certain men of modest and discreet appearance feel perfectly at ease in the midst of the most brilliant speakers and the deepest thinkers. They speak only when necessary, and find the exact word to express what they wish to say. They maintain their position, and every day inspire more esteem, more affection, and sometimes even admiration.

In the history of art Eugène Boudin was and will remain one of the men who had his share of talent, tact and purpose. A painting by him is never out of place: it delicately reduces the rowdy to silence, and remains precious even next to the strong. Even though he is a minor master, Boudin is a man of the first order, and a delightful artist, whose reputation will increase even more. He has no vast ambitions and no dazzling rewards. He was at the antipodes of academic art, and his discretion and delicacy are ill-suited to the vulgar crowd. But what a splendid man, and what a good painter he was, and how he regained his eloquence and value in the studio, and on the beach, his rather more spacious studio. Or more accurately, as true artists do, he made his studies in the open air, and his pictures in the studio. Whatever the theories and schools may prescribe, the artist is always more or less governed by this law: without it, the painters who have achieved the most in the open air would have no studio, and they do have one in which they always have passages to repaint or complete.

Those who have had the honour of watching Boudin in his studio have described his strange fashion of working: the clumsy board he used as a palette and which he balanced on the ledge of his easel, wedging it as best he could; his two free hands, the brushes passing from one to the other, constantly wiped, fiddled with, and tormented, while he talked, walked round, and pondered; then a tone picked up on the end of the brush and put down, progressing successively a little at a time all over the canvas; and the picture itself was always complete and charming in all the stages of its development. In the course of his conversation appeared all sorts of very sharp perceptions, seasoned with mischief and veiled with modesty. Death at last came to this deeply serene and pure tempered man: feeling himself to be lost, Boudin had himself taken to Deauville, to finish his days in suffering, but to have before his eyes the sea, sky, boats and human beings that he had loved so deeply.

In the work of an artist there will remain an element of the immaterial and incalculable. One cannot with impunity be a clearsighted spirit, an indefatigable worker, an eye sensitive to the harmony of things, a trained hand; but the result of all this will conserve, for a long time to come, and to the great profit of mankind, a charm, a beauty and a value that cannot but become more intense and rare, as have the works of so many perfect and modest men, Dutch or French, whom Boudin has gone to join, leaving his beautiful paintings to those who will love them, and a good example to those who will have the wisdom and energy to follow him. (Preface to catalogue, Boudin's studio sale, Paris 1899.)

Source material

LETTERS FROM BOUDIN

1. *To M. Martin.* There are 235 of these letters, the first dated 20 February 1861 and the last 25 December 1890. The correspondence was uninterrupted during this period of thirty years, and thus documents virtually the whole of the artist's intellectual and emotional evolution.

2. *To Louis Boudin.* There are 119 of these letters from Boudin to his brother, the first dated 21 February 1853 and the last, from Paris, 28 May 1898. In contrast with the continuity of the correspondence with Martin, this one is frequently interrupted; probably a certain number of letters have been lost or destroyed. No letters at all have been found for the years 1854, 1855, and 1856, and the correspondence is interrupted from 1858 to 1861, from 1871 to 1874, and from 1880 to 1893.

It will be noted that by a strange and happy chance the gaps in this correspondence are covered by the letters to Martin, and the painter's life can be followed almost without interruption from February 1853 until his death, that is, over a period of forty-five years.

I was told of the existence of these letters by the recipient, M. Louis Boudin, who later bequeathed them to me. His kindly consideration and his exceptional memory for any fact concerning the life of Honfleur and Le Havre made easy a task which would have been impossible to do well without his help. I deeply regret that his death in 1918 limits my thanks to grateful remembrance.

3. *Two letters to Claude Monet.* These letters, dated 28 July 1892 and 14 July 1897, were brought to my notice by Monet himself.

4. *A letter to Le Havre town hall.* This letter, dated 1872, requests a copy of the municipal decision of 1851 to grant him a pension. It is in the town archives of Le Havre, series R.I., box 34, bundle 8.

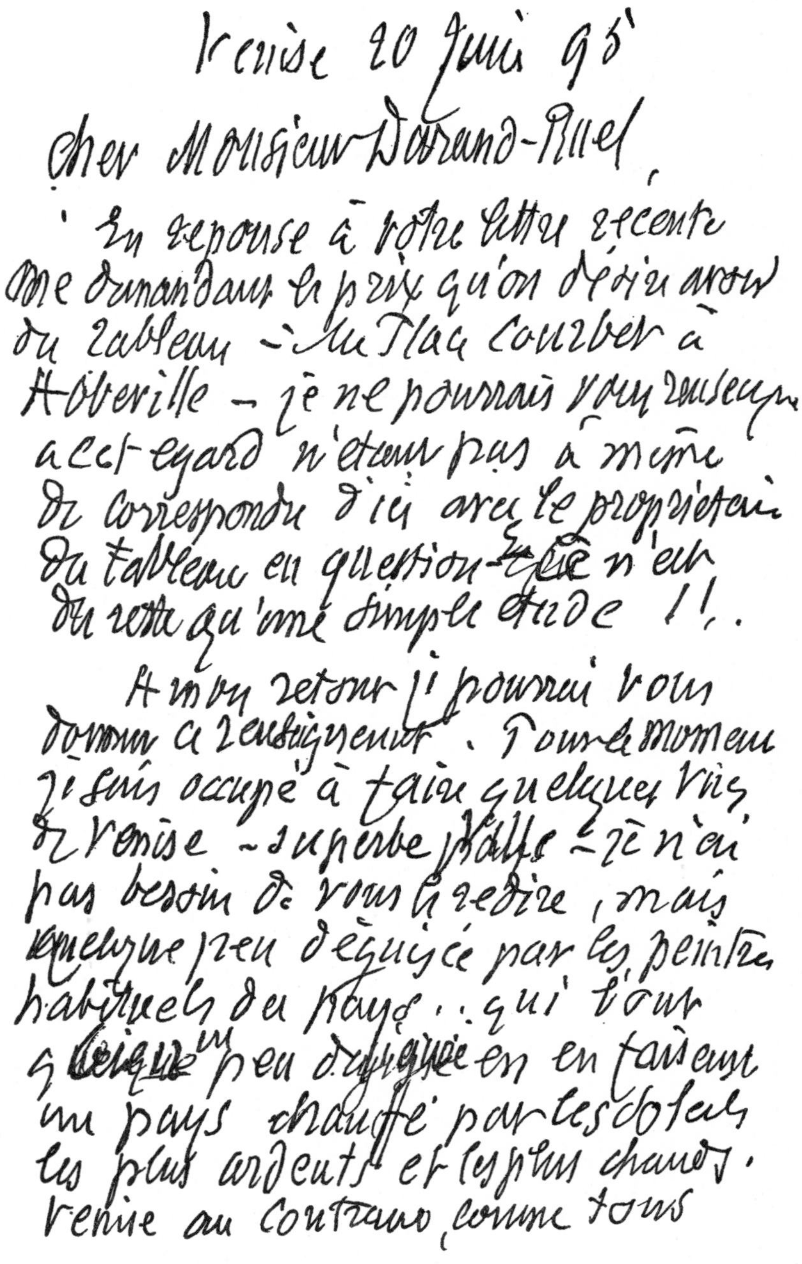

Venise 20 Juin 95

Cher Monsieur Durand-Ruel,

En réponse à votre lettre récente me demandant le prix qu'on désire avoir du tableau — une Plage Courbet à Hôberville — je ne pourrais vous renseigner à cet égard n'étant pas à même de correspondre d'ici avec le propriétaire du tableau en question — elle n'est du reste qu'une simple étude !!.

A mon retour je pourrai vous donner ce renseignement. Pour le moment je suis occupé à faire quelques vues de Venise — superbe — je n'ai pas besoin de vous le redire, mais quelque peu déguisé par les peintres habituels du pays... qui l'ont quelque peu déguisé en en faisant un pays chauffé par les soleils les plus ardents et les plus chauds. Venise au contraire, comme tous

MISCELLANEOUS DOCUMENTS

1. *Written by Boudin:* notebooks covering the years 1847, 1854, 1855, 1856, 1859 and 1860; account books kept by the artist between the years 1851 and 1866; several rough drafts of letters.

2. *Letters to Boudin,* from Troyon, Bonnafé, Dubourg, Couveley, official agencies and collectors.

G. JEAN-AUBRY

ces pays lumineux est d'un coloris
gris : l'atmosphère en est douce
et brumeuse . et le ciel .. d'y
toute parée de nuages comme un ciel de
nos contrées normandes ou Hollandaises
Quoique la chaleur y soit assez
dure par moments .. d'ailleurs
depuis que j'y suis il a toujours
été orageux et l'est encore en ce
moment ! ..

Néanmoins c'est un ravissant
pays rempli de belles choses qui
attestent un passé artistique bien
supérieur .. En ce moment on y
expose une Exposition de tableaux !
— c'est la première et nous y voyons quelques
uns de nos peintres en renom.

Je regrette de n'avoir plus les
années de jeunesse qu'il faudrait pour
créer une belle série de vues de ce pays
d'ailleurs assez difficile à représenter
à cause des monuments qui
exigent une grande science de
dessin et de longues stations dans
la cité comme en a fait Ziem
autrefois.

Agréez, cher Monsieur
Durand-Ruel mes plus ardents
souhaits pour votre santé
et mes cordiales salutations.

amitiés à votre fils E. Boudin

Chez Mr Placco
Calle St Zaccario 4688.
Riva dei Schiavoni – Venise

Encore pour une quinzaine
à cette adresse.

Letter from Boudin in Venice to Charles Durand-Ruel, 20 June 1895. Archives of Galerie Durand-Ruel.

List of illustrations

COLOUR PLATES

Inscr. b. r.: E. Boudin Trouville 73
Collection: Mr and Mrs Paul Mellon, Upperville, Va.

115
On Trouville beach, 1874
Oil on panel, 19×33 cm
Inscr. b. l.: E. Boudin 26 août; b. r.: 1874 Trouville
Private collection

117
On Trouville beach, storm effect, 1894
Oil on panel, 15·5×24 cm
Inscr.: E. Boudin à mon ami Morlot 1894
Collection: Mr and Mrs Paul Mellon, Upperville, Va.

121
Gathering on Trouville beach, 1874
Oil on panel, 17×35 cm
Inscr. b. l.: E. Boudin; b. r.: Trouville 74
Private collection, New York

123
Figures on beach, *c.* 1875
Oil on panel, 17×30·5 cm
Inscr. b. r.: E. Boudin,
Private collection, New York

129
View of Rotterdam roadstead, 1880
Oil on canvas, 78·5×111·5 cm
Inscr. b. r.: E. Boudin
Private collection, New York

137
Sailing boats off Deauville, *c.* 1882
Pastel, 18×27 cm
Inscr. b. r.: E. Boudin
Private collection

139
Berck beach: setting sail, 1883
Oil on canvas, 54·5×74·5 cm
Inscr. b. l.: E. Boudin 83; b. r.: Berck
Formerly in de Beriot collection

142
Sailing ships on the Meuse at Dordrecht, 1884
Oil on canvas, 46×65 cm
Inscr. b. r.: E. Boudin 84
Private collection

145
Landscape: the river Touques, 1883
Oil on canvas, 55·5×75 cm
Inscr. b. l.: E. Boudin 83, la Touques
Private collection, London

151
Deauville beach at low tide, *c.* 1885
Oil on canvas, 36×58 cm
Inscr. b. r.: E. Boudin; b. l.: Deauville
Private collection

156
Trouville beach: the nursemaid, 1885
Oil on panel, 13×23 cm
Inscr. b. r.: E. Boudin; b. l.: 85
Collection: Jack Lasdon, New York

159
House and garden of the painter Braquaval, 1885
Oil on panel, 30·5×40 cm
Inscr. b. l.: 1885; b. r.: A Madame Braquaval souvenir de E. Boudin
Collection: Mr and Mrs Paul Mellon, Upperville, Va.

161
On the beach: the yellow sunshade, 1887
Oil on canvas, 14×24·5 cm
Inscr. b. r.: E. Boudin; b. l.: 87
Private collection, Detroit, Mich.

163
Entrance to Trouville harbour, low tide, *c.* 1890
Oil on panel, 32×41·5 cm
Inscr. b. r.: E. Boudin
Private collection, New York

165
Berck beach, low tide, 1890
Oil on panel, 31·5×42·5 cm
Inscr. b. l.: Berck; b. r.: à Mr Matheron E. Boudin 1890
Private collection

167
Bénerville beach, low tide, 1892
Oil on canvas, 50×75 cm
Inscr. b. r.: Bénerville E. Boudin 92
Private collection, France

169
Fécamp docks, 1892
Oil on canvas, 40×55 cm
Inscr. b. r.: E. Boudin 92 Fécamp
Private collection

171
The de Beriot children on Trouville beach, 1892
Oil on panel, 14·4×23·9 cm
(reproduced original size)
Inscr. b. r.: E. Boudin à Mlle Jeanne de Beriot 92; b. l.: Trouville 8
Formerly in de Beriot collection

175
Le Havre: La Barre dock, 1892
Oil on panel, 35×27 cm
Inscr. b. l.: Havre 92 E. Boudin
Private collection

178
Fisherwomen on Berck beach, low tide, 1894
Oil on panel, 22·5×33 cm
Inscr. b. l.: E. Boudin 94 Berck
Collection: E. G. Buhrle foundation, Zurich

179
Landing-stage and jetty, Deauville, 1895
Oil on panel, 32×45·8 cm
Inscr. b. l.: E. Boudin 95; b. r.: Jetée de Deauville
Private collection, New York

181
Venice: the Dogana, the Salute, the entrance to the Grand Canal, 1895
Oil on canvas, 32·5×45·8 cm
Inscr. b. r.: E. Boudin Venise 95
Private collection, New York

187
Sailing barges off Trouville, *c.* 1892
Oil on panel, 17·3×27 cm
Inscr. b. l.: E. Boudin
Collection: Fred Uhler, Neuchâtel

189
Still-life: flowers and basket of fruit, 1869
Oil on canvas, 53×43 cm
Inscr. b. r.: E. B.
Private collection

MONOCHROME ILLUSTRATIONS

Endpapers
On Trouville beach, 1866
Watercolour, 18×29 cm
Unsigned, inscr. b. r.: 1866

13
Three figures in the harbour
Pen and ink drawing, 18×11 cm
Unsigned

17
Shepherds
Pencil, 16·5×11·5 cm
Unsigned

19
Fishermen and laundresses
Pencil and wash, 13·7×18·5 cm
Unsigned
Louvre, Cabinet des dessins

20
Breton costumes
Pencil and wash, 18·8×28·8 cm
Unsigned
Louvre, Cabinet des dessins

25
Le Havre: town hall, glacis, Tour François Ier, Porte du Perrey, 1852
Oil on panel, 16×38·5 cm
Inscr. b. l.: E. Boudin 1852
Musée du Havre

Le Havre: Tour François Ier, 1852
Oil on panel, 16×38·5 cm
Inscr. b. r.: E. Boudin; b. l.: 1852
Musée du Havre

26
The Pilgrimage of Sainte-Anne-la-Palud, Finistère, 1858
Oil on canvas, 28×115 cm
Inscr. b. r.: E. Boudin 1858
Musée du Havre

Study for the painting 'The Pilgrimage of Sainte-Anne-la-Palud', *c.* 1858
Pencil, 19×29·5 cm
Inscr. b. l.: E. B.

35
Study for the painting 'Breton Festival', 1864
Watercolour, 16·5×25·5 cm
Inscr. b. l.: E. Boudin 64

38
Study of figures, 1865
Pencil and wash, 11·7×22·7 cm
Inscr. b. r.: 1865
Louvre, Cabinet des dessins

55
The Crinolines, *c.* 1865
Watercolour, 13·5×18·5 cm
Unsigned and undated

56
Trouville pier, 1864
Oil on panel, 29·5×46 cm
Inscr. b. l.: E. Boudin 64

58
Bathing machines, 1866
Watercolour, 16×22 cm
Inscr. b. r.: 1866

63
Groups of Breton peasants
Pencil and wash, 22×30·9 cm
Unsigned and undated
Louvre, Cabinet des dessins

Market scene in Brittany
Charcoal and wash, 17·9×23 cm
Unsigned and undated
Louvre, Cabinet des dessins

64
Harvest at Le Faou, *c.* 1871
Watercolour, 13·5×19 cm
Inscr. b. l.: E. Boudin; b. r.: Le Faou

Breton women at Plougastel, *c.* 1870
Watercolour, 14·5×21 cm
Inscr. b. r.: E. B.; b. l.: Plougastel

69
Gathering on the beach, 1865
Watercolour, 13·3×23·8 cm
Inscr. b. l.: E. Boudin; b. r.: 1865

Groups of strollers on the beach, 1869
Watercolour, 15×25 cm
Inscr. b. l.: E. Boudin; b. r.: 1869.
Stamp b. r.: E. B.

70
Pilgrimage in Brittany, *c.* 1867
Watercolour, 26×21 cm
Inscr. b. r.: E. B.

77
Conversation on Trouville beach, 1865
Watercolour, 19×30 cm
Inscr. b. r.: E. Boudin 1865 A Mr Hte Fortin souvenir de Trouville

78
View of Antwerp, the Tête de Flandre, 1871
Oil on panel, 33×62 cm
Inscr. b. l.: E. Boudin Anvers 1871

85
View of Antwerp harbour, 1871
Oil on canvas, 51×77 cm
Inscr. b. r.: E. Boudin Anvers 71

86-7
Camaret harbour, 1873
Oil on canvas, 54·5×90 cm
Inscr. b. r.: E. Boudin 73 Camaret

88
Rotterdam: the Beursbrug, 1870
Oil on canvas, 45×65 cm
Inscr. b. l.: E. Boudin Rotterdam 1870

91
View of Bordeaux harbour, 1874
Oil on canvas, 70·5×102 cm
Inscr. b. r.: E. Boudin Bordeaux 74

92
Market in Brittany, 1869
Watercolour, 21×26 cm
Inscr. b. r.: E. B.

97
Entrance to Le Havre harbour, squall, west wind, 1887
Oil on canvas, 65×90 cm
Inscr. b. r.: E. Boudin 1887 le Havre

98
Sailing ships at anchor in Deauville harbour, 1878
Oil on canvas, 31×46 cm
Inscr. b. r.: E. Boudin 78 Deauville

103
Dordrecht: windmills beside the canal, 1885
Oil on canvas, 50×61 cm
Inscr. b. r.: E. Boudin 85

104
Harbour mouth, Le Havre, *c.* 1891
Oil on canvas, 46·5×65 cm
Inscr. b. r.: E. Boudin Havre

105
View of Antibes, 1893
Oil on canvas, 55×90 cm
Inscr. b. r.: E. Boudin 93

119
Villefranche quay, 1892
Oil on canvas, 45×64 cm
Inscr. b. r.: Villefranche E. Boudin 92

120
Juan-les-Pins: view of roadstead, 1893
Oil on canvas, 33×43 cm
Inscr. b. l.: E. Boudin 93

125
Six pencil and wash drawings

126
Boats on Scheveningen beach, *c.* 1875
Watercolour, 21·5×32 cm
Inscr. b. l.: E. Boudin Scheveningue

Boats on Scheveningen beach, 1876
Watercolour, 22×33 cm
Inscr. b. l.: E. Boudin Scheveningue 76

131
Saint-Valéry-sur-Somme: moonrise over the canal, 1891
Oil on canvas, 46×66 cm
Inscr. b. r.: E. Boudin 91

132
Venice: the Salute and the Piazzetta, 1893
Oil on panel, 27×41 cm
Inscr. b. r.: E. Boudin Venise 93

Venice: the Dogana, the Salute and the Giudecca canal, 1893
Oil on canvas, 50×74 cm
Inscr. b. l.: E. Boudin Venise 93

134
Ships at anchor in Camaret bay
Pencil, 18×31·5 cm
Unsigned
Louvre, Cabinet des dessins

144
Flock of sheep
Pencil

147
Three fishermen
Charcoal, 21·9×27·2 cm
Unsigned
Louvre, Cabinet des dessins

148
Boats on Trouville beach, 1870
Watercolour, 13·5×25·5 cm
Inscr. b. l.: E. Boudin; b. r.: Trouville 70

153
Honfleur: sailing ships at the harbour mouth, *c.* 1860
Pastel, 20·5×30·5 cm
Inscr. b. r.: E. Boudin

154
Still-life: game, *c.* 1856
Oil on canvas, 72×98 cm

Inscr. b. l. : E. Boudin
Musée du Havre

191
Gleaners returning from the fields, 1850
Oil on canvas, 61×82 cm
Inscr. b. r. : E. Boudin 1850

Hunters returning from the chase, 1850
Oil on canvas, 62×82 cm
Inscr. b. l. : E. Boudin

192
Fisherwomen near Honfleur, *c.* 1852
Watercolour, 17·5×25 cm
Inscr. b. r. : E. Boudin

Women sieving grain, *c.* 1858
Oil on cardboard, 19×24 cm
Studio stamp b. l.

193
Pear tree by a pool, Normandy, *c.* 1856
Oil on panel, 44×70 cm
Inscr. b. l. : E. Boudin

Norman meadow, *c.* 1858
Oil on canvas, 66×90 cm
Inscr. b. l. : E. Boudin

194
Seashore at Honfleur, *c.* 1860
Oil on panel, 26·7×39·8 cm
Inscr. b. l. : E. Boudin

Near Honfleur, *c.* 1860
Oil on panel, 27·7×39·8 cm
Inscr. b. l. : E. Boudin

195
Still-life with oysters, *c.* 1862
Oil on canvas, 40·5×59 cm
Inscr. b. l. : E. Boudin

Still-life with mushrooms, *c.* 1862
Oil on canvas, 30×46 cm
Inscr. b. l. : E. Boudin

196
Meadow near Honfleur, 1864
Oil on canvas, 63×84 cm
Inscr. b. r. : E. Boudin 1864

The farm of Saint-Siméon, Honfleur, 1860
Pastel, 19×29 cm
Inscr. b. r. : E. Boudin 60

197
Gathering on the beach, 1864
Oil on panel, 35×54·5 cm
Inscr. b. r. : E. Boudin 64

Crinolines on Trouville beach, 1865
Watercolour, 16·5×26 cm
Inscr. b. l. : E. Boudin; b. r. : Trouville 65

198
Le Havre docks, *c.* 1867
Oil on panel, 23×32 cm
Inscr. b. r. : E. Boudin

Beach scene, 1868
Oil on panel, 21×35 cm
Inscr. b. r. : E. Boudin 1868

199
Fish market, Trouville, 1868
Oil on panel, 24×31 cm
Inscr. b. l. : E. Boudin 68; b. r. : Trouville

Old fish market, Trouville, 1871
Oil on panel, 27×41 cm
Inscr. b. l. : E. Boudin 74

200
Landscape in Brittany, 1870
Oil on canvas, 45×64 cm
Inscr. b. r. : E. Boudin 70

Le Havre harbour, 1870
Oil on canvas, 45×65 cm
Inscr. b. l. : E. Boudin 70

201
On Trouville beach, 1871
Oil on panel, 22×45 cm
Inscr. b. l. : E. Boudin 71; b. r. : Trouville

Groups of figures on Trouville beach, 1871
Oil on panel, 22×45 cm
Inscr. b. l. : E. Boudin 71; b. r. : Trouville

202
Market, Le Faou, 1870
Oil on panel, 31×42 cm
Inscr. b. r. : E. Boudin 70

Market in Brittany, *c.* 1870
Oil on canvas, 30×41 cm
Inscr. b. r. : E. Boudin

203
The Canal de Louvain, Brussels, 1871
Oil on panel, 38·5×58·5 cm
Inscr. b. r. : E. Boudin 71

Dock, Brussels, 1871
Oil on panel, 21×34 cm
Inscr. b. l. : E. Boudin Bruxelles

204
Boats at Portrieux, 1873
Oil on canvas, 36×58 cm
Inscr. b. l. : E. Boudin 73 Portrieux

Bordeaux harbour, 1874
Oil on canvas, 36×58 cm
Inscr. b. r. : Boudin 74 Bordeaux

205
Fishwives at Berck, 1874
Oil on canvas, 85×151 cm
Inscr. b. r. : E. Boudin 1874 Berck

206
Crinolines on Trouville beach, 1874
Oil on canvas, 19×33 cm
Inscr. b. r. : E. Boudin 74

Scheveningen beach, 1875
Oil on canvas, 56×90 cm
Inscr. b. r. : E. Boudin 75 Scheveningue

207
Near Bordeaux, 1876
Oil on canvas, 48×73 cm
Inscr. b. r. : E. Boudin Bordeaux 76

Seashore at Berck, 1877
Oil on canvas, 45·8×75 cm
Inscr. b. r. : E. Boudin Berck 77

208
Boats beached at low tide, 1879
Oil on canvas, 85·5×150·5 cm
Inscr. b. r. : E. Boudin 1879

209
Deauville harbour, *c.* 1880
Oil on panel, 26·5×35 cm
Inscr. b. l. : E. Boudin

Deauville docks, 1881
Oil on canvas, 40×55 cm
Inscr. b. r. : E. Boudin 81

210
Meadow by the river Touques, 1880
Oil on canvas, 72×100 cm
Inscr. b. r. : E. Boudin 80

Meadow by the river Touques, 1886
Oil on canvas, 55×75 cm
Inscr. b. r. : E. Boudin 86

211
Etaples : La Canche, low tide, 1883
Oil on canvas, 36×58·5 cm
Inscr. b. r. : E. Boudin 1883

Inner harbour, Trouville, 1884
Oil on panel, 32×45 cm
Inscr. b. r. : E. Boudin 84 Trouville

212
Gathering on Trouville beach, 1862
Oil on canvas, 68×104 cm
Inscr. b. r. : E. Boudin 1862

213
Sunshades on the beach, *c.* 1882–4
Oil on panel, 15·5×27 cm
Inscr. b. l. : E. Boudin

Berck beach, *c.* 1885
Oil on panel, 15·5×24 cm
Inscr. b. r. : E. Boudin

214
The Chemin des Bœufs, 1884
Oil on canvas, 46×65 cm
Inscr. b. r. : E. Boudin 84

214
The garden of the Mareile residence, Oisème, near Chartres, 1888
Oil on canvas, 48×67 cm
Inscr. b. r.: E. Boudin Oisème 1888

215
Deauville races, 1885
Oil on panel, 19·5×33·5 cm
Inscr. b. l.: E. Boudin 1885; b. l.: 19 août Deauville

Fisherwomen on Berck beach, *c.* 1888-90
Oil on panel, 16·7×29·7 cm
Inscr. b. l.: E. Boudin; b. r.: Berck

216
Street at Caudebec, 1884
Oil on panel, 35×26 cm
Inscr. b. l.: E. Boudin 84

Street at Dordrecht, 1889
Oil on panel, 41·5×33 cm
Inscr. b. l.: E. Boudin 89

217
Sailing ships in Dunkirk harbour, 1889
Oil on canvas, 36×58 cm
Inscr. b. l.: E. Boudin 89; b. r.: Dunkerque

The Seine at Caudebec, morning effect, 1889
Oil on canvas, 46×65 cm
Inscr. b. l.: E. Boudin 89

218
Deauville pier, 1890
Oil on panel, 32·5×41 cm
Inscr. b. r.: E. Boudin 90; b. l.: Deauville

Capstans at Etretat, 1890
Oil on panel, 54×65 cm
Inscr. b. l.: E. Boudin 90 ; b. r.: Etretat

219
Canal at Saint-Valéry, 1891
Oil on canvas, 36×58 cm
Inscr. b. l.: E. Boudin 91; b. r.: Saint-Valéry

Canal at Saint-Valéry, 1891
Oil on canvas, 40×55 cm
Inscr. b. r.: E. Boudin 91

220
Entrance to Saint-Valéry harbour, 1891
Oil on canvas, 36×58 cm
Inscr. b. r.: E. Boudin 91

Saint-Valéry-sur-Somme, 1893
Oil on panel, 40×55 cm
Inscr. b. r.: E. Boudin 93

221
Road to the Citadel, Villefranche, 1892
Oil on canvas, 40×55 cm
Inscr. b. l.: E. Boudin 92 Villefranche

Old road, Villefranche, 1892
Oil on panel, 50×74 cm
Inscr. b. l.: E. Boudin 92; b. r.: Villefranche 4 mars 92

222
Landscape, Oisème, near Chartres, 1894
Oil on canvas, 61×50 cm
Inscr. b. r.: E. Boudin 94

Oisème valley, 1891
Oil on panel, 46×38 cm
Inscr. b. r.: E. Boudin 91; b. l.: Oisème juin

223
Nice harbour, 1892
Oil on canvas, 40×54 cm
Inscr. b. l.: E. Boudin 92 ; b. r.: Nice 16 mars 92

Juan-les-Pins, 1893
Oil on canvas, 55×90 cm
Inscr. b. l.: E. Boudin Juan-les-Pins 93

224
View of Antibes, 1893
Oil on canvas, 18·8×25.5 cm
Inscr. b. r.: E. Boudin 93 environs d'Antibes 14 mai

Antibes harbour, 1893
Oil on canvas, 40×55 cm
Inscr. b. r.: E. Boudin Antibes 93

225
Abbeville square, 1894
Oil on panel, 46×38 cm
Inscr. b. l.: E. Boudin 94; b. r.: Abbeville

225
High street, Abbeville, 1894
Oil on panel, 46×37 cm
Inscr. b. l.: E. Boudin 94; b. r.: Abbeville

226
Old town, Touques, 1893
Oil on canvas, 40×55 cm
Inscr. b. l.: E. Boudin Touques 93

Bordeaux harbour, 1894
Oil on canvas, 32×46 cm
Inscr. b. r.: E. Boudin Bordeaux 94

227
Venice: Isola di San Giorgio, 1895
Oil on canvas, 36×55 cm
Inscr. b. centre: E. Boudin Venise 95

Venice: The Mole and the Salute, 1895
Oil on canvas, 36×58 cm
Inscr. b. r.: E. Boudin Venise 95

228
Venice: the Mole, the Piazzetta, the Salute, the Dogana, 1895
Oil on canvas, 20×39 cm
Inscr. b. r.: E. Boudin Venise 95

Venice: the Mole, the Doges' Palace, and the Tower, seen from San Giorgio, 1895
Oil on canvas, 22×38 cm
Inscr. b. r.: E. Boudin 95

229
The Côte Sainte-Catherine, Rouen, morning mist, 1895
Oil on canvas, 40×55 cm
Inscr. b. l.: E. Boudin Rouen 95

Piers in Trouville harbour, 1896
Oil on panel, 33×41 cm
Inscr. b. l.: E. Boudin 96 ; A son petit ami Georges Sporck

230
Beaulieu bay, 1897
Oil on canvas, 45×64 cm
Inscr. b. r.: E. Boudin 97

Regatta in Deauville harbour, 1897
Oil on panel, 33×41 cm
Inscr. b. l.: E. Boudin 97 ; b. r.: 31 août

Bibliography

MONOGRAPHS

1899 Arsène Alexandre, *L'Œuvre d'Eugène Boudin*, Paris 1899.

1900 Gustave Cahen, *Eugène Boudin, sa vie, son œuvre. Préface d'Arsène Alexandre*, Paris 1900.

1922 G. Jean-Aubry, *Eugène Boudin, d'après des documents inédits*, Paris 1922.

1927 Claude Roger-Marx, *Eugène Boudin*, Paris 1927.

1928 Louis Cario, *Eugène Boudin*, Paris 1928 (2e éd., coll. *Maîtres de l'Art moderne*, No 24, Paris 1930).

1937 L. Ruth Benjamin, *Eugène Boudin*, New York 1937.

1959 Charles L. Cunningham, *Some still-lifes by Boudin*, London 1959.

1961 José Roberto Teixeira Leite, *Boudin no Brasil*, Rio de Janeiro 1961.

CATALOGUES

1908 Jean Guiffrey et Pierre Marcel, *Inventaire général des dessins du Musée du Louvre et du Musée de Versailles. Ecole française*, Paris 1908, vol. II, nos. 1426–9, repr.

1955 Reynold Arnould, *L'Œuvre d'Eugène Boudin au Musée des Beaux-Arts du Havre. Supplément au catalogue 1952-1953*, Le Havre 1955.

1958 Charles Sterling and Hélène Adhémar, *Musée national du Louvre. Peintures. Ecole française. XIXe siècle*, vol. I, nos. 121–9, repr., Paris 1958.

1959 Jean Dries, *Guide du Musée municipal de Honfleur*, Honfleur 1959.

1965 Robert Schmit, *Eugène Boudin 1824–1898*, Paris 1965.

1966 John Rewald, *French Paintings from the Collection of Mr and Mrs Paul Mellon and Mrs Mellon Bruce*, Washington 1966.

Index

PHOTOGRAPHIC
ACKNOWLEDGMENTS

Bibliothèque Nationale, cabinet des estampes, Paris; M. Christ, Paris; Galerie Durand-Ruel & Cie, Paris; Galerie Robert Schmit, Paris; Galerie Wildenstein & Co., Paris et New York; M. Guilbert, Paris; M. Lalance, Paris; Les Beaux-Arts, édition d'études et de documents, Paris; Musée du Havre, Le Havre; Musée du Louvre, cabinet des dessins, Paris; M. Sirot, Paris.
Documentary picture research by
Karin Hallberg.

Printed in Switzerland